BEGINNINGS is a powerful historical drama played out over millennia where genetic memories revive moments when life and death choices are made and raise questions about their impact in the future. Although these crucial events from the past occur in various parts of the Iberian Peninsula, the central story is set around the Basque country of Spain and France over two decades of Spain's murderous civil war, nazi occupation, cynical liberation, recriminations and social division.

Powerful and troubled characters play out an ancient cycle of murder and revenge which seems to follow down from ancestor to descendant over the centuries and returns to haunt a young woman in the mid-20th century as she desperately seeks to escape war and violence and to find a new life for herself and her young daughter; only to realize there can be no escape from the irrevocable events in their past.

## About the Author

Gary Heilbronn has written on diverse subjects, from aviation, criminal trials and terrorism to tourism, piracy and weather modification. He has a fascination with the human condition, criminology, science and metaphysics as well as with ancient and recent Mediterranean history; all facets of this novel.

Gary was born and grew up in Australia. He was a student during the social revolution of the nineteen sixties and seventies Vietnam War years, travelling widely in those years and becoming a lawyer and later, a law professor. He wrote his doctorate on aviation law. Gary pursued a career in Australia, Switzerland and in Hong Kong, writing a couple of dozen law-related academic and educational books, especially in the fields of aviation and criminal litigation and also dozens of academic articles.

Though he changed his life focus to sailing the high seas and raising horses in south-west France over the last two or three decades, Gary continued with some academic writing, eventually returning to his first passion, literature. He has written some one-act plays but his first significant published novel is BEGINNINGS: *Where A Life Begins* which was completed in 2013.

Gary Heilbronn is now based in rural south-west France and is writing the second historical novel in this two-part series and a *memoir* focussing on his early years growing up in Australia in the 1950s and early 1960s.

# BEGINNINGS

## WHERE A LIFE BEGINS
Tales of Survival and Revenge

GARY HEILBRONN

Copyright © 2013 HPEditions

All rights reserved. No part of this book may be reproduced, stored in a retrieval system, transmitted in any form or by any means without the prior written permission of the publishers, except by a reviewer who may quote brief passages in a review to be printed in a newspaper, magazine, or journal. Enquiries should be addressed to the publisher.

Printed by IngramSpark 2016
**Australasian paperback version**
Available from Amazon and many other book stores
Also available as an e_book on Kindle and other devices in many online bookstores

ISBN 13: 978-0-9875212-9-3
ISBN 10: 0-9875212-9-2

Historical Fiction – Murder & Revenge – Genetic Memory

Heilbronn, Gary

Length: 123,780 words approx.

Published by HPEDITIONS
Australia
The author and publisher wish to express their gratitude to many people who have assisted in the preparation of this and the serialized version of this book.

# Table of Contents

About the Author ............................................................... ii
Title Page ......................................................................... iii
A two-part series ........................................................... viii
    Foreword ..................................................................... ix
    Cast of Characters ........................................................ x
    ESCAPE FROM SAN SEBASTIAN ..................................... 1
Map of Basque Country around San Sebastian ............... 2
    One ............................................................................... 3
    Two ............................................................................... 7
    Three ........................................................................... 12
    Four ............................................................................. 16
    Five .............................................................................. 20
    AMBUSH ON THE BORDER ......................................... 23
Map of the Border near Bayonne .................................. 24
    Six ................................................................................ 25
    Seven ........................................................................... 28
    Eight ............................................................................. 31
    Nine ............................................................................. 35
    PALAEOLITHIC VENGEANCE ........................................ 38
Map of Cantabrian Mountains ...................................... 39
    Ten ............................................................................... 40
    Eleven .......................................................................... 45
    Twelve ......................................................................... 50
    Thirteen ....................................................................... 54
    COMING OF THE PHOENICIANS .................................. 65
Map of Phoenician World: Western Europe .................. 66
Map of Phoenician World: Eastern Europe ................... 67
    Fourteen ...................................................................... 68
    Fifteen ......................................................................... 71
    Sixteen ......................................................................... 75
    Seventeen ................................................................... 80
    Eighteen ...................................................................... 87

| | |
|---|---|
| Nineteen | 94 |
| Twenty | 100 |
| Twenty-One | 106 |
| Twenty-Two | 112 |
| Twenty-Three | 120 |
| Twenty-Four | 127 |
| Twenty-Five | 134 |
| BIRTH AND THE BEGINNING OF WAR | 142 |
| Map of France Occupied Zone and Free Zone | 143 |
| Twenty-Six | 144 |
| Twenty-Seven | 151 |
| Twenty-Eight | 156 |
| Twenty-Nine | 161 |
| Thirty | 166 |
| SIEGE OF SAGUNTUM | 172 |
| Map of Carthaginian Empire 3rd Century BC | 173 |
| Thirty-One | 174 |
| Thirty-Two | 178 |
| Thirty-Three | 183 |
| Thirty-Four | 190 |
| Thirty-Five | 196 |
| AN UNCERTAIN PEACE | 202 |
| Thirty-Six | 203 |
| Thirty-Seven | 206 |
| Thirty-Eight | 210 |
| Thirty-Nine | 214 |
| Forty | 217 |
| Forty-One | 222 |
| Forty-Two | 227 |
| TROUBLE IN TOLEDO | 230 |
| Map of the Kingdom of Tolosa, 5th Century | 231 |
| Forty-Three | 232 |
| Forty-Four | 235 |
| Forty-Five | 238 |
| Forty-Six | 243 |
| Forty-Seven | 248 |
| Forty-Eight | 252 |
| Forty-Nine | 256 |
| DISSENT AT HOME | 262 |

- Fifty ..................................................................... 263
- Fifty-One ............................................................. 267
- Fifty-Two ............................................................. 272
- DEATH COMES TO TOWN ................................... 276
- Map of Spain and Zaragoza, 15th Century ................... 277
  - Fifty-Three ......................................................... 278
  - Fifty-Four .......................................................... 283
  - Fifty-Five ........................................................... 287
  - Fifty-Six ............................................................. 292
  - Fifty-Seven ........................................................ 297
  - Fifty-Eight ......................................................... 301
  - TRACKING DOWN EXILES ................................ 306
- Map of Spain and France ............................................. 307
  - Fifty-Nine .......................................................... 308
  - Sixty .................................................................. 312
  - Sixty-One .......................................................... 317
  - Sixty-Two .......................................................... 322
  - Sixty-Three ....................................................... 328
  - Sixty-Four ......................................................... 331
  - Sixty-Five .......................................................... 335
  - Sixty-Six ............................................................ 338
  - DAYS OF RECKONING ..................................... 342
- Map of France and Spain ............................................. 343
  - Sixty-Seven ....................................................... 344
  - Sixty-Eight ........................................................ 350
  - Sixty-Nine ......................................................... 355
  - Seventy ............................................................. 359
  - Seventy-One ..................................................... 362
  - Seventy-Two ..................................................... 365
  - Seventy-Three : Epilogue .................................. 370
  - Background: Science and History ..................... 374

## A two-part series

This is the first part of a two novel series exploring the inner lives of otherwise ordinary people caught up in extraordinary dramas that have occurred at different times in history. A vivid context of violence, revenge and political intrigue also reveals insights into the special bond that can exist between mother and daughter. The storyline develops these insights by exploring the boundaries of what may be described as genetic memory, a natural extension of on-going scientific research into genetics which highlights the unique culture, politics, history and genealogy of people native to the Basque territories in Spain and France. It ranges through the lives of women connected genetically who find themselves more or less involved in significant but lesser known historical events affecting this part of the world. Though grounded in the nineteen-forties and nineteen-fifties, these events take place over millennia, from pre-historical times, through biblical, Carthaginian, post-Roman, medieval and even modern times during the Spanish Civil War and before and after World War Two when modern Basque political activism developed.

The second novel in the series continues the historical and genealogical themes involving the delicate links between human lives through countless generations and focuses on events in the lives of certain of the characters in the first novel during the nineteen-sixties and nineteen-seventies. Its world is extended outside the Franco-Spanish parts of Europe to encompass social and political activism in the "new world" especially Australia during the Vietnam War years and those decades when the music revolution and student political activism threatened to tear apart the social fabric and the bond between parent and child.

# Foreword

At first sight, BEGINNINGS, *Where A Life Begins* is about several significant but less well-known events and undercurrents in the long history of Spain and its people, as well as the impact that other cultures have had on their development over millennia. Basque culture provides unique backdrop and theme. Events unfold around the lives of participants.

On another level, this story is about murder, revenge, life and death, but mostly about life and if an individual life has any significance, especially when seen in the context of lives lived through a hundred and fifty generations or more. It is inspired by the subtle but scientifically verifiable genetic links between generations and the possibility of a generational or genetic continuum within which birth, life and death are events that have as much meaning as science allows.

The inspiration for the historical themes and part of the underlying subject of this story is the research into Mitochondrial DNA: that type of DNA which is only passed on from mothers to their children. Thus, it is a peculiarly female phenomenon and variations and markers in MtDNA are used by scientists to trace maternal genealogy down through centuries and indeed through millennia.

In this tale, which is as much about human identity and what makes each and every individual who they are, as it is about the grander themes mentioned above, there are appearances by a number of the great personages from history, both ancient and modern. Likewise, there are references to places, events and peoples which are or were once real, though sometimes little-known or now almost lost in the mists of history.

For more discussion, have a look at the section *Background: Science and History* at the end of this book.

# Cast of Characters

Fictional characters are marked with *

## Characters in the Escape from San Sebastian and Elsewhere

| | |
|---|---|
| **Anna Abene*** | Maria's daughter – born with unusual insight into her ancestors' lives |
| **Alberto Perea*** | Husband of Maria and father of Anna – killed by Franco's forces in 1939 |
| **Alphonso Zuidilla*** | Republican sympathizer who shot Toma's killer on the Hendaye bridge as Maria tried to escape in 1939 |
| **Helena*** | midwife and friend of Maria, witness to Anna's difficult birth |
| **Maria Abene*** | A young widow and mother escaping from war-torn Spain – traumatised and full of doubts about her values and her purpose in life |
| **Mysterious Gardia officer** | An unpleasant character who returns later, known as Juan Herrerro |
| **Thomas Abene (Toma)*** | Maria's first born son – tragically killed as an infant during Maria's escape; an event that returns to haunt the family's future |
| **Yann Zuidilla*** | Young son of Alfonso, with him at the Hendaye bridge and re-appearing as a young man to aid Anna's escape |

## Upper Palaeolithic Era Characters

| | |
|---|---|
| **Ara*** | Uuna and Toa's father – the spiritual leader of his tribe |
| **Chnn*** | An angry tribal hunter, a loner, rapist and murder, killed by Uuna while defending her mother – he is perhaps the distant ancestor of Juan Herrerro |

| | |
|---|---|
| **Ran*** | Uuna's mother and Ara's husband – almost murdered by Chnn |
| **Suma*** | Tribal Goddess of fertility |
| **Toa*** | Uuna's young brother, carelessly killed by Chnn during Uuna's rape |
| **Uuna*** | Twelve year old daughter of Ara and Ran; avenger of her brother, Toa, and saviour of her mother's life – a likely ancestor of Anna Abene |

## Phoenician and Celto-Iberian Characters

| | |
|---|---|
| **Alda*** | Chief of a Celto-Iberian tribe living on the northern coast of Spain near modern-day Santander in 900BC |
| **Amilca*** | Phoenician trader from Tyre (near Jerusalem), father of Daavid, future husband on Hannh. They eventually settle on the east coast of the Mediterranean; ancestors of Alia |
| **Hannh*** | Daughter of Alda, a woman warrior – an early source of genetic mixture of the Phoenicians and the Celto-Iberian peoples, a likely ancestor of Anna |
| **Jaan*** | Younger sister of Hannh and eventual tribal chieftain |
| **Manno*** | Servant of Amilca |
| **Chnnta*** | Chief of a vicious mountain tribe living in the foothills at the eastern end of the modern-day Cantabrian Mountains |
| **Zum*** | Son of Chnnta and a young warrior, consumed by pride and arrogance, but destined for an early death – a likely descendant of Chnn |

## Characters in the Beginning of War and Resistance
(as well as characters from Escape from San Sebastian)

| | |
|---|---|
| **Théo*** | Son of Georges (a colleague of Maria) and associate of Jean Moulin |
| **Jean Moulin (Max)** | Emissary of Charles de Gaulle to the resistance in nazi-occupied France – a legendary figure assassinated in 1943 |
| **Klaus Barbie** | Nazi Gestapo officer, responsible for the death of many French resistance operatives – tried in France in 1983 |

## Characters in the Siege of Saguntum

| | |
|---|---|
| **Alia*** | Daughter of Leontius, a wealthy merchant, and wife of Quintus – she comes of age under Hannibal's siege of Saguntum – a likely descendant of Hannh and ancestor of Alba and Anna |
| **Alorcus** | Historical figure, inhabitant of Saguntum, often considered a traitor but who as an emissary of Hannibal, tried to save the Saguntines before they were all massacred |
| **Hannibal Barca** | Carthaginian General, famous and significant historical figure at the time of the Second Punic War between Carthage and Rome |
| **Leontius*** | Alia's father, a wealthy merchant of Phoenician ancestry and an important city elder in the city of Saguntum in about 200BC |
| **Polybius** | A famous Roman historian |
| **Quintus Gaius*** | Alias's young husband, a coward who deserts her to save himself |
| **Titus Livius (Livy)** | A famous Roman historian |

## Characters Concerned with the Trouble in Toledo

| | |
|---|---|
| **Alba*** | A young serving maid in the home of the Kingdom's Deputy Administrator Zocodover in Toledo in the 6$^{th}$ century AD – a likely ancestor of Anna |
| **Alaric II, King** | Son of Visigoth King Euric, himself the grandson of Alaric I who had attacked and sacked Rome in 410 AD – killed by King Clovis in battle |
| **Amalaric** | Son of King Alaric II and Theodegotha, daughter of Theodoric the Great, the King of the Goths and of Italy |
| **Antonius*** | Captain of the Guard, a conspirator with Eneco Zigora |
| **Armando*** | Son of August Zocodover and eventual husband of Alba |
| **August Zocodover*** | Deputy Administrator of the Visigoth Kingdom of Tolosa (Toulouse) based in Toledo in the 6$^{th}$ Century AD – a fair and decent but strong administrator |
| **Clovis, King** | Considered founder of the modern nation of France, King of the Gauls and Franks in South West and Central France in the 6$^{th}$ Century AD, great-grandson of Merovech – first Merovingian King of France. Legend has it that the Merovingian Kings had a bloodline link direct to Mary Magdalene and the mythical son of Jesus Christ |
| **Eneco Zigora*** | A greedy, power-hungry official – perhaps a distant descendant of Chnn and ancestor of Juan Herrerro, officer in Franco's army and secret police |

| | |
|---|---|
| Gesalic | Natural son of Alaric II – an incompetent leader and unsuccessful pretender to the Visigoth throne |

## Characters from Death Comes to Town

| | |
|---|---|
| Alfonso Montesa* | A member of a wealthy Jewish family imprisoned and tortured at the same time as Azena de Valdés |
| Alcaide | Gaoler in charge of feeding the inquisition tribunal's prisoners – and generally enriching himself at their expense |
| Alguaçil | Torturers and gaolers of the Royal Inquisition tribunal, late 12$^{th}$ century |
| Pedro de Arbués | A protégé of Toma de Torquemada, the Inquisitor-General, and the first Inquisitor of Aragon, murdered allegedly by 'conversos', Jews who pretended to convert to Christianity |
| Azena de Valdés* | Woman in her mid-thirties married to Rodrigo de Carvajal and living in Zaragoza – perhaps the mysterious assassin of Toma de Torquemada and a likely ancestor of Anna Abene |
| Calificador | Official whose role was to advise the inquisition tribunal on religious matters |
| Dominquito de Var | A choirboy supposedly murdered by Jews to perform a weird ritual – a false charge invented to stir up hatred of Jews |
| Fiscal | Officer responsible for prosecutions in the inquisitorial tribunal |
| Toma de Torquemada | Infamous Inquisitor-General of all Spain under Isabella I, Queen of Castile and her husband Ferdinand II, |

| | King of Aragon – a sadist, mentor and close companion of Pedro de Arbués; he died mysteriously |
|---|---|
| **Rodrigo de Carvajal*** | A descendant of an old Zaragozan family, and a senior office-holder in the Aragon administration at the end of the 12th Century AD |

## Characters in Tracking Down Exiles and Days of Reckoning
(as well as characters from Escape from San Sebastian)

| | |
|---|---|
| **Javier Ibarrin*** | Son of Markesa and Karlos Ibarrin, school friend of Anna |
| **Juan Herrerro*** | Mysterious nationalist army officer at the bridge in Hendaye, later member of Franco's secret service – and possible descendant of Chnn and Zigora |
| **Karlos Ibarrin*** | Basque refugee, father of Javier, school friend of Anna, who later helps her to escape |
| **Markesa Ibarrin*** | Basque refugee, mother of Javier, school friend of Anna, who later helps her to escape |

# ESCAPE FROM SAN SEBASTIAN

*San Sebastian, north coast of Spain, May 1939*

## Map of Basque Country around San Sebastian

## One

It's dim and cramped in the womb. But it feels safe. Unborn but awake, she senses a growing tension in her mother's limbs and feels the cold edge of fear as it creeps into the young woman's pounding heart. It's unpleasant yet somehow familiar. For a moment, she focuses on holding back her mother's mounting fear as it threatens to invade her own tiny heart. The fear recedes. Gradually, she slows down her heartbeat to match the cushioned shock of her mother's regular footfall. The movement is comforting. A sense of calm returns.

The very pregnant young mother makes her way steadily along Calle San Juan. She's carrying a small child and a suitcase, and heading in the direction of San Sebastian's downtown bus terminal. It's in a temporary location, half hidden amongst the less salubrious and somewhat dilapidated buildings that populated the west bank of the Urumea River at the end of the 1930s. Dismal places are an all too common choice for bus stations. It's the same the world over. Not just in small Spanish towns in the far reaches of a country ravaged by three years of a vicious and unforgiving civil war.

But few thoughts of the bus station's dingy location enter the young woman's mind. Right now she feels like a fugitive on the run; and not for the first time. Yet she's strangely pre-occupied by the past.

"How easily fortunes change" she says almost aloud. She sighs inwardly and thinks longingly of her childhood. She was born into a family of wealthy and respected Basque landholders. But today all that is gone. She's just another young woman on the wrong side of Spain's turbulent political history. But she harbours no bitterness. If those feelings come, she just assumes them, then lets them go. Her grandmother taught her that. Her heart is kind and despite recent hardship and suffering, she accepts the life she's been given. It's just that these days, feelings of anger and resentment are sometimes so hard to repress.

Her married name is Maria Abene y Perea. But she's not even sure if she's still married. Maria is a little over twenty-four years old and now heavily pregnant; for the second time. She is petite but blessed with the slim, strong body; perhaps the body of a dancer. She carries her rather too battered alligator skin suitcase with relative ease and a hint of elegance. Her delicate fingers take pleasure in the worn leathery smoothness of its handle. She smiles a little.

"... a relic of a past era", she says softly, almost lovingly; "and once the cherished possession of my dear grandmother".

In her mind's eye, she glimpses the outlines of the imposing old lady's face. She recalls her grandmother's strong voice telling her that the suitcase had been brought home from the colonies. It was a gift for the old lady's own maternal grandmother. For five generations it had served the women of the family.

Abruptly, she remembers her present plight and glances around furtively as she steps confidently but cautiously along the pavement.

Her muscular left arm holds close to her breast her angelic looking young son. Her eyes meet his and she is almost overcome with his beauty. He's heavy for his age, but her arm is not aching. She's used to carrying him. He could walk himself; but not as quickly as she needs right now. He's just twenty-two months old. His name is Thomas, pronounced 'Toma'. It's an unusual name in this part of the world, but Maria and her family were well-educated and knew much about the world outside of their Basque-country homeland. The little boy smiles happily back at his mother, unaware of just how precarious life is and how close he may be to seeing his short time on earth brought to an end.

Maria's mind flits briefly to her unborn child, unaware that it is wide awake and attentive to all its mother's thoughts and feelings. The young mother imagines her unborn baby is sleeping peacefully. For a second her thoughts flash back to her maternal grandmother and to that distant era of fearless foreign exploration and places so far away.

"Not now!" she whispers sternly to herself. Her mind is racing. Everything had happened so fast since she woke that morning.

§

It is springtime, and it's 1939. It had been daylight for only a short time. The sun is low but already strong, and the far corners of the neat but rather dingy rooms they live in are brightened by shafts of sunlight streaming in through the windows. The light is misty with millions of tiny dust particles; though the faded almost nostalgic beauty of the scene is all but lost on the young mother. She is awake and busy tending to the needs of her infant son when she hears a gentle tap-tap-tapping on the solid front door. She freezes and the blood drains from her cheeks. For a brief few seconds she feels a deep emptiness in the pit of her stomach. Fear threatens to overcome her. Yet she has no choice but to answer.

No sooner was she handed the note with the words 'salir en seguida': 'Get Out. Right Now!' scribbled on it in Spanish – not in euskara, her native Basque tongue – than the messenger had disappeared. He was little more than a child. As Maria read the scrappy little note, she drew in a sharp breath. She felt a constriction in her throat as panic began to take hold.

"Stay calm. Breathe deeply" she told herself.

She bowed her head, as if in prayer, then spoke quietly.

"Holy Mary, Mother of Jesus, blessed and most merciful" she whispered, praying for the messenger's safety "keep from harm this young boy who has risked his life to warn us of danger".

Her prayer was in vain. She would never know it, but by the time the dreaded message had been delivered, the old family-friend who was Maria's would-be protector, was already suffering the agonies of torture and was near death. He died without a whisper. He did not betray her. And a similar fate awaited his grandson, the young messenger, on his return home later that morning. It was a dangerous time in a cruel world.

Maria knew she only had a few minutes to arrange her affairs and leave. She had no time to waste. But she must make sure that no sign of where she was going was left in the little apartment. She regained more self-control with each passing second as she quickly packed her few sparse belongings. It didn't take long.

She hurriedly donned her well-used navy and white floral cotton dress. Its slightly worn, double-stitched hem fell just below her slim suntanned knees and billowed out over her bulging belly – though she didn't look eight months pregnant. The dress was stylish in a traditional, even somewhat old-fashioned way – a little reminiscent of the carefree 'twenties. But she had few clothes to choose from now; so unlike her childhood.

She quickly adjusted the triangular shoulder pads of the comfortable summer dress; brushed her long auburn hair, its dark red lights shimmering in the morning sunbeams filtering through the bleached lace curtains. She then took up the modest, navy blue felt hat with its finely-woven, almost transparent dark blue veil and set it primly but firmly on her head.

Dressing carefully cost her precious seconds. But Maria knew that in sunny, slow-moving San Sebastian, a young woman with a too casual appearance out so early would likely draw undue attention to herself; especially on the still empty streets leading down to the waterfront. It wouldn't matter that she was a young mother with a babe-in-arms and another one heavy in her belly.

Little Thomas smiled sweetly at her as she quickly finished dressing her fair-haired infant son and prepared to move on to yet another safe house. This time it would be across the border, in France or *Frantzia* in euskara. At least, she would still be in the Basque-country – but on the free, French side of the border.

As she hurried with her tasks, she consciously recalled the addresses of several such safe houses and the passwords needed to obtain admission. She'd been given them discreetly in a dingy tapas bar several weeks ago and had meticulously committed them to memory. She'd done the same with the brief directions on how to find them, before gulping down all the grubby chits of paper on which they were scribbled. It seemed the best way to be sure they'd not be found.

Weeks had passed peacefully here in San Sebastian but now, all of a sudden, it was time to leave again; and quickly.

## Two

Maria and her young family slipped silently out of the faded, aging red-brick tenement house situated high up in the old town, near the top end of Calle San Juan. In euskara, the street was called *San Juan Kalea*, though since their defeat by the nationalists, local people tried to use Spanish rather than Basque names. She was sure that no-one had noticed their departure. No clue to her destination was left behind her. She had done this before. Feeling a little relieved, she headed quickly in the direction of the riverside bus terminal in downtown San Sebastian. The bus station was some distance away and out on the narrow streets of the old town, Maria moved inconspicuously with the controlled pace of an experienced fugitive. It was a role that didn't come naturally to her. She was an idealist and a dreamer. But she had no choice.

She felt a tinge of regret as she left the no-longer 'safe house' that had been her home for some weeks. The last two months of her pregnancy had been much calmer than the first six. The much-needed rest and sunshine had been a godsend for her. She'd been feeling healthy and almost at peace; the best she had felt since early autumn last year when her soon-to-be second child had been conceived. That was in the tiny seaside village of Celorio. She thought of the little village with fondness. She pictured it now; nestled in a cove on the coast. It was about half-way between San Sebastian and Santiago de Compostela at the far western end of the north coast of Spain. They went there in June '37, just a month before Thomas had been born and just before Bilbao fell to the nationalist forces. In Celorio they had lived safely for well over a year.

Later, on leaving Celorio, they had travelled eastward about two hundred kilometres back to Bilbao. But so much had changed there. It saddened her.

"Bilbao ... that wonderful old city" she thought.

**BEGINNINGS**  Gary Heilbronn

---

"... It had seen such greatness ... and now so much of it lying in ruins". The sadness entered her heart as she continued on her way. She recalled that in '36, Bilbao had been officially named as the capital of the Basques Autonomous State, that short-lived dream of all her people.

"Back then there had been hope..." she said almost choking on the words. "But almost three years have passed since then."

Now, that brief moment of celebration seemed like it was in another lifetime.

"That was before the war," she thought almost aloud, "and before the arrival of all those other fascists; the Germans and Italians with their aircraft and troops and their unstoppable engines of war. ... It was before the relentless persecution of so many people ... and not just the Basques; but all the others who supported the Republican cause."

Indeed, it was before she had lost Alberto ... but she could not yet speak those words; nor even bear to think them. A hint of the pain she felt creased her brow and her thoughts turned quickly quite bitter.

"No-one had been able to stop the fascists" she said under her breath, "...not even the International Brigade with its idealistic young volunteers. They'd come so bravely from so many parts of the world to help us; ... unlike the governments of the world's democracies."

She fought back tears as her bitterness turned to grief.

"And look at us now!"

"How is it that evil so easily overcomes 'good'?" she reflected sadly; and not for the first time.

Maria spoke to herself so much these days. She lived in her own thoughts. She had no friends, no adult company and certainly no confidantes. Even most of her family were gone.

She looks lovingly at Toma.

Her young son with the angel's face smiled generously up at her, but he couldn't understand her thoughts, even if she'd been able to express them clearly. Only the unborn one, still part of Maria's flesh and nurtured by her life's blood had heard her unspoken words and

BEGINNINGS  Gary Heilbronn

understood. But she did not share her mother's anguish. Nor did she share her pain. Such frail sentiments were not part of her nature.

Maria walked on.

"Thank God I still have my children": the young mother whispered with relief. It was as if the unborn one was already there, with her; and in a sense she was. Maria spoke half-aloud this time but to no-one in particular as she continued along the empty alleyway.

Unsurprisingly, her thoughts turned to the four thousand Basque children whose anxious parents had sent them off with hope but fearful heartache to what had seemed like safety in distant England. Maria had read in the newspaper that they had left from the Port of Santurse, Bilbao on the steamship "Habana". That was in May '37, after the bombing of Guernica and just before the fall of Bilbao. And others had been sent away since that time. No-one then imagined that many would end up staying so far away from their families for so long: seven long years and more, until what would soon be known as the Second World War had run its grisly course. Some would never return. There would be nothing for them to return to. Others had been sent to Mexico or to the Soviet Union and for decades would be forbidden to return.

In Maria's mind, the 26th of April 1937 was the day that her life as a fugitive had truly begun; and she could not forget it. It was the fateful day the Germans bombed nearby Guernica almost to oblivion. It was so unexpected and had such a devastating impact on the civilian population. It was the moment of fascist madness so soon afterwards immortalised on canvas by the artist, Pablo Picasso. His eight by four metres black and white painting depicting the horrors of war at Guernica was unveiled later that year at the Paris World's Fair's International Exposition. From that time onward, the hated nationalists and the even more feared pro-fascist, Falangist spies were everywhere.

Within weeks of Guernica's destruction, Bilbao came under attack. Alberto had fled with Maria, then heavily pregnant for the first time. They travelled westwards along the coast before finding refuge in the seaside village of Celorio. She remembered it so clearly. The little family had been in hiding since then. At first Maria had felt that it was a bit like a child's game, even though she already had her baby son to look after. He was her priority. More than a year passed while the focus of the war was elsewhere. But as the end of 1938 approached, the rapidly increasing reach of General Franco and the fascist forces meant that nowhere would be safe for Republicans, idealists and dissidents.

From the quiet sandy beaches of sleepy Celorio, Alberto had taken Maria, pregnant again, and young Thomas back to bustling Bilbao. It was where, as a newly married couple just a few years before, they'd spent hours upon hours in cafés and smoky bars in deep discussions with other young idealists and members of the various Basque Youth movements. The better-known was *Euzko Gaztedi*. It had annoyed Maria how its members seemed to have been forever in conflict with other youth movements and the Basque Nationalist Party itself. She didn't like conflict. But by the time of their return, the meetings had gone underground and Maria's main concern was survival.

She had felt fairly safe back in Bilbao with Alberto and little Thomas; at least for a while. But it wasn't long before she'd been forced to flee again, and this time without her beloved husband. Again she fled eastward; but just another hundred kilometres or so along the Cantabrian coast to her next hiding place in San Sebastian. There, she was almost within sight of the frontier; though the border with France and the gates to freedom would still be a bumpy bus-ride away.

By then it was early 1939. And things began to happen so quickly; too quickly for their impact to be properly absorbed by anyone, let alone a young mother with an infant son to occupy her time. First there was the military collapse of Barcelona, over on the east coast. There had been a valiant offensive struggle by the Republicans along the historic Rio Ebro that flows eastwards all the way from the Basque country in the north-west right across to the Mediterranean Sea, south of the Pyrenees Mountain range. But Barcelona had fallen to the nationalist forces on January 26. The fall of Madrid, far away to the south, followed a little later, on March 28. By April 1 of that same year – just four days later – the civil war came to an end, officially bringing peace to Spain.

Thinking of that date, she smiled grimly to herself.

"That so-called peace ..." she whispered. There was a quiet anger in her voice. "It had been the fascists' practical joke". Her lips tightened, turning the wry smile almost into a scowl. "Instead of finding peace at the end of the war, the persecution and executions only multiplied."

It seemed to Maria that her whole world had fallen apart. Everything had gone completely wrong. The Basque Autonomous State was no more, the fascists had won the war, executions and reprisals were endemic in Franco's Spain and the Basque people had not been spared. Alberto was gone and now she was here alone, in San Sebastian, pursued to the far reaches of her homeland, with fake 'official papers' and little money.

"But God willing, there is hope," she said aloud. There was some relief in her voice. "We're less than twenty kilometres from safety".

That safety was just over the border, in the south-west extremity of neighbouring France. The fashionable old cities of Biarritz and Bayonne were less than a few hours away, as was her desperate dream of sanctuary and maybe even a new life.

"Alberto's gone, forever." She sighed with the pain, finally being able to say it aloud.

"Have I not already paid a heavy enough price for some safety?"

Without thinking, her pace had quickened and she instantly knew it could attract unwanted attention.

"Wait. Slow down! Just take your time" she whispers to herself. For the moment she is still in mortal danger on the streets of sleepy, sun-drenched San Sebastian.

## Three

Maria had been born in December, 1914. It was the early days of the Great War in which Spain had thankfully remained neutral. All her young life had been spent in her beloved Basque country where she'd passed a sunny, carefree childhood and adolescence. That was followed by a few all too short and tumultuous years as a beautiful and passionate young woman. She married at twenty-one, just before the civil war began. And she'd always lived in this fertile, yet wild and isolated region at the eastern end of Spain's northern coastline; at the very corner of the vast triangle of waters known to the English as the Bay of Biscay.

As a child, Maria had been educated with great care. That was when her parents were alive and still wealthy. She had flourished under the guidance of private tutors and had been taught much about Spain's history and even its pre-history. She had learned of the many foreigners who'd passed through or invaded the Iberian Peninsula. There were the Phoenicians and their Carthaginian descendants; the Romans; Vandals; Visigoths and Moors. Later came the Christian fanatics. They exterminated the simple, pious Cathar people in the early thirteenth century Crusade against what they called the 'Albigensian heresy'; they welcomed in the Inquisitions and later fostered the nineteenth century conflict known as the Carlist Wars and more recently, the hated Fascists' dictatorship.

Secreted in San Sebastian, she found that her thoughts often turned to her own family and how she now viewed them in a different light. Her ancestors and her careful affluent upbringing had been unequivocally Basque, monarchist and fiercely Catholic. But were not these people the stalwart supporters of Franco's nationalist party? The people who now saw her as the enemy!

§

BEGINNINGS                                   Gary Heilbronn

Maria's path to the downtown bus station in San Sebastian led through the narrow streets of the old town and down past the port, before crossing the newer central district between the beach and the river. The city was called *Donostia* in euskara, the distinctive Basque language. As she walked, she thought about the old town. She recalled that it had been founded back in the twelfth century and was a thriving seaport since 1524. That was during the reign of Charles I of Spain; known more widely in Europe as Charles V or *Charles Quint*. He had even been crowned Holy Roman Emperor, like his namesake 'Charlemagne' back in 800 AD.

Her mind buzzed with these thoughts. It wasn't a bad thing, as it helped to mask the agonizing, almost debilitating fear hidden just below her outwardly composed exterior.

She looked around her; worried that she might be the subject of scrutiny. "I must be more careful!" Maria chastised herself quietly; "try to think of other things". Had other people been out on the streets of the old town so early that morning, they might well have noticed this heavily pregnant young woman, so pre-occupied by her thoughts and seemingly talking to herself, or perhaps to the infant she carried. Though in reality, it was her unborn child who took most notice as it listened to its mother's words and thoughts.

Maria knew she must take charge of her emotions. She did not want fear to overcome her. Her eyes looked ahead but she allowed her thoughts to go elsewhere.

She turned into Calle de 31 Augusto – in euskara, it was called *31 de Agosto Kalea* – and trod lightly but surely on down towards the port; her eyes taking in cautiously what she thought may well be her last sights of San Sebastian.

The old town had been built on a sandy isthmus connecting the mainland with a rocky outcrop, called Monte Urgull. It was just uphill to her right. It was where the great sixteenth century fortress: Castillo de Santa Cruz de la Mota had once stood. Now even its ruins were all but gone.

"Time passes so quickly": she murmured to herself, "and so much changes ... but is it only on the surface?" she wondered aloud.

**BEGINNINGS**  Gary Heilbronn

She recalled that the whole city had been rebuilt after being destroyed in the great fire of 1813. It had been ignited by an explosion following a barrage of cannon fire from the English and Portuguese troops under the command of the Duke of Wellington. They were there to oust the occupying French forces during the siege of San Sebastian in July and August of the same year. The victorious troops had then ransacked and burned the city.

"Only the street I now walk on had escaped destruction. ... Was that a good omen?" she wondered.

She immediately scolded herself for such a silly thought.

Her mind turned again to San Sebastian's chequered past.

By the late eighteen hundreds the city had become the summer residence for the Bourbons, the newly-restored Spanish royal family ... with, and she smiled at her old history tutor's words: 'their rather suspect and ambiguous English connections'. Indeed, Queen Maria Cristina had used the designs of an English architect to build the Miramar Palace during the reign of the Bourbons. It still stood down at the other end of the main beach. In the late eighteen and early nineteen hundreds, San Sebastian was a fashionable seaside resort attracting visitors from all over Europe.

"But that was then and now is now" she reflected with a sudden change of perspective, "in these dark days, no elegant and wealthy foreigners visit this town ... only displaced people and refugees. Not even Spanish families take seaside holidays here now; not since this horrendous war has divided communities and families alike". Indeed, her own family had broken apart and lost everything. Now all but her were dead.

Maria's thoughts of San Sebastian's past and those rather genteel nineteenth century times began slowly to subside as she pressed on, though not so quickly as to draw attention to herself.

She was calmer now. Yet the bus station was still a distance away and it would still help if she could to try to take her mind off her almost desperate situation. She glanced around her at the neat houses that crowded together along the street as she turned into Calle Campana – *Campanario Kalea* in euskara – leading from the church bell tower down parallel to the port.

# BEGINNINGS

The narrow, normally spotless alleys of San Sebastian's old town were a refuge for Maria; or at least they had been until now. It had always pleased her to see how the residents there diligently cared for their own little section of sidewalk and gutters. They were swept clean and either washed by regular rain or, in its absence, by sprinkling about the precious water brought in clay pots from the nearest fountain. Not all the people living in the old town had water supplies piped to their houses.

Even this early in the morning, the street corners were clean and bathed in warm sunlight, though shadows still partly hid the comings and goings of the few people out and about on those less frequented cobblestone alleyways and lanes of old town Donostia.

# Four

Maria walked on towards the port. Just down the hill, the sea was like crystal, calm and sparkling in the morning sun. Her plan was to skirt along the beachfront past the *Hotel de Londres y de Inglaterra*, then turn inland zigzagging her way in the direction of the Maria Cristina Bridge that spanned the Urumea River. It was a longer, but safer route at this time of the morning.

Although it was still early, she could see a few foreigners, or at least they appeared to be foreigners, strolling across the shimmering white sands of La Concha, the city's vast and sandy main beach. One or two were wearing those fashionable dull-white canvas shoes. Others sported rougher locally-made leather sandals, carelessly flipping streams of fine white sand rhythmically up behind them as they walked. Eventually and inevitably, their casual paths reached the old port at the north-eastern end of the beach. They passed by several local fishermen; their heavily weather-beaten faces bent in concentration over the worn, salt-stiffened fishing nets that they never seemed to finish mending. The old men sneered and joked in euskara about the crazy unwelcome foreigners as each of them passed affably by.

Most visitors and short-term residents, just like the better dressed tourists of earlier years, gullibly took the gapped-toothed grins of these aging mariners to be jovial and friendly. They smiled back foolishly, serving only to deepen the hatred harboured by these often cruel old men. In more recent times, some of the foreigners passing through had grown more wary of the old fishermen. A few had learned to trust no-one after having fought with the International Brigade; that loosely knit coalition of loyalists, communists, adventurers and idealists that had supported the Republicans. It counted amongst its numbers, committed young men such as Ernest Hemingway and George Orwell.

Maria too, knew the various portside inhabitants for what they were. She too had learned to be suspicious. Over the past weeks, many had eyed her malevolently as she strolled along the port and she knew that for a few pesetas or even just to curry favour with their new masters, most would betray her and her young family – even her unborn child – to her feared and hated enemies.

"There are those amongst them" she imagined vividly, "who looked so cruel that they'd violate even a pregnant woman with pleasure and without so much as a thought use their highly sharpened knives to gut her young body like some still flapping fish." She shivered. What horrific thoughts were rising in her consciousness?

"But these are such cruel times" she sighed.

Maria again felt the cold emptiness of fear in her breast as she trod on, willing herself to be as invisible as she could to the increasing number of eyes around her.

Her unborn child sensed its mother's quickened heartbeat; the clammy stabs of fear and intermittent surges of adrenalin as her anxiety rose and fell. It touched a familiar chord in vague but vivid memories buried deeply in her blood and bones; perhaps not all the way back to their ancient roots, but still far, far into the past.

In her ageless mind, and it was not an empty vessel as some might suppose, the unborn babe saw or imagined things – or did she 'remember' them – and in so much more detail and from a perspective so different to that of her mother. In those days past, survival was also an ever-present concern. At least that was how she remembered it.

Her enemies had been many. There were the relentless armies of the Carthaginian conquerors and the legions of Roman invaders who by the first century BC had imposed, from afar, their well-organized rule over most of the Iberian Peninsula. She felt in her bones the civilized cruelty of the Roman administrators, rather than having learned of it from tutors and books as her mother had. And later, but was it that much later ... in the fourth and fifth centuries, it was the tribes of Vandals, Alains, Sueves and their ruthless henchmen and followers who had ridden down from the north-east to conquer, pillage and slaughter all who stood in their way. They were the enemy that spread across the peninsula like a plague.

Yet before long, they in their turn were pursued and ousted leaving only a few remaining Suevi tribesmen in the far north-west, around the Galician coastal foothills and low mountains to the west of the Basque homeland. This time it was the Arian Visigoths who invaded. They were led by King Euric to whom Rome ceded control of a vast empire in Western Europe in return for ridding a distracted Roman Empire of its enemies. Euric established a mini-kingdom with Tolosa – or as it was later known, Toulouse – as its capital; and it stretched from the Loire river valley in the middle of Gaul down to Gibraltar in the far south of the Iberian Peninsula. But after King Clovis of Gaul defeated Euric's great-grandson, the young Visigoth King Alaric II in 507 AD, the Goths' days too were numbered. Within a century those who remained had forgone their heretic Arian beliefs and blended in with the locals.

After a time, the unborn child's thoughts or, more accurately, this stream of semi-conscious images that she experienced, turned slowly on to the next set of invaders of the fertile Iberian Peninsula. Once again, they came from the south. It was the turn of the Moors, whose grand civilization and gilded culture, accompanied as it was by a casual almost unintended violence, dominated much of Spain. They remained until the 12th century or so, and at its apogee, their rule briefly extended into the southern part of Gaul where traces of Sarasin architecture remained. Then, as their civilization finally decayed in the early centuries of the second millennium, they were chased away by the same Catholic Kings who brought the darkness and torture of the Spanish Inquisition to the land.

The unborn child's pulse-rate rose and took several moments to subside before the stream of images continued. They became gradually less vivid. Soon they petered out and her heart calmed.

"The futile comings and goings of great empires... and how many lives had passed?" the unborn babe wondered in a dream. She could not articulate these thoughts, but the long lost images of those times trickled back into and out of her semi-consciousness, as her mother approached the bus station.

"But never" the unborn child felt more than thought, "never did any of these invaders conquer my homeland." With those words, she felt with a pride that echoed her mother's own feelings.

There was in her heart, a subtle awareness of having travelled the length and breadth of the land over more generations than could be said and having fought many enemies. The unborn child's heartbeat steadied with a knowledge locked in its bones, of having endured and survived the hardships and horrors of those times; of having battled with numerous oppressors and experienced both victories and defeats during so many centuries of violence and aggression.

## Five

The passenger bus destined for the Spanish-French border with a connecting service on to Bayonne was scheduled to depart at 8.40am. Buses often left late but Maria had to make sure she was on board. It was her last chance to escape and she knew it.

Since the previous year she had been continually on the run, going from safe house to safe house every few days. And it was during that difficult time after they had returned to Bilbao that real disaster had struck. That was before she found a welcome respite in the old town of San Sebastian. On a cold evening in late February, just a few months ago, she was making her way to meet her young husband. He was to be waiting in front of Bilbao's fourteenth century Gothic Church of Santiago. She was carrying little Tomas in her arms when what she saw stopped her in her tracks. There was a commotion up ahead. Fortunately, she was still at a safe distance.

"What's going on?" she had wondered. And then a terrifying emptiness had invaded her gut.

For several seconds, she stood and watched in shock as Alberto was grabbed and searched by Guardia troops. They then threw him roughly into the back of an army truck. He had been taken away to prison and God only knew what fate. Though trembling with fear, she could not stop herself going to Guardia headquarters. They denied they even knew of her husband's existence. What more could she do? Once again, there must have been a betrayal. She did not know who it was and didn't care then or now. What good would it do to know?

She broke off the memory of that horrible moment.

"All that matters now" she thought, steeling her resolve, "is to reach the bus terminal and board the bus destined for the border and Bayonne. ... Then, I must talk my way through Franco's frontier police at the Hondarribia-Hendaye border crossing".

She knew that the local French immigration police were not a concern. She'd been told that they would allow her to cross to their side even without the correct papers, provided she spoke to them in euskara. And she knew her Basque mother-tongue well enough.

With a silent sigh of relief, Maria arrived at the small makeshift bus terminal; and in good time. It was on the opposite side of the river to the railway station – *la estación de Amara*, and a little nearer to the ocean. The bus terminal was virtually empty. She moved carefully but with a confident step across the dusty waiting room, betraying none of the fear festering in her heart, and stopped in front of the single dingy ticket counter. The floor around was littered with ticket stubs and grubby papers thrown away by travellers the evening before.

She spoke quietly through the steel mesh to the unfriendly attendant. He was unshaven and stunk of garlic. Cash and a single one-way ticket changed hands. Maria then sat silently in the shadows to await the departure of the Bayonne-bound bus. It was a tense but uneventful wait and the unborn one had easily fallen back into unconsciousness, sleeping peacefully through this time. Her big brother sat quietly beside his young mother on the hard wooden bench. He was a well-behaved child.

Within the half hour, Maria was aboard the bus with her young son sitting on her lap and her battered suitcase placed on the seat beside her.

"... best discourage any fellow passengers and their conversation," she said silently to herself.

It hardly mattered as there were so few passengers anyway.

Maria stared absently through the closed, almost opaque and dust-caked window as the ancient, battered Mercedes-Benz bus rumbled along the road towards the north-east. The frontier was only a few dozen kilometres away and the tension mounted in her bones as she rehearsed her story, first in perfect Castilian for the Franco authorities and then in euskara for the French. That done, she sat back and breathed in regularly, slowly, trying to calm her nerves. She thought again of Alberto, the father of her son and her as yet unborn child. Maria knew instinctively it would be a daughter. She would be called Anna-Maria after Maria's own grandmother.

If only she could believe that Alberto was still alive. Then there would be some hope that Anna-Maria would know her father. But she'd heard so many stories of what happened to the young men seized like Alberto – taken off the streets, from corner cafés and bars and even from their beds. Few had been seen again and those that had, recounted chilling tales of their capture and mistreatment.

She had been told too, of the fearful screams that people had heard coming from many of the Guardia barracks in the depths of the night and the rumble of military trucks through the towns in the early hours of the morning. There were rumours of mass burial grounds on the outskirts of many towns and cities but most chose not to believe them. Maria prayed that Alberto had not ended his days in such a place; with no grave nor tombstone to bear witness to his short, passionate and loving life.

Anna – she now knows her name – senses her mother's sadness and despair; but those sentiments seem to just wash off her. They are not hers and somehow lack the force to touch her inner being; and she knows instinctively how much stronger she is than her mother. She feels her mother's sadness and despair, but it is no more than a fine film over the granite-like surface of her ageless soul.

## AMBUSH ON THE BORDER

*Spanish-French Border near Biarritz, May 1939*

## Map of the Border near Bayonne

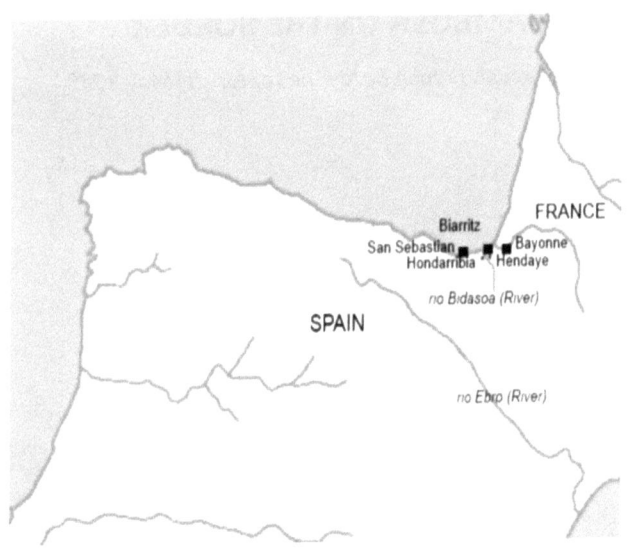

## Six

Maria took out a delicate gilt-edged pocket-watch from her sensible handbag and peered intently at its tiny face. She did it more to avoid looking elsewhere than out of any real interest in the time or in the antique time-piece itself. Over an hour and twenty minutes had elapsed by the time the Bayonne-bound bus slowly ground to a halt at the border. It quickly began to disgorge its bedraggled group of thirteen passengers at the bus company's Spanish-side terminus somewhat to the south and outside of the township of Hondarribia. The bus had stopped a lot along the way and the trip had been very slow. The delays only intensified the stress Maria was feeling.

The Hondarribia bus terminus had been built haphazardly just a few metres from the barbed-wire encased guardhouse on the edge of Spanish frontier. It was some thirty or forty metres from a neat but similarly dusty brownstone building clearly visible across the metal-frame bridge at the entrance to the French border town of Hendaye.

A cold chill crept down Maria's spine when she saw near the guardhouse, the pair of young and brutish looking men belonging to the Guardia Civil. Half of the Guardia Civil police forces had been loyal to the Franco nationalist forces during the Civil War and those loyal to the Republic were called the Guardia *Nacional Republicana*. But now there was just one Guardia. These Guardia soldiers were lounging around a few metres behind a short, more smartly dressed immigration official. Gleaming pointed bayonets were fixed into sockets on the barrels of their aging manual-reload Lee-Enfield rifles. The thought flashed through Maria's mind that the bayonet was a Basque weapon. It had been invented in the mid seventeenth century in the town of Bayonne, her hoped-for destination not so far from the border.

A shiver of fear shot through her as her eyes moved across to a leathery-faced young officer standing several paces further away. He stood there, cleaning his fingernails with a short blade dagger.

Maria's eyes were drawn to the dagger's almost feminine beauty; its slightly curved double edged and subtly gleaming bronzed blade, no more than ten or twelve centimetres from its point to a thick base. She could see part of the base. It was inlaid with gems on either side, and flanked by an ornate protective bar just above what seemed to be a walnut and gold-plated handle all but hidden within an unexpectedly delicate hand. It was a very uncommon piece; but strangely familiar.

Momentarily entranced, Maria found her mind racing off to another time and place. But on this occasion it was not her conscious mind. As her mind's eye penetrated the mist, she thought she saw that same blade plunging deep into the breast of a dark, garishly dressed Arab-looking official. It was gripped tightly by a woman with a vaguely familiar face; a young powerfully built dark-haired woman. A fierce commitment flashed in her deep angry eyes as she was dragged away by palace guards, leaving behind the dagger planted in her enemy's chest. Maria felt a deep sense of loss. Was it for the dagger? She'd no idea where the vision came from or why she felt that way – an over-elaborate feeling of déjà vu perhaps?

At that instant, she became aware that the leathery-faced officer had raised his eyes slightly from his mundane task and was returning her stare.

"Madre Dios", she gasped. She had looked at him for too long. The blood drained from her cheeks and her heart stopped beating for what seemed to be an eternity as fear and loathing wrenched and tore at her gut. She felt nausea almost overcome her as if she could foresee the pain and heartache to come, or, perhaps, she relived it from a time hidden deep in her past.

Maria somehow found the strength to stand up from the bus seat. She gathered her young child and battered suitcase, walked the few paces to the doorway and stepped hesitantly down from the bus. She was last to descend and forced her eyes toward the dusty street directly ahead of her, avoiding the cold regard of the leathery-faced officer. She strode purposefully towards the small wooden cabinet that housed the immigration official on the Spanish side of the border.

# BEGINNINGS    Gary Heilbronn

It was less than a minute or two's walk from there to the more elaborate stone structure on the French side of the frontier and freedom. In her mind, she quickly went over once again the story she would tell. She was just going to visit family and friends for a few days. She had been told that the lazy officials at this border post rarely bothered travellers and if they did delay you, a hundred peseta note would speed you on your way. Maria had the note ready in her hand along with the somewhat tattered and creased documents proving she was born Dominique Crasson, daughter of Elodie and Didier Crasson, horticulturists and residents of Bayonne.

The false papers had been given to her several weeks beforehand in a dingy little tapas bar in Bilbao. Her contact was an unnamed member of a cell of Basque republican sympathizers and activists. He had also slipped to her the details of those safe houses that she had also committed to memory. She'd later heard that the cell had been exposed and the burned and mutilated bodies of its members had been found dumped on the outskirts of the city. She could not even remember their faces. But wasn't that what always happened after people die, even when you lose a loved one.

"Maybe even more so," she thought. "Gradually, the precise details and lines of their appearances fade and disappear. Try as you will, the image just drifts deeper into the haze and only returns for a momentary glimpse then fades again."

She tries to remember the tender expression on Alberto's' face. She knows it is his face that she has conjured up and holds persistently in her mind but the features are unclear. She lowers her gaze to chance a glance at the angelic face of the little boy-child in her arms. Thomas' bright blue eyes gleam back at her. He does not smile. He senses his mother's tension.

## Seven

In less than a minute Maria is standing at the immigration post. She looks up into the heavily tanned and unshaven face of a middle-aged man. He is dressed in a neat but dusty immigration uniform and looks at her with bored eyes. She mouths the words earlier committed to memory and holds out her papers. The man is not that tall and so she shrinks herself to seem smaller than him. He looks from her papers to her face sensing her tension. He shrugs. Tension is common on the faces of ordinary people having dealings with government officials in these dangerous days. Seconds pass. He looks at her papers again.

The immigration officer smiles slyly, inwardly relishing that little bit of power he exercises daily over the lives of his fellow man and particularly the women. As he hesitates, Maria reaches over. She carefully takes hold of the top of the papers and gently moving her index finger and thumb, slides the hidden hundred peseta note so that its edges show out the side underneath her documents. A slight grin creases the corners of the man's mouth as he gestures with a nod that she can pass, permitting in a well-practised way, her documents to slip from his hand while deftly retaining the banknote.

Maria resists the impulse to surge forward and starts to advance at a careful pace across the bridge, her heart pounding.

She had taken several purposeful steps and was beginning to breathe more slowly when she hears a slightly raised voice call out.

"Aguarde usted! ... Arretez s'il vous plait" ...the words spoken much too politely in both Spanish and in French, but with an undertone of wry mischievous humour or was it just plain meanness; commanding someone – "was it me" she thought, "it must be" – to please stop. "Please stop, he says!"

The words had come from the thin twisted lips of the officer with the ornate knife. And now he was approaching her quickly from behind, accompanied by a large nasty-looking soldier carrying a bayoneted rifle. Maria's mind raced.

# BEGINNINGS                                    Gary Heilbronn

"Can I pretend that he's calling out to someone else?" she thought. But there was no-one nearby. She kept walking. They were now at least fifteen metres behind her and she was already on her way to the French immigration post on the other side of the bridge and certain safety.

"Could I outrun them? Should I even try?" she thought almost hysterically.

Many eyes were now turned towards her. Once half way across the bridge the French would certainly come to her aid, but until then she is still in Spanish territory.

All of a sudden, she saw that she was running, clumsily, as if in slow motion; as if in a dream. But heavily pregnant and carrying a small child and a suitcase, she is no match for her pursuers.

They are upon her little more than a metre before she can reach the middle of the bridge and the possibility of help from the French officials. The officer seizes her left arm from behind, spinning her around and loosening her hold on Thomas. Maria, losing her balance, begins to fall towards the ground as the heavy-set soldier's rifle butt surges down upon her, striking a glancing blow on her right shoulder and landing with a sickening thud on the side of her small son's soft skull ending his brief life in that instant.

The boy's warm blood splatters in dark red spots and sprinkles over her fading navy and white floral cotton dress as a short shallow cry of heartfelt desperation and pain wrenches from her throat. For a moment the Guardia soldier and the officer with the knife seem to be struck mute and immobile by the unexpected sight before them. The consequences of their impulsive acts had not been envisaged. Time seems to stand still. Though barely a second or two had passed, a lifetime of maternal agony and grief and self-reproach plays itself out in Maria's mind.

"Thwwack!"

The eternal moment was cut short by the crack of a gunshot followed immediately by the grunt of the rifle-wielding soldier as the unseen bullet strikes his back and rips through his uniform penetrating the chest cavity, tearing through lung and heart tissue before bursting through his breast and ricocheting off one of the steel struts supporting the metal bridge. Maria imagined she saw, or did she really see, the distorted lead slug leaving the soldier's body, gleaming, twisted but darkly stained with his life's blood and tinged with fragments of muscle from his heart and lungs.

He had barely started to crumple to the ground before the second round rang out. It grazes the right side of the Guardia officer's head and, with blood beginning to trickle from a scratch on his temple, sends him reeling in a slow circular motion back towards the Spanish immigration post where the middle-aged dusty official stands gap-jawed. For several seconds, the immigration official looks as if he is rooted to the spot before he dives for cover behind the building. The shots had obviously come from the Spanish side of the border; but from where? Anything else would give rise to an international incident. And shootings were common in a Spain so recently ravaged by a bitter civil war.

In the confusion and sudden excitement of the Guardia and immigration officials, no-one seemed to notice the two French soldiers sprint to the middle of the bridge and half carry and half drag a numbed and inert Maria, still clutching her suitcase and the lifeless and bloodied body of her tiny son, into French territory and back towards the guardhouse behind the immigration control point.

As they lie there, small crowd gathered quietly around the crumpled forms of Maria and Thomas, but there is mayhem on the Spanish side of the border. Soldiers shout orders at each other and scan the surrounding buildings and riverbank, waiting for another shot to be taken.

A priest in a dusty frockcoat had run to the fallen guardsman and was crouching down whispering the last rites over the blood-soaked, bloated body. Where had he come from? Had he been on the bus as well? Further back and now on his knees, a little groggy and bleeding steadily from his wound, the leathery-faced officer's dark eyes burns with fury and pain. He is still clearly in the land of the living but he feels deeply humiliated by this woman and somehow knows that this is not the first time; and that this burgeoning hatred of her has forever been his religion.

# Eight

A man who looked to be in his mid-forties moved stealthily through the dense undergrowth along the steep southern bank of the Bidasoa River quickly putting as much distance as possible between himself and the scene of the shooting at the metal bridge. His name was Alphonso Zuidilla. He was accompanied by his seven-year old son Yann, who shadowed his every step. His left hand gripped his aging single-shot, bolt action rifle, though today, it had served its purpose well enough. He had not intended to engage the enemy on this occasion but events had taken their own course. His primary mission had been observation and reconnaissance. That was his daily brief. It had become more difficult over time as it seemed that more and more of his countrymen and women were fleeing into France as refugees.

He would likely have joined them in their flight had he known that within the next several months as many as half a million Basques, Catalans, Republican fighters and the foreigners who had fought alongside them in the International Brigade would make their way across the border to France. They'd escape either over the mountains or through one or another of the border control points along the ragged Spanish-French frontier that stretched all the way from the Mediterranean Sea in the east to the Atlantic Ocean in the west.

But it was perhaps better that he did not know about the coming exodus, as large numbers of those escapees, including his wife and young son, would soon find themselves exiled and in deplorable conditions in hastily built internment camps across the border. There they would suffer and starve until, if they had the chance, fortune turned in their favour and they would be released. Others were not so lucky. Their hardships continued throughout the long years of the Second World War in the company of Jews, gypsies, dissidents and others who the Nazi occupiers considered to be undesirables. Many people were sent to these camps as 'first ports of call' before being

BEGINNINGS                                    Gary Heilbronn

train-loaded to labour or extermination camps back in Spain, in Germany and in Eastern Europe.

Zuidilla swore under his breath as he and his young son hastily retreated away from their hiding place near the old bridge, hunching their bodies to be closer to the ground and slipping quickly from one bit of camouflage to the next. He was furious that he had put his son in unnecessary danger, though he had known almost from the moment that the young pregnant woman started to run across the bridge that her destiny was in his hands.

"What else could I do?" he asked himself in desperation, as he scrambled along the riverbank.

He knew that the woman could expect no mercy from that Guardia officer and his men. He had seen them in action before. A pretty young woman like that, even though heavily pregnant, would have been whisked away and secreted in the barracks for the eventual enjoyment of the officers then passed on to the enlisted men until they tired of her and she disappeared quietly and completely. Nor should he or his son expect anything other than torture and mistreatment if they were to be caught by their enemy.

And here he was, shooting the enemy as if the war was still on. But in a sense it was still on. Republican sympathizers were still being hunted down, executed or persecuted despite all the talk of reconciliation, fair treatment and the freeing and rehabilitation of war prisoners. Yes, the war was supposedly over, but even if that was true, it wouldn't have mattered. War prisoners, ex-soldiers and even non-combatants who did not support the victorious nationalists could expect only persecution, torture and an unhappy death at the hands of the fascists.

"It had not been like that after the Great War" he thought aloud, "war prisoners went home when it was over". Spain had of course been neutral in that war but had played an important role in facilitating communications between prisoners of war and their families.

"This is not how it's supposed to be!" he complained bitterly.

Alphonso was not an educated man but he had heard talk of the Geneva Convention and the rights of prisoners of war to humane treatment. On those rare occasions when leaders of the International Brigade had visited his sector, he heard them discussing it with the foreign intellectuals and communists accompanying them. It seemed that this supposedly esteemed legal document was barely worth the paper it was written on, at least insofar as the victors and vanquished in the Spanish civil war were concerned.

Now that he and his son were well out of sight of the bridge Alphonso slowed down so they could rest for a bit. He crouched down beside Yann who was breathing heavily from the exertion.

"What a joke is this Geneva Convention that is supposed to protect us!" he whispered bitterly to his son. The boy really had little idea what he was talking about but he could see the effect it was having on his much-loved father.

"There's a world of difference" Alphonso said, "between the words of the politicians and lawyers in their meetings and what happens on the field of battle!" Alphonso turned to the side and spat; then went on. "They tell you one thing and then do another."

After a couple of seconds, the father and son resumed their escape alongside the riverbed towards safety.

Of course, Yann did not reply to his father's comments about the failure of the Geneva Conventions to protect soldiers in the civil war. Indeed he did not really understand what his father was talking about. However, in his mind, seeds were being planted that would later bear fruit. On that day and in purely practical terms, the lacunae in the Geneva Conventions' protections for combatants and non-combatants were all too clear to Alphonso. And it was perhaps ironic that in the not so distant future, his son would come to scrutinize every word of these conventions closely and in detail in the course of his studies in Paris after the end of the next world war that would transform all of Europe. But that would be in the future.

Alphonso, would not himself live to know it, but before the end of the next decade, despite or perhaps because of the several years of war horrors that lay ahead, a new Geneva Convention of 1949 would replace the three earlier documents and would extend, not only to captured and injured soldiers but also to civilians, like him, all these wartime protections that prohibited murder, torture, hostage-taking and any extra-judicial sentencing and executions – at least in theory! Nor would he ever know of the 1949 Geneva Convention's eventual adoption by almost every nation, though still some of the stark disparities he saw then, in 1939, between the law of nations and practical realities of armed conflict and grubby politics would remain and haunt humanity for generations to come.

## Nine

As Alphonso and Yann rushed to escape from the scene of the shootings at the old metal border bridge near the Hendaye-Hondarribia border, what would lie ahead of them was beyond their imaginations. As was the possibility that one day, years in the future, the paths of some of the actors in this brief scenario at a far-flung outpost on the Spanish-French border might again cross and change the course of all their lives.

The pair's escape route took them eastward along the rugged southern banks of the Bidasoa River. The river flowed slowly in the opposite direction to their flight. It spread around the barren *Isla Santiagoaurra* and the more fertile *Isla Iru Kanale* before broadening into the Bay of *Txingudi* and then following its course out into the vast Bay of Biscay. Luckily, the planned construction of the airport to the north of both the old metal bridge and railway line on the Spanish side of the smaller bay had been suspended several years beforehand and there was no activity and few buildings around the river. There was just dense undergrowth with occasional clearings and both father and son knew the terrain like the backs of their hands.

They had quickly moved well clear of that desperate border post by the time the Guardia soldiers stationed there had even thought about giving chase.

§

That night, Alphonso sat in silence at the family dinner table after they had all finished eating. His mind returned to what would have happened if he and Yann had been captured that day. He was horrified at the danger he had put his son in. He thought again of the Geneva Conventions and what those intellectuals and leftists had said about it. What he had learned from their discussions had surprised him. He went through it all again in his mind. It seemed that the 'Geneva Convention' was in fact a series of international law agreements, but he didn't know if Spain had signed up to them or not. The agreements set out legal principles designed to protect wounded combatants as well as civilians in times of conflict. They also did things like establish the International Red Cross –

"... how wonderful the Red Cross is!" he said half-aloud, startling his young son who was reading in silence, seated beside his father.

"Yann..." He spoke softly, looking intently at his son. "You know I cursed a thing called the 'Geneva Convention', when we were out today".

Alphonso did not want to say too much about what had happened earlier in the day; certainly not in front of his wife. He was of another generation; some years older than his wife and he spoke rather formally, especially to his children.

"But it is important. And I'm told" he continued, "that the inspiration for the Geneva Convention came from the suffering of wounded soldiers on the battlefields in northern Italy; that was during the Battle of Solferino in June 1859." He paused.

"The first Convention was agreed in 1864 and was to provide protection for sick and wounded soldiers on the battlefield. The next Convention of 1868 extended that protection to sailors wounded in battles at sea." Alphonso looked at his son. The boy did not reply but his father could see that he was listening. So he spoke again.

"But it was not until six decades later, after the Great War and millions of casualties, that the League of Red Cross and Red Crescent Societies were founded in Paris. That was just twenty years ago, in 1919. Wounded soldiers of course need assistance from doctors and nurses without them all being subjected to military attack and it is the Red Cross and Red Crescent that were supposed to provide it."

He went on.

"The last Geneva Convention was in 1929." Alphonso had himself read in the newspapers about the third and most recent version of the Convention. "It declared that prisoners of war were not to be regarded as criminals, but should be treated humanely and released when the war is over. They should be freed and able to go home to their own countries after the end of the war." He grimaced and would have spat on the ground had he not been inside the house. "But that hasn't happened here in Spain."

Alphonso paused, looking down at the table. Indeed, the civil war in Spain had been no ordinary war where professional armies from different countries faced each other in battle. He spoke again.

"It's crazy, when you think about it," he said. "Spain's present troubles are not even 'a war' under the Geneva Conventions, but an internal, civil dispute. So these rules don't apply."

He spoke just audibly with a cynical smile; more like a scowl.

Yann just looked at him.

"But what happened here is not so different to so many of the wars that occurred in the past!" he said.

"There were armies and there were battles. Yes, there was also guerrilla activity. And it was all fuelled by personal and class hatreds and flavoured by a heavy dose of religious fervour. It sounds like most wars to me," he said barely restraining himself from spitting the bitter taste from his mouth.

Yann listened but said nothing. He was just a boy and his destiny was yet to unfold, but his involvement in the escape of Maria and his father's criticisms of the Geneva Conventions set the scene for the roles he was yet to play in the unravelling of all these events.

§

The lives of Alphonso, Yann and the wounded and deceased Guardia soldiers were forever changed by the events on this day, as were those of little Thomas, Maria and her unborn daughter. But to the other soldiers, the shots that had been fired were little more than another banal and futile act of terrorism by the vanquished Republicans and no further thought was given to Maria and her son.

Though there was an exception: the officer with a smouldering hatred in his deep dark eyes and an unusual, ornate dagger tucked into his belt. He had stood there, looking across the border, glaring at the distraught and crumpled object of his hatred, his soul too deeply scarred to forget what he perceived as yet another humiliation; a humiliation that demanded a terrible vengeance.

# PALAEOLITHIC VENGEANCE

*Altamira, Cantabrian Mountains, North Coast of Spain,
circa 10,000 BC*

## Map of Cantabrian Mountains

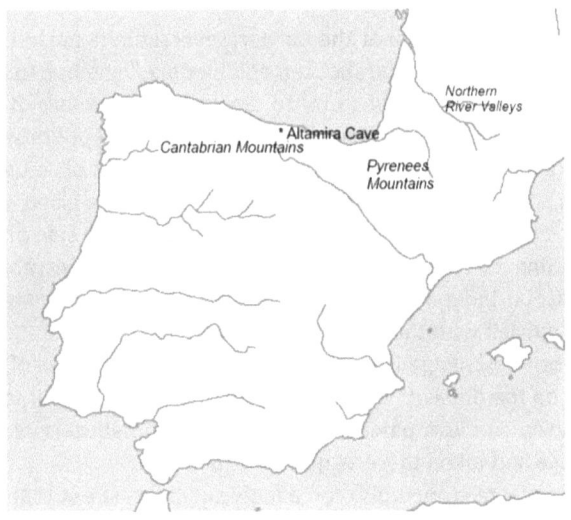

## Ten

After the brutal incident at the border, several hours passed in a waking dream for Maria. Still shocked and bloodied, she had fought through her grief and despair to try to remember the details of her safe-house destination and to communicate them surreptitiously to her rescuers on the bridge. With the increasing exodus of refugees from Spain, it was usual for there to be sympathizers allied with different social and political groups waiting on the French side of the border crossing; to contact new arrivals. That day was no exception and the Basque independence contact pressed in close to Maria, identifying himself with the usual words and signs.

After a brief exchange in euskara, Maria gave the address of the safe house on the outskirts of Bayonne, and though it was still some distance away, she was passed over to other sympathizers of the Basque cause and taken there as quickly as possible.

It was in a large stone house on a leafy suburban street that she now found herself. The distraught and pregnant young woman had been greeted kindly by a short, slim old lady with a tanned face, much wrinkled by exposure to the sun. The old lady called herself Jeanne and she was dressed humbly in a peasant's work clothes. She whispered that she was a friend and helped Maria to a room at the back of the building where she could rest.

Maria was trembling and sweating profusely. Her tiny son, pale and cold, wrapped now in a blood-stained blanket, was still in her arms. His life force was long gone; forever.

Maria had been brought up in the Catholic faith and although she had remained rather religious, she rarely entered a church these days especially as they were almost always under covert surveillance by the fascists. She believed her son's innocent soul was now in heaven with her own parents and the little boy's father, her cherished Alberto. It was precious little comfort but it was all she had, apart from the child-to-be waiting quietly in her belly.

BEGINNINGS                                    Gary Heilbronn

The unborn one, unseen and a little neglected of late, passed those numbing hours in a different manner; a manner that Maria could have not even imagined. Though she lay motionless in her mother's womb, her excited little mind raced.

Back on the bridge she could not herself see what was happening but had sensed the presence of extreme danger, heard the muffled sounds of violence and perceived an ancient image of the cruel mouth and cold eyes just like those now residing in the visage of the young Guardia officer. It was an image passed down through time and it gave her a shock that she had not been prepared for. Moments later, the unborn one felt her heartbeat slow and subside as her mind leapt back almost a dozen millennia.

§

*End of the Upper Palaeolithic Era, 10,000 BC;*
North Coast of Spain

She was elsewhere yet in a strangely familiar place that much later her mother would know as the nearby Cantabrian Mountains, on the sunset edge of the Basque country, at the eastern end of the north coast of Spain. She sat there on her haunches at the entrance to a cave on a rocky hillside, strenuously rubbing the edge of a sharp angular stone against another flat, dense granity one. There were hills in the distance behind which the sun would soon dip in a fierce glow of gold and orange, opening a door to the many fearful sounds and other uncertainties of the night. But for the moment, the warming rays of the late afternoon sun shone through to her place at the cave's entrance. She could feel the agreeable sensation on her shoulders, although her matted reddish-brown hair was impenetrable to its warmth. There had been rain earlier in the day. Lots of it and the fresh smells of abundant springtime vegetation were everywhere.

She was strong and no longer a little child reliant on her mother. She had lived for almost twelve summers and had quickly learned how to survive and live off the land. Her mother and her mother's man called her "Uuna", but only occasionally did other members of the group speak directly to her even though she was now considered

BEGINNINGS                                          Gary Heilbronn

to be almost a young woman. Uuna spent most of her time helping her mother gather berries and bitter fruit, or using sharpened stones, like the one she was now making, to scrape the insides from the skins of animals, mostly buffalo and deer, that the menfolk had hunted down and speared to death.

The skin of one young deer had been fashioned into the cloak she wore and was secured around her waist with a narrow strip of softer deerskin from along the animal's underbelly. It kept the cloak from getting in her way when she bent to pick up objects or foodstuffs from the ground. The cloak was still stiff in parts and chafed her young skin when she moved. Only the soles of her feet and the palms of her hands were toughened from her chores and trekking through the rough mountainous terrain. The rest of her body was a little dusty, but clean and as smooth as that of a baby reindeer.

Some members of the group were using special stones and bone tools to make these animal-skin clothes and carrying bags, but she had not yet been permitted to use these implements. They were guarded jealously by those who possessed them. To do her work she mostly had to use bone scrapers and occasionally those long flat narrow flakes of stone which she had sometimes seen the men strike with the blunt end of an axe as they chiselled away at huge lumps of bone. The floor of the cave was dusty but cleared of debris and swept relatively clean using leafy branches. There were the still glowing embers of a large cooking fire just in from the entrance of the cave and around the walls were stacked piles of dried bones. Here and there, stretched between crossed sticks were the drying skins of bison and deer, though fortunately with the dryness of the cave, the smells of any remaining putrefying particles of flesh had quickly disappeared.

Both those majestic beasts, the bison and deer, lived and grazed in the surrounding woods, often in the company of wild pigs and other game. But the bison, with its dark brown coat with long, coarse hair on its head, neck and shoulders was a prized kill. At the shoulder, a male animal was taller than a man and weighed as much as ten of the clan's biggest men. After a successful hunt it would take most of the group of hunters just to drag the dead animal, by leather thongs attached to its thick horns, back to the cave to be skinned and butchered. To butcher it out in the open was to invite the attentions of dangerous carnivores. Moving the slain animal to the safety of the cave as quickly as possible was a necessity. Once there, skilfully, the skin was removed and butchering of the flesh was quickly effected by the few clansmen expert at the task. As these jobs were carried out, the open eyes of the animals stared blankly at the young children who watched the grisly task half in fear and half in fascination. Antlers, horns and tusks were carefully removed and stored, some for tools and some for carving or fashioning into ceremonial apparel.

After careful scraping, the skins were thoroughly washed in the stream below and pounded on the rows of smoothly rounded grey rocks that were the size and shape of rabbit skulls and lined the banks of the stream. Some skins were too tough to be fashioned into clothes or even sleeping covers for the cold winter nights and were put to good use as covers to be hung as roofing over the rapidly erected stick frame canopies used by the clan when they wandered off towards cooler places or bivouacked when out on a distant hunt.

Uuna had heard some of the older clansmen talk of the furry almost impenetrable skins of the giant mammoth and of the tough but strangely beautiful white material harvested from its huge tusks, but she had never seen one. Gripping stories were told around the evening fires of mammoth hunts that the clan had carried out in a time long before she could remember; and the exciting images and frightening sounds born out of those hunts were vivid in her imagination and rung like the roar of a mountain lion in her ears. After all, her people's language and vocabulary were still limited and much was communicated through eye contact, signs, imitation of animal cries and lively body movements.

The crouching girl's imaginings of hunts and thoughts of wild animals were broken by her mother's words and gestures:

"Uuna, take Toa to wash in stream," she said. In part, she communicated by stroking the air in a downward motion with her roughened hand in the direction of Uuna's young brother.

Two other children between Uuna and Toa had died when very young and she and her youngest brother were the only two remaining. The young boy's name was symbolic of a hunter of the fierce and powerful mountain lions that sometimes preyed on those members of the clan foolish or careless enough to venture alone too far from the camp.

Uuna obediently took Toa's small grubby four-year old hand and smiled at him.

"Uuna ... stream" he said. He spoke to her with evident pleasure. He stood up from the rocky recess where he'd been playing in the thick red clayish mud their mother's man had gathered from the hillside and stored in various recesses in the cave. There, just enough water trickled through cracks in the rock wall above, to keep the ochre clay humid and soft. Uuna and Toa ran out towards the stream a hundred paces or so downhill from the mouth of the cave.

This was home and other members of the group were around, though only one turned his head a little from his work and surreptitiously squinted his cold dark eyes in their direction as they ran. They felt safe within sight of the clan members and allowed a youthful exuberance to overcome the permanent watchfulness they usually showed when outside the cave on trips to gather fruits and berries with their mother and the other women and children. But Uuna's senses and instincts were raw and unhoned. She was oblivious to the malevolence just then streaming silently in the direction of Toa and her.

# Eleven

Uuna's mother was called Ran and her man was known as Ara and though not a hunter, he had nonetheless secured an exalted place within the group. It was he who led the menfolk in many of their ceremonies and rituals held deeper in the cave in the flickering light of burning torches fuelled by tightly bound reeds soaked in animal fats.

From an early age when other boys had followed the men of the clan on hunting expeditions, Ara had been fascinated by the drawings on the walls in the depths of the cave the group had then inhabited. The skill and right to make these drawings was usually passed from father to son. As Ara's father had done before him, Ara had studied his own father's careful actions; mixing the deep red ochre clay with water to form a dark reddish paste and slowly singeing the wooden sticks to form black charcoal before diluting it into a thick mulch using boiled down animal fats.

Sometimes he had been permitted to follow his father deeper into the cave and sit silently as the older man studied the contours and shadows on the rockface before fastidiously applying his pastes and powders to create the outlines of buffalo, wild boar, horses and deer which seemed to move and came almost alive in the shimmering torchlight inside the darkened cave. After about twelve summers, when boys were initiated into manhood and full membership of the group, Ara had become skilled in the techniques of cave painting and in particular, depicting horses, which had become more plentiful in recent years. But he had accompanied the group on very few hunts and had not tested his strength against the animals on the lowlands or, for that matter, against the other young men of the clan, not to mention their familiar-looking but heavily-browed two-legged enemies who roamed in small bands through the mountains and plains.

For a long time Ara had been ignored by the others and only found his place in the clan after the death of his father, when he took over his father's cave-painting duties; creating on the walls and ceilings of the cavernous interior of their home, complex hunting scenes and evoking shadowy beasts that the other menfolk admired and feared. He had even inspired friendship and awe in the hearts of some of the older hunters by standing them close to the cave wall, placing their outspread hands tightly up against the moistened rock and throwing or blowing handfuls of red dust or black soot across their hand before they withdrew it, startling the model with an image of his own hand immortalized on the rock wall. The womenfolk smiled good-humouredly at the pride and arrogance of their men, though in their hearts, they sensed the presence of the spirits of these wild animals in and around the walls of the cave.

In time, Ara had taken Ran as his woman. She was attractive and strong and some of the other young men were jealous of Ara's position in the group; none more so than Chnn, two summers Ara's elder. He was a clan-member who had from an early age proved his cunning and courage in the hunts and in the regular skirmishes with the groups of men and women that inhabited and wandered though that area of land from the dry mountainous region of what would later be known as Asturias and Cantabria in northern coastal Spain. They even strayed up as far as the more fertile river valleys of south-west France. Most of these clans of people were semi-nomadic though many returned regularly to the same caves of their birth, sometimes after many seasons away.

Ara and Ran's group had tended to stay put for rather longer periods of time in this cave surrounded by forests and plentiful game, except for one long journey to the northern river valleys when a serious drought had dried the stream and driven the animals away. At that time, Ara's father had led the clan to the better hunting grounds in the north and back again two seasons later. Though still young, Ara and Ran had both survived that journey while many others in the group, including Chnn's parents, had not. Most of the time since then, the hunting had remained good and the members of the group, especially the women who treasured these more stable times spent in the same place, in some ways came to believe that the paintings of Ara and his ancestors on the walls and ceilings of their caves kept the animals abundant and in close proximity to their home.

However, Chnn had resented Ara's father and on the older man's death, Chnn's anger at having never been able to maim or kill the man he saw as responsible for his parent's deaths only intensified his hatred of Ara and his small family. But with the instinct and cunning of a hunter, he bided his time watchfully.

§

Several sunsets before this day, Chnn's eyes had burned and watered as he entered the depths of the cave. Visibility was not good but in the half light of the flickering, splattering animal fat torches, he saw that his moment for revenge had finally come. Ara had set down on a stone near him, a small highly polished figurine carved in ivory; its wide hips with a flattened "v" crease between the short legs and body were prominent as were the large breasts bulging between the narrow shoulders. This cherished symbol of fertility known to the group as "Suma" was part of the paraphernalia of the spring fertility ceremonies. The fact that it was here in the possession of Ara was not in itself unusual but what Chnn saw Ara doing had chilled his heart and excited his instinct for revenge.

Chnn's eyes blazed fiercely in the semi-darkened cave.

"... No draw Suma! ... Kill Suma spirit!" Chnn rasped.

Ara, startled and wide-eyed, turned his face away from the rock wall where he had begun outlining in charcoal the form of Suma around a mound in the stone wall representing the midsection of the figurine. The general form of the idol was already becoming apparent on the wall. He faced Chnn, incomprehension showing in his eyes.

Other members of the clan, hearing Chnn's raised voice, had quickly entered and their bearded scruffy faces were showing astonishment at what they heard and saw outlined on the wall there.

Some joined in the wailing chorus: "Aaahhiiiiie...Aaahhiiee" half in fear and half in amazement. Never before had they seen the human-like figure of a fertility idol depicted on the cave wall along with all those beasts. They were afraid. Several of them clenched in their hands spears and clubs and one or two were beginning to shake their weapons and stamp their feet as if in preparation for battle.

Chnn saw his chance for revenge before him and began shouting:

"No draw Suma! ... Evil! ... Chase away bison and deer."

These words coming from such an accomplished hunter seemed to carry a great deal of authority with the menfolk of the group.

"No draw!" he threatened again.

"Suma angry! .. Kill our women!"

The crowd was growing and the men were becoming increasingly agitated when Ran entered the chamber. Immediately sensing the worsening atmosphere, she knew she must act decisively. She mustered all her strength and calm loudly proclaiming:

"Suma happy ... Suma on cave wall always protect home from wild beast. Suma spirit stay here always on wall and bring many children to clan living here."

It was a direct challenge to the words of Chnn.

The agitated menfolk looked back and forth from Chnn to Ran as other females in the clan surged into the chamber, curious and half-afraid of the angry voices. As they saw the outline of the figurine they associated with their fertility on the wall, many of the women began to smile and chat amongst themselves happily, seeing it as a good omen.

Chnn was furious. He was losing control of the group and sensing the loss of his moment for revenge, he screamed more shrilly:

"Suma kill you! ... Suma kill your children!"

But Ran began to laugh breathlessly and the other women started to laugh too, dragging breaths into their lungs. One or two got down on their knees and began to raise their arms in worship towards the still unfinished image on the cave wall. The men looked back and forth from the wall to their women unable to decide what to think. Then slowly, one by one, they too knelt down and raised their arms towards the image.

The anger had departed from all but Chnn who visibly shook with rage, it was taking all his self-control to stop himself from running at Ara and tearing at his flesh with the sharp tool he had already drawn from under the rough skin belt tying the bison pelt robe around him. He fought back the tears of anguish and hatred beginning to well in his eyes over his frustration and anger at seeing his chance pass by. He had failed to destroy his enemy and remove him from a place of power in the clan.

"Aaarggh!" A bestial growl heaved from his throat and he spat heavily towards the floor of the cave to cover his humiliation, before hunching his shoulders and moving slowly out of the room avoiding the eyes of the clan members, many still worshipping and gesticulating happily towards the outline of Suma on the cave wall.

Ran moved towards Ara taking care not to come between the worshippers and the image of their idol on the cave wall.

"Watch out for Chnn," she said softly to him in a somewhat guttural voice, looking in the direction of the departed enemy and shaking her head up and down.

Ara was one of the wiser clan leaders but had still been taken completely by surprise when Chnn had entered the chamber and started yelling at him. He had been in a reverie of his own, creating the outline on the cave wall using the figurine beside him as a model. Until then, he had clearly no idea of the depths of Chnn's hatred and desire for revenge. For the moment, he added no further details to the image of the figurine. Best leave that to another day.

The following few days were quiet in the clan's cave. Chnn was rarely seen except when he came to take away his share of the butchered meat and eat it brooding by himself on the extremities of the clan's encampment.

## Twelve

As Uuna and Toa now raced towards the stream below the cave, Chnn followed their course with his eyes and rose slowly, slipping quietly off into the bushes behind where he'd been crouched over his work.  He moved stealthily and noiselessly through the undergrowth calling on all his skills as a hunter, afraid to alert either the clan or the children.  Within a few moments he was hidden in bushes beside the stream watching Uuna and Toa splashing and playing at the edge of the water.  Uuna was washing the dirt from her young brother's skin and hands, bending over him at the edge of the stream.

Chnn seized his chance and jumped behind Uuna grabbing the back of her neck with his right hand and holding her forward with his powerful right arm fully outstretched.  With his left knee he separated her already slightly spread legs and with his left hand grabbed under her left buttock inserting his greasy forefinger and middle finger into the crack between her legs, pulling it open and pushing them up into her cavity to make space for the hard member which he then started thrusting into her.  It was dry and a bit rough for a start but, that changed quickly and it took only a few quick thrusts to penetrate her fully.

Uuna was taken totally by surprise and cried out.  But her attacker's left hand now came round to cover her face and mouth.  She could barely breathe and smelt the overpowering stink of the skin of the reindeer Chnn had only a few minutes before been skinning and trimming.  The initial stab of pain was subsided as juices began to flow but the roughness movement of his member inside her young body was still numbing.

It was a few moments before Toa turned to witness the attack on his sister and despite his tender age he ran towards Chnn flailing his fists.  Chnn's left hand flashed from Unna's mouth striking a stunning blow on the side of Toa's head even before the child could touch him; maintaining his rough thrusting all the while.  It was over quickly.  When Chnn had finished, Toa was lying lifeless on the edge of the stream, blood pouring from wounds on both sides of his little

# BEGINNINGS  Gary Heilbronn

head, caved in on crashing against the large smooth stones on the edge of the river bank. Uuna was still held doubled over by her attacker whose left hand had been brought back to cover her mouth, although through wide, terrified eyes she could see the blood gushing from her brother's head and snaking off down the stream in the direction of the current.

Moments later she felt her attacker's grasp on her face and neck release. His thumb had dug deeply into the left side of her neck and it hurt. She collapsed towards the lifeless body of her brother wailing: "Toa...Toa... not dead ...not dead!" and trying to cradle his broken body in her arms. She did not see Chnn slip unhurriedly into the undergrowth and idle with satisfaction back towards the encampment. Indeed she had not seen Chnn at all but had smelt his odour and knew without a doubt that it was he who'd attacked her and who'd murdered her young brother.

Uuna's wailing grew in intensity and it was only moments before other clan members arrived at the edge of the stream. When Ran saw Toa's broken body she collapsed to his side screaming in grief clutching her last son to her breast and calling his name:

"Toa, Toa not dead... not dead."

After a few seconds, Ran turned her head slightly and she sniffed the air two or three times in the direction of her daughter. The odour of sex was unmistakable and she sensed as well as smelt her daughter's recent rape.

Ran's mind worked slowly as she considered the scene around her. It was not uncommon for a female entering womanhood to be taken roughly from behind by a dominant member of the clan. Sometimes it was the beginning of a permanent mating arrangement. That was a female's role in the clan, but there were strict rules and given her parent's high status, Unna was to be taken only by one of the most valued of clan members. Quickly Ran's instincts told her the essentials of what had happened at the edge of the stream. It was always potentially dangerous for a sibling or other infant to interfere with mating but generally clan members would do no more than push them roughly away. The men were used to it. This was more violent; as if the clansman had sought to do the most harm he could to the child.

# BEGINNINGS

**Gary Heilbronn**

Only one person in the clan would do this, she thought to herself, and that is Chnn. And there he was. He had returned and was standing smiling, just a little to the rear of the group of clansmen and women who were now edging tentatively towards the grieving family, many of their heads moving from left to right sniffing the air for the telltale odours to confirm the circumstances and sequence of events.

But knitted brows, frowns and head-shaking betrayed their uncertainties. In a society where verbal communication was still very limited, there was heavy reliance on other senses, especially smell and instinct.

The blood spilled by Toa and the musky male semen smells were there but something was missing; there was no hint of the female sexual pheromones which would normally have triggered the mating instinct of the male attacker and all its tragic but perhaps not that uncommon consequences. Guttural noises and short grunts showed their uncertainty was turning into suspicion. Some codes of the clan were not to be broken. While forced copulation with a young female physically ready for childbearing was accepted, there was something unnatural to them about the same occurring with girls not yet ready or with boys or even young men.

Chnn said nothing but all the clan and especially Ran could smell his involvement and while some looked downwards, seemingly embarrassed, casting furtive glances towards him from the corners of their eyes, others stared at him sniffing their disapproval. Chnn was known as a great hunter and powerful member of the clan. He was not to be accused lightly.

Ran lay Toa's body gently down and slowly turned her head towards her enemy, her eyes blazing.

"Arrghhh...Chnn die!" the now furious mother shrieked with hatred and anger as she threw herself towards Chnn.

He grabbed her wrists while fending off the blows from her clenched fists and struggling forward with her as the crowd separated around them. All of a sudden they both fell, Chnn on top of the screaming woman close to the stony riverbank where Toa still lay silent. By now Chnn's strong hands were around Ran's throat squeezing the life out of her.

## BEGINNINGS             Gary Heilbronn

He seemed sure of finishing her off when he felt a searing pain through his shoulderblade and into his left lung, followed by an explosion of light as the sharp wooden spear Uuna had grabbed from another clansmen punctured Chnn's heart. Thick red fluid coughed up through his mouth as his lungs filled with blood pumping in from his wounded heart. His head turned slowly to face his young killer, his eyes burning with a fierce unquenchable hatred that froze Uuna's soul as he collapsed lifeless on top of the choking squirming body of the older woman, Ran. The blunt end of the wooden spear pointed towards the heavens. Chnn's body reacted slowly, shaking once, twice, three times as the last bursts of life escaped through his open, bloodied mouth.

§

The unborn child shivered in the safety of her mother's womb. She felt the adrenalin surge from the kill and knew of her part in the dream. Slowly, she separated herself from the bloodied people on the bank of that glistening stream so long ago in the Cantabrian highlands. She gave no thought to Uuna's future, or if a new life resulted from that rough copulation; or its future. As if from a vantage point on a cliff top, images of scenes below flashed before her eyes and she viewed them without emotion as if untouched by the pain and suffering, the love and warmth.

She saw innumerable hunts for mammoth, bison and wild boar; violent skirmishes with animal-skin clad beast-like tribesmen; bone-crunching blows from stone axes and clubs; more peaceful agricultural scenes of family groups in small clearings tilling the soil with rudimentary tools in the bright sunshine; women crushing grains in deep stone bowls with children playing noisily nearby; village folk gathered in circles in fields praying to the Sun God as blood gushed from the slit throats of small animals sacrificed by shamans on slabs of stone; battlefields drenched in the blood of brightly clad warriors whose severed limbs and heads lay littered amongst the carcasses of horses and camels.

The images grew more distant and faded as she increasingly sensed the comfort of the womb.

## Thirteen

Maria watched sadly as her little son was buried in a small shaded cemetery just south of *le Petit Bayonne* district, near the centre of Bayonne city. The cemetery was on a little lane just off the *Allée Grand Paradis*. The street name itself confirmed Maria's conviction that her child was now in a better place.

There had been a brief and tearful service in the *Funérarium* on the nearby *rue Dominicaines* where Maria and a few of her new friends and protectors had said their goodbyes to the little boy. It was a quiet and mournful affair. For some time Maria had been walking around as if in a trance. She had to be led by others, but they had almost to drag her away from her young son's graveside. They then took her back to *Chez Jeanne* and she was alone once again.

The minutes and hours passed slowly for Maria in her rooms at the back of Jeanne's modest hostel and she tried to sleep a lot. It helped her to escape a little from the pain of her loss. First Alberto, then baby Thomas. The heartache was unbearable. She kept revisiting in her mind the funeral service and the tiny grave. As the days passed, the full realization of the horrific events surrounding her Thomas' death had returned to her. She reproached herself with such vehemence for having run from the Guardia officers. But to have done otherwise would have been suicide. She knew that. But it didn't help.

At times she fell into such fits of self-loathing and shame that only the blessed refuge of sleep allowed her any respite. After some days alone, she sometimes imagined she could hear a tiny voice responding to her self-recriminations:

"It wasn't your fault", it said. "It was God's will. Some things are meant to be".

As several more days passed by, the voice took on a sterner tone:

"You had no choice. You know what fate would have awaited you at the hands of the Guardia. You were right to run. There was no more you could do. There is no more to be done. Revenge has been taken and that is all," the voice whispered.

Gradually, Maria found herself in dialogue with the voice. There was in fact rarely anyone else there for her to talk to. At first she thought it was her son's spirit that spoke to her. But he was gone; and slowly she realized that the voice was coming from within her but was not her own. It was stronger and braver and, perhaps, even crueller, than she could be. It could only be coming from within her womb. It had to be the voice of her unborn child. It *was* the baby within her; it was the reason she would wake every day and force herself to eat and drink and try to return to the day-to-day world; the land of the living.

Days passed and the young woman's strength slowly returned. Life did not improve for Maria; it just became slowly less unbearable.

Although she tried to rest, there were so many times when sleep escaped her. Then her mind sought refuge in the past. Her thoughts returned to her family, all now departed, and especially her maternal grandmother. Though the old lady had been distant and aloof at times, Maria had loved her. She had been a gracious and kind woman. She'd inherited considerable lands; then with determination and strength had expanded her father's claim to thousands of hectares of grasslands, running enormous herds of beef cattle. Their land had extended south and west from Amurrio, almost forty kilometres south of Bilbao on the north coast of Spain, into the fertile foothills of the Cantabrian Mountains. It was vast. But that was more than a generation ago and what now felt like several lifetimes away.

Back in the present, the anguish and recriminations resurfaced in Maria's mind. Once again the voice from within returned to comfort her. It made her feel better. She smiled as her eyes drifted around the room, finally alighting on the dusty alligator skin suitcase that carried her few possessions and had been handed down through generations from mother to daughter or granddaughter, and now to her. The suitcase had been brought back from the sometime Spanish colony of Florida – a land that seemed to be a world away both then and now, but for different reasons.

## BEGINNINGS  Gary Heilbronn

"Florida" she sighed and images of a land overgrown with flowers flashed into her mind. "Was it really like that?" she whispered.

She now recalled from her childhood lessons that it had been given that colourful and optimistic name on a brilliant Easter Sunday in 1513 by Juan Ponce de León, one of Spain's most intrepid explorers. He'd even accompanied the great Genoese adventurer Cristoforo Columbo on his second voyage to America, back in 1493. Her thoughts played with that date.

"1493 and 1943" she said aloud. "What will that year bring?" Maria wondered. And she thought of 1943.

"Still almost five years in the future. Will we be safe? Will life be better then?" After all, what she wanted now was a safe haven.

Her thoughts drifted back to her memories and Florida.

Maria had been well educated. She had learned that Florida had proved too difficult for Spain to colonize; and it had passed from Spanish to British hands and then back again to the Spanish over the centuries. Then, in 1819, it was finally surrendered forever to the emergent United States of America under the Transcontinental Treaty. That treaty set out the boundaries between the USA and what was then called New Spain, a conglomerate of Spanish colonies in North America, but governed from Mexico City. And over the century that followed, most of those territories were lost; a bitter disappointment to the Spanish people. But it was just another one of those all too common reversals of fortune that the proud and partisan people of Spain had had to endure.

Abruptly, her feelings of loss dissolved in sleep.

§

Maria stayed several more days at *Chez Jeanne*, but the people who had become her protectors wanted her to blend as quickly as possible into the local community. They said that she could be too easily traced to that safe house. The story of the horrific escape across the border had spread quickly through the Basque community and many wanted to help. They hastily found Maria her own place to live. She took up residence in a bright, spacious two-room apartment on the second floor of a three storey seventeenth century building in rue Marengo. The thick walls were built of local stone and there were open fireplaces in each room.

She lived there alone although the baby was just about due. Her new friends also organized a midwife, a refugee from Bilbao, to check on Maria twice each day. Her name was Helena and she lived just around the corner, on the Quai des Corsaires.

On her regular visits, Helena insisted that Maria leave the small apartment and come with her for short walks. As grief-stricken as she was, Maria knew she had to get out and take her mind of her loss, if not for herself, then for the unborn baby who would soon change her life so completely. She could not bear to bring a new child into a world steeped in grief.

She vowed to make the effort to live again.

Maria and Helena often walked along the wide shaded avenues of central Bayonne as well as in the tiny backstreets and riverside walks of the old town. Maria liked Bayonne. It is an attractive city and she began to feel its charm. Helena was thrilled to see that with each day as they explored Bayonne, a spark of life was being rekindled in Maria's soul and she was amazed when Maria started to tell her what she knew about the city's history.

"You know Helena, though Bayonne has become the major centre of Basque culture in France," she explained, "the city started its life in the first century AD as a Roman military camp known as Lapurdum. It wasn't until a millennium later, in the eleventh century, that it became known as Bayonne."

"I had no idea. You must tell me more, Maria!" Helena replied. She wanted to encourage the younger woman to talk and think of anything other than her grief.

"If you wish," Maria went on. She, herself was feeling the therapeutic effect of their walks and Helena's companionship.

"Bayonne prospered during the following three centuries when it was under English domination. This had come about as a result of the marriage of Eleanor of Aquitaine with Henri Plantagenêt, King Henry II of England."

"As you probably know, Helena," Maria said kindly, though she doubted that Helena had received much of this kind of education, "Eleanor had previously been Queen of France through her fifteen year marriage to, Louis VII, King of France. But in 1152, that marriage ended in annulment and without a male heir to the throne of France. Afterwards, she married 'Henry, Count of Anjou', who became King Henry II of England. Henry's reign as King of England endured until 1189 when Eleanor's son Richard, who was known as 'Richard the Lion Heart' acceded to the English throne."

"I have heard of him" Helena responded happily.

"Eleanor did not seem to have much luck with her husbands," Maria said with a slight smile, "... and this did not seem to be a happy marriage either. For years before Henry's death, Eleanor and Richard spent most of their time here in Aquitaine, particularly in Bordeaux, where Eleanor had acquired a reputation as a patron of poets. In fact, Bayonne and much of western France remained under English control throughout that time and were only fully returned to France in the 1450's, after the drawn-out horrors of the Hundred Years War."

Maria became silent. The thought of a war lasting a hundred years only depressed her and stifled further conversation.

§

Days passed. Maria rested most of the time. Her pregnancy was close to full term. It was getting towards the end of May 1939 and now three weeks since little Toma's funeral. She spent a great deal of time at home. Maria's modest apartment was located just beyond the Musée Basque which was housed in the mediaeval Maison Dagourette, also situated in *le Petit Bayonne* district, within the old fortified part of the city.

Maria had been told that as soon as she was ready, after the birth of her baby, there would be a post on the small museum staff for someone of her education and knowledge of Basque history and culture. On hearing this offer, even through the veil of all her suffering, she had felt that the light of providence had smiled upon her. In truth, she should not have been surprised by this glimmer of good fortune as her family was well-known for its culture and erudition. And the involvement of her lost husband in the Basque youth movements had not gone unnoticed by its sympathizers.

Yet, she had not visited the museum and was beginning to be curious about it. So when Helena next came by suggesting another short walk, Maria instead proposed a visit to the museum, telling her how keen she was to find out what it was like.

The Basque Museum was quiet. A middle aged lady sitting rather idly behind the museum's reception desk did not appear to be busy. She seemed happy to explain to them how the museum had been decades in the planning but it was not until 1922 that the old Maison Dagourette had been bought for the museum by the city of Bayonne. And then it had been opened to the public in 1924.

The two women walked around some of the displays on the ground floor. Maria could see that the museum was already well established.

As they left after their short visit, Maria turned to look at her companion, a quizzical expression on her face.

"You know, Helena" she said "I find it a little strange that there's nothing in the museum on the pre-history of the Basque people."

"What do you mean?" Helena replied unsurely.

"Well, you know that the Basque country has always been a place apart from the rest of Spain. The coming of civilization is said to be a comparatively recent story. Supposedly, it didn't occur until some two thousand years after several ancient trading ports had been founded by Phoenician seafarers. That was around 800 BC on Spain's eastern Mediterranean seaboard and even earlier, around 1100 BC, on its southern coast at Gades, or what we now call Cadiz, near Gibraltar."

Maria thought for a few seconds.

"But the Phoenician traders had settlements all around the Mediterranean. They are even supposed to have sailed south down the coast of Africa and all the way north to Britain. It just seems strange that they didn't try to establish trading centres or settlements on the west coast of Iberia and follow the coastline all the way into the Bay of Biscay and up the coast of France. Of course there's no archaeological record of them because they didn't build temples and carve statues like the Greeks and Romans who came after them. They were really only interested in trade."

She thought some more.

"The Phoenicians seemed so like but also so unlike the Basques," she said. She was a little distracted. She spoke half to herself and only half to her companion. It was as if somehow, despite the three millennia that separated them, she felt there was a close connection between those courageous seafaring people from the eastern end of the Mediterranean and the Basque people who had for centuries lived quietly and isolated in this far corner of the vast European continent.

Maria spoke again.

"All their trading ports around the coast developed with the co-operation of the primitive Celto-Iberians who lived here. And apparently, they traded peaceably with their foreign visitors. ... Of course, for many centuries before that, the Phoenicians had traded widely throughout the whole of the eastern Mediterranean region."

Helena said nothing. Maria paused for a moment to be sure that her companion was still listening. She seemed to be.

"You know, some three thousand years ago when the Phoenicians were ruled by a King Hiram, they even supplied the ships and great cedar timbers needed by King Solomon of ancient Israel to build his legendary Temple; the first great place of worship in ancient Jerusalem. This was several centuries before the Roman Empire and before the Carthaginians, the descendants of those early Phoenicians, came from North Africa and settled more permanently here on the Iberian Peninsula."

Other thoughts flashed through Maria's mind. She began to feel more and more enthusiasm for these ideas.

Maria and Helena walked on slowly towards home.

"It makes me so happy" Helena said to the younger woman, "to see you so animated and hear you talking about all these historical things that I never really learned anything about. Please tell me more."

But Maria's mood had changed. The talk of religion and early Jerusalem only made her a little more pensive and the grief that she had momentarily let slip to the back of her mind had found its way back to the surface. Though she had been brought up a strict Catholic, the horrors of the civil war in which the church had been so partisan and the loss of both Alberto and Thomas had shaken her belief in Catholicism and even in Christianity, but not her faith in God.

"How complex is the role of religion in our lives and our history ..." Maria said more softly, as they walked along, "and how ironic that the Temple of Solomon, this wonderful religious monument, was to be destroyed and rebuilt time and again as a holy site for Jews and Christians and then claimed by Islam ... the religion of the Moors."

These words started a new train of thought for her as she reflected on those Arab peoples who had made such an impact on so much of Spain, but not on the Basque country and her own people.

"Of course, it wasn't until much later; in the 7th century that the Moors' began their six centuries-long occupation of the Iberian Peninsula" she said.

"That was centuries after the Carthaginians and the Romans had left, not to mention those less civilized Arian tribes from the north who left so little trace of their passing. The Moors were different. They left behind them so many remnants of their Islamic beliefs, their culture and architecture, though not in this part of the country."

"But you know Helena," Maria looked intensely at her companion, her heart glowing with a tiny spark of pride, "none of them could ever conquer our Basque homeland."

She walked on; but the glowing smile slowly slipped from her face as she thought of the recent years of civil war and how the nationalists had invaded and forced the Basque people to their knees.

"But that was the past." She spoke softly. "Now things are so different in Franco's Spain."

Maria sighed visibly. The pain and grief had returned to her heart.

§

**BEGINNINGS**  Gary Heilbronn

The sky was blue from one horizon to the next. It was another beautiful sunny day in Bayonne, though unusually, the morning had begun with a light shower of rain. Now those brief clouds had cleared and the air was fresh. Maria's midwife, Helena, let herself into the little apartment with the key she'd been given in case she needed to gain access urgently. She had knocked loudly but there had been no response. It was just after eight-thirty in the morning on Friday, the 26th of May 1939.

Helena was a little surprised that the apartment was so quiet. Maria had recently been an early riser.

"Perhaps she's not slept well" Helena thought aloud to herself, "after all, the weather was humid and hot yesterday, indeed abnormally hot for late May."

"Maria! Are your there Maria? ¿Cómo estás?" she called. She moved carefully across the still curtained living room and past the tidy little kitchenette situated in the corner nearest the door. The two women had adopted the habit of speaking in Spanish rather than risk being overheard speaking euskara. They thought it might draw unnecessary attention to them. Helena paused as she knocked on Maria's bedroom door; but there was no answer.

"¿Qué pasa Maria?" she said softly as she pushed open the heavy oak-framed door to the little bedroom. Maria seemed to be still sleeping. She lay on her side in the unmade bed. She was still; very still. She was facing the wall, but her shoulders were moving slowly up and down rhythmically; so it was clear that the heavily pregnant young woman was breathing. But the drawn and crumpled white sheets were a testament to a restless night. There was also a slight stain and wetness on the bed around where her hips lay.

Helena shook Maria's arm gently in an attempt to waken her.

"Maria! Maria, can you hear me? Your waters have broken." The words were exhaled with increasing anxiety.

So that she could see the sleeping woman's face, Helena turned Maria a little. She now lay half on her side and half on her back. Air was being inhaled and exhaled regularly through her nostrils. She was breathing and seemed fine; just unconscious.

"Thank God! She's still breathing" Helena mouthed these words almost soundlessly as she reached for Maria's wrist to feel for her pulse. It was strong; though her pulse was a bit slower than normal. It was as if Maria was in a trance. But from the grimace on the sleeping woman's face, it appeared to Helena that contractions had begun. She'd never before seen a mother-to-be having contractions while still asleep or unconscious.

"Perhaps it's not impossible ..." she murmured. "Babies can be born when the mother's under anaesthetic".

But she had no idea what to do. Eventually, she decided that it was best to sit with Maria until she awoke. She pulled up an uncomfortable kitchen chair and sat down. At that moment, she was startled by a shiver running down Maria's still unconscious and swollen body, from her shoulders to her thighs.

The unborn child felt it too. It happened just as the little one winced at the heavy contraction. It grabbed at the top of her skull as she reposed way down at the bottom of mother's womb near the cervix at the entrance of the birth canal. The pain was intense and it sent her mind racing to a haven so far away. Almost three thousand years were swept away in that instant.

# COMING OF THE PHOENICIANS

*Coastal Northern Spain, circa 900 BC*

## Map of Phoenician World: Western Europe

## Map of Phoenician World: Eastern Europe

## Fourteen

Around 900 BC; coastal Northern Spain

For some time a young woman had been lying almost asleep on the soft sandy beach. Her tanned skin seemed to glow from soaking up what heat there was left in the late summer sun. Its warmth had a soothing soporific effect and she'd been feeling that life could not get much better.

She exhales heavily, blinks once or twice and opens her eyes wide. Her whole body feels warm and she revels in the sensation.

"Time to cool down!" she sighs. She speaks quietly but firmly as if giving herself an order. It helps shake her quiescent body out of the reverie that the warm sun had induced. She raises her head a little and she peers towards the sea. The calm, sparkling blue waters look so tempting.

She rises effortlessly from the sandy beach with a measured feline elegance. Fleetingly, here and there beneath her light brown skin, ripples of muscular contraction and release offer a glimpse of a considerable physical strength almost completely hidden within her smooth almost perfect young body. Its only defect, if it could be called a defect as it was hardly noticeable, is a slightly darker patch of skin, like a birthmark about the size of a thumbprint, on the left side of her throat. Her grandmother bore almost the same roundish birthmark; at least that's what her mother had once told her.

For a moment, she stands tall and still on the sandy beach watching the sun sink leisurely towards the darkening sea. Beads of sweat mixed with occasional grains of fine sand trickle slowly around the tiny lines at the corners of her eyes and over her high cheekbones. Then they roll quickly down the side of her face and neck, across her tanned breast and into the crease of her armpits before attaching themselves to the almost invisible strands of fine fair hair hidden there. Their glistening fairness is a stark contrast to the thick mass of dark curls falling loosely from her head and bouncing heavily around her shoulders. Her hair is casually separated and tied on each side of her head by thin chords made from deer-hide tightly interlacing a dozen or so perfectly matching little shells. The shells had been lovingly harvested by her young sister from the far end of

## BEGINNINGS
## Gary Heilbronn

the beach where it butts up abruptly against a rocky promontory. Masses of them accumulate there.

The young woman surveys the sea before her as if it were her own domain, without haste, absorbing the blueness and the flashes of sunlight on its mirror-like surface. No waves crash noisily on the shoreline today. She waits a moment, drinking in the pleasure of the soft sea breeze as it gently caresses her body. There is no cause for haste. The beach is still deliciously warm and she is enjoying the sensation of the fine grains of golden sand caressing the white undersides of her brown-skinned feet.

This day had been hotter than she could remember for the season, she observes to herself, though she had not yet lived twenty summers. She recalls the old people's tales of times long-past; of endless battles to survive the cold, the biting cold; and the magnificence of vast ice rivers snaking through the distant high mountains where the morning sun rises, before bringing its warmth to the earth in this place she calls home.

"How different it is now" she says. It's as if she is determined to shut out those unpleasant thoughts.

"... but what happened to those long and arduous winters of the past?" she wonders aloud. "Where did all that cold and those ice rivers go? Did they leave with the ancestors? Was it their burden to bear? Not ours?"

She shrugs off such thoughts and runs down the beach towards the inviting waters of the calm sea. Diving in, she feels its salty sting on her face and shoulders. Her thin deerskin tunic clings to the curves of her lithe young body. She bursts up through the surface beyond the almost imperceptible shore break and slowly propels her body forward upon the surface by reaching both arms out in front of her and pulling herself through the cooling waters. She does this several times and stops. Her floating body feels the 'to and fro' of the gentle swells; first pushing her towards the shore then dragging her out in the direction of the open sea. The tide was still going out and the water was not deep. If needed, her feet could easily touch the only slightly sloping sandy bottom.

From her vantage point out in the water the young woman can now see further around the rocky promontory. She glances in that direction. Her eyes widen. What she sees sends a slight shiver down

BEGINNINGS                               Gary Heilbronn

her spine; but she is unafraid. After all she is Hannh, the daughter of Alda, the chief of the tribe, its wisest and most feared warrior: the tribe's protector. Under his guidance they had rebuilt their village on high ground just below the crest of the hill facing the open sea. It looks back down the fertile valley where most of the villagers now till the soil, cultivating grain and root vegetables which soften and sweeten when boiled with herbs and berries. Of course, there are also several hunter-warriors who keep the village supplied with fresh meat, especially wild boar and deer. Bison were a rare treat now, but deer were abundant along the coastline as were smaller mammals, in particular large grey rabbits. They afford a plentiful source of food for the village.

The sea also provides handsomely for them. Young boys from the village usually spend early mornings and evenings on the rocky promontory, hopping from pool to pool at low tide with short sharpened sticks ready to spear the smaller fish and soft-shelled crabs left there by the receding waters. The older boys trail fine vines into the sea, with sharpened rabbit bones attached to the ends. They sometimes return to the village with basketfuls of fish of all sizes, shapes and colours, still flapping sporadically until they are gutted clean, skewered and roasted over open fires. The village people eat well and their children grow strong and healthy. Hannh is no exception.

The young woman now stands in almost chest-high water and stares out towards the open sea. Strange dark objects seem to be floating out there on the surface; like huge sea animals swimming slowly towards the shore. As the objects come closer, she can distinguish three of them; now approaching more rapidly than before. They soon take on another form; like long, low wooden huts with squarish grey clouds above each of them; and here and there she sees flashes of purple beneath. The striking colour takes her by surprise. It's somewhere between animal blood and the skins of the sweet berries that the women collect.

The dark objects seem to be heading for where she stands.

Hannh can see that the boys from the village who'd been spearing fishing and gathering shellfish along the rocky promontory have noticed the objects too and are running off at full pace towards the hut of the chief to warn of the objects imminent arrival.

## Fifteen

Those strange floating objects that had so surprised Hannh were sturdy wooden longboats. On board the first of them stood a well-travelled Phoenician trader known as Amilca of Tyre and his son Daavid. The son had been named after the great Hebrew King who had not so long before the boy's birth led the Judean and Israelite tribes to a decisive victory over the warlike Philistines. The battle had taken place some years after that ungodly race had attacked and devastated the Canaanite people who lived quietly on the coast close to Amilca's own homeland. The same King David had then gone on to vanquish the belligerent Jebusites, another nearby tribe. It was said that after his conquest of the Jebusites, King David brought the Ark of the Covenant, the most holy relic that the Israelites possessed, back to Jerusalem; then newly renamed the "City of David".

These victories brought peace to the fertile lands neighbouring those ruled by Abibal, then King of Tyre. At that time, Tyre was the foremost Phoenician city and the place where Amilca had been born. Tyre was situated on the sunny shores of the far eastern coast of the Great Sea, as the vast Mediterranean Sea was then known. It was in an area making up much of the land later to be known as Lebanon. The early Greeks had referred to the peoples of Tyre and Sidon as 'Phoenicians' but later they were called Sidonites in the writings of the Old Testament. The Phoenicians were perhaps the greatest seafarers and merchants of the millennium immediately preceding the birth of Christ and they kept close trading and friendly cultural ties with their Israelite neighbours immediately to their east. During the preceding several centuries, they had also maintained good relations with the Mesopotamians living to their north-east and with the Egyptians to their south, prior to the decline of those two ancient civilizations.

The Phoenicians were also reputed to be the most capable shipbuilders of ancient times. Their ships were larger and more effective than any of those built by the Egyptians whose vessels had evolved from the smaller reed boats developed several centuries beforehand. They functioned well in rivers but much less so out on the open sea.

Although the Phoenicians did build warships, as those were indeed dangerous times, they mainly built merchant vessels capable of carrying large cargoes. They were called 'round boats' because they were unusually broad-beamed, providing much larger cargo-space than the earlier narrow galleys. These 'round boats' depended for movement principally on large squarish sails, though windpower was normally supplemented by oarsmen, usually arranged in two tiers of 11 and 13 men on each side of the boat.

It was the longer and narrower version of this craft that was now approaching the distant shore where just a few minutes before, Hannh had stood like a queen, breathing in the soft warmth of the late summer afternoon. These were boats that had been built for exploration and possible minor skirmishes rather than purely for trade, and each boat came equipped with a long battering ram protruding from the bow.

§

Hannh watches as the Phoenician longboats finally round the promontory and close on the shoreline. She wonders at the squarish clouds above the approaching boats, turning and flapping loosely before being lowered down onto the deck from each side, then efficiently wrapped and tied to a long pole which was then hoisted and turned vertically to point towards the heavens. It was as if a long branchless tree grew up from each of the boats.

With calm curiosity, her eyes follow as the longboats continue towards her and the nearby village under oar-power alone.

Aboard the first vessel and in command, Amilca raises his right hand. With it, he makes two quick motions, signalling to the helmsmen of the other two boats to stop their crews rowing. They know they are to stay some twenty oarstrokes from the shore. This is their standard tactic so as not to appear too menacing when approaching the occasional villages found along such undiscovered coastlines. Over the years, they had visited and established coastal settlements in several places, most importantly on the far western side of the Mediterranean between their larger bases at Massalia

(Marseilles), to the east of the other side of the vast Iberian Peninsula, and Gades (Cadiz) on its southern side. But this time they had ventured much further westwards round the coast of Iberia into unknown territory where a vast expanse of ocean lay out towards the setting sun.

At that moment, Hannh's father, Alda, appears on the beach. He is surrounded by a dozen powerful looking tribesmen, all armed with long flint-tipped spears and large wooden-framed shields covered with thick dried and doubled bison-skin. Alda is himself an impressive sight despite his advancing age. He is taller than most of the other tribesmen. His arms are thick and muscled as are his thighs and lower legs. His powerful neck, sitting on broad tanned shoulders, is framed by long dark curls and his head is covered with a thick leather protective bonnet that he wears only when he foresees possible danger or battle. Other villagers remain behind in support and armed with whatever spears, wooden clubs and slingshots they could find.

Hannh still stands well out in the water watching the approaching vessels. To all who see her, she shows no fear.

Alda called to his daughter. "Hannh! Return to shore. They may attack us" he shouted.

Hannh turned to look at her father briefly and threw back her head with youthful arrogance. Showing apparent disdain for his words, she stood her ground, now a little over waist-deep in the cool salty water.

"Damned fool girl" Alda seethed through clenched teeth. He knew that pride and bravado, as well as curiosity would stop her returning too quickly to her father's side. After all she was his own first born and trained as a warrior. She feared no man.

Alda, the village chief had fathered seven children although two had died young; the last in childbirth some seven years before, taking with it to the grave Alda's beloved wife Luna. His eldest child was Hannh, the older of the two surviving daughters. Alda's three teenage sons were now at his side and each carried two spears; a long and a short one. Years of practice had already assured their accuracy and speed but they shuffled uncomfortably from foot to foot and you could see from their less confident appearance that they had little experience of real combat. That was unsurprising as few persons, friendly or otherwise, lived near or ventured into this region.

Alda looked to his left, his eyes settling on his other daughter, Jaan. She stood tall and was armed with a slingshot and a bag full of small stones that were attached to her side by a deerskin chord tied tightly around her waist. She also carried a short spear.

"What warrior she looks!" he thought to himself, impressed by her demeanour. Her hair was much fairer that her older sister's and her eyes danced with curiosity and playfulness.

But she was more than a pretty face. She had become an expert shot with the weapon she carried, as was her older sister who had tutored her in the skill. She wore the same knee-length deerskin tunic as Hannh and the curves of her young adult body had already attracted the attention of more than a few of the young men in the village. But none took any liberties; and not just out of the respect that was owed to the family of their chief.

The villagers stared with apprehension at the approaching vessels.

Alda carefully calculated the strength of this potential enemy. Each of the longboats housed forty-eight warrior-oarsmen, twenty-four on each side. They sat in banked formation, one lower and one higher in each row, with one man to an oar. But what he could not see was that as they approached the coastline, they kept their short bronze swords and wooden shields close at hand, placed near to their feet on the galley floor. When preparing for battle the shields were slung over each side of the boat, but this was not the case now. Also within reach but out of sight were their wooden spears of the shorter variety, tipped with pointed flattened bronze spearheads. They were lighter and more suitable for transportation on lengthy voyages and for quick, easy use on rapid hunting forays or occasional skirmishes with any aggressive local tribes that they might encounter on such voyages.

The Phoenician visitors were never sure of the reception awaiting them.

## Sixteen

Amilca and Daavid stood in the prow of the first longboat; one each side of the solid cedar-wood bowsprit. It was a solid extension of the ship's keel and at the bow, it curved upwards to rise vertically more than a man's height above the deck. The two men were unarmed so as to exhibit their non-hostile intentions to any local tribes they may meet. Over their tunics, they had donned rich purple cloaks that were held together below the neck with large shiny bronze clasps, inlaid with precious stones. They stood with the cloaks thrown back over both shoulders and their hands placed on their sides just below their thick leather belts. Their elbows pointed out from their sides, holding open the purple cloaks to show that there were no weapons hidden underneath.

From well offshore they had seen the few individuals on the beach and around the rocks and had watched without surprise as some had raced off inland and returned with armed re-enforcements and what they took to be the chief or a tribal elder.

Amilca had ordered his trusted servant, Manno, to bring onto the deck some small glass trinkets and other items. There were beads and an unguent flask, a small roll of cloth dyed purple and a bronze dagger. At the beginning of the voyage, Manno had been designated as keeper and controller of all the trinkets and precious objects. These had been brought with them for the purpose of impressing the locals and offering gifts with a view to establishing trading links.

It was not often that the seafarers encountered tribes of local inhabitants on their visits ashore. But it was precisely these encounters they had been seeking. The Phoenicians were not a warlike people. Their intention was to find and develop new trading posts in the lands around the Mediterranean Sea, or the Great Sea as it was then called. This voyage had however seen them travel much further afield than in the past. From the Great Sea they sailed westward through the waters between the town of Abila, situated at the north-western tip of the Berber lands on the vast African continent, and the Pillars of Hercules, as the Greek Athenians and

Mycenaeans called the great rocks of Calpe (later known as Gibraltar) at the southern end of the Iberian Peninsula.

Then, after stopping at the ports of Gades (Cadiz) and a few more isolated villages around the southern Iberian coast, they had taken advantage of brisk southerly winds and favourable current to turn and follow the North Star, heading up the rocky western coastline for several days. Unlike a few earlier Phoenician adventurers who had continued north further out to sea and had returned much later with precious tin from a land they called Baartan (later known as Britain), Amilca had decided to hug the coastline. He kept the midday sun behind them, but then followed the coastline when it turned eastwards. They had heard of other vessels being lost in stormy conditions when attempting this voyage, but they had experienced nothing but clear sunny weather and favourable winds.

The lead longboat was now the only one being pushed along by the regular slap of its oars on the calm waters, though the lower tier of oarsmen had been ordered to stop rowing and to keep at the ready in case hostilities began.

As the longboat neared the beach, Alda called again to his daughter, telling her to return. This time Hannh obeyed and strode gracefully out of the water and towards the other villagers. They stood some twenty paces up from the fine, wavering streak of salty foam that traced a ragged line along where the sea lapped against the sandy beach.

She never once took her eyes off the figures on the longboats. Though she had no reason to believe that the visiting seafarers meant any harm, she still carefully surveyed their movements, attentive for the least sign of hostile intent. Of course, Amilca had earlier ordered his oarsmen not to make the slightest move towards their weapons unless the local villagers on the beach attacked them first.

Amilca and Daavid stood on the deck of the lead longboat, seemingly transfixed by the beautiful young woman as she left the water and joined the men on the beach. She showed no apparent fear of them or their longboats and her controlled movements comforted their hopes that the locals would greet them not with hostility but with curiosity or at worst, just a healthy suspicion.

The first longboat on which Amilca and Daavid stood was only a half dozen oar-strokes from landing on the beach when Amilca ordered his helmsman to change direction.

"Follow along the shore at this distance and pass slowly by the spot where the villagers are gathered and in full view of them" he commanded. "... And make no abrupt movements."

Aside to Daavid he confided: "We want them to see that we mean them no harm." Daavid had understood the tactic but said nothing.

Amilca and Daavid now kept their eyes fixed on the villagers as they glided slowly by them, ever aware that hostilities could come from the shoreline at any moment.

"Their weapons are primitive but they seem to be a formidable tribe." Daavid observed quietly to his father.

Amilca leaned towards his son without taking his eyes of the group on the beach.

"I'm not too concerned," was his father's quiet reply.

"We outnumber the fighting men at least four-to-one though some of the women do look fierce. Our warriors are experienced and they know what they have to do" he said.

After the longboat had passed slowly by Alda and his group — all members of the tribe had followed its progress with their eyes — it neared the beach some twenty paces further along. Daavid, standing slightly behind and to the right of his father signalled slowly to the oarsmen to stop rowing and raise the long wooden oars, which were smoothly slid from the water, lifted to the vertical and slipped into place behind wooden latches below semi-circular rowlocks set regularly along the longboat's gunwales. The oarsmen knew they had to remain still, quiet and make no quick or suspicious movements and above all show no weapons. The other longboats stayed well out from the beach.

The helmsman of Amilca's boat turned the rudder ninety degrees and the longboat slid silently towards the shore, slowing with a start as its keel ran up the sandy beach about thirty paces further along from where the villagers had gathered. The group of villagers on the beach visibly tensed but waited on the order of Alda who they trusted implicitly and knew would lead them courageously into battle; but only if it were necessary. Alda had no illusions about their situation. They were very likely facing a well-trained and experienced force and if battle did ensue there would be very many casualties.

Amilca and Daavid held tightly onto the bowsprit to keep their balance as the boat pulled to a stop and did not rush to disembark. The villagers now tightened their grips on their weapons, though none were yet raised against the strangers. Amilca slowly stepped over the gunwales and onto the beach, purposely half turning his back to the villagers as he landed on the shore. Daavid passed him the bolt of cloth and trinkets. Amilca held his two hands open in front of him with the flat roll of cloth parallel to the ground and the coloured glassware and bronze dagger and scabbard placed upon it. Daavid also stepped stealthily to the ground and stood behind his father.

"Keep just behind me and carry these gifts in front of you" Amilca said quietly to him. He passed back the goods and they both began to walk carefully and slowly towards the assembled villagers. They showed no fear and carried no weapons but had their eyes riveted on the village leaders.

The villagers' eyes were all upon the two strangers. At this time, according to the plan Amilca had worked out beforehand, the oarsmen in the lead longboat aground further along the beach were no longer the centre of the villagers' attentions. So they carefully, and without being noticed, brought their weapons and shields within easy reach in case they needed to protect themselves and their leaders, who by then had come to within several paces of the unknown villagers.

Alda and Hannh were at the front of the group of villagers, now numbering several dozen. Alda was tall, powerful and imposing and Hannh had inherited his physical presence. They watched the approaching strangers without a move.

Amilca came to within five paces of the group and stopped. He held out both his hands, palms facing upwards and slowly turned towards his son, gesturing at the goods he carried and bringing his opened hands back to face Alda to show that the gifts were for him.

Alda took a step forward and there was a murmur in the crowd behind him. Keeping his eyes on the two strangers, he half turned to the villagers and brought his right hand to about waist high in a gesture which told them to hold and stay quiet. He then slowly raised his hand across his body and slapped the left side of his chest.

"Alda. I am Chief". He stated firmly in a tongue Amilca could not comprehend though the meaning was clear. He then gestured with his right hand again towards his older daughter standing just behind him to his right side with her gaze fixed on Daavid.

"Hannh. My daughter" he said.

Taking his cue from Alda, Amilca mimicked his gestures and introduced first himself, then his son Daavid, who still stood calmly carrying the cloth, the dagger and trinkets being offered as gifts. Hannh stepped forward as did Daavid, who carefully passed to her the gifts he was carrying and stepped back behind his father once again. So far the encounter was passing off just as Amilca had hoped. The gifts had clearly made an impression. They had been accepted and the tensions of the villagers seemed to be easing a little.

§

A sudden stab of pain wracked Maria's unconscious body and although she did not waken, it shook Helena out of a light sleep. The pregnant woman's back arched and her mid-section lifted from the bed before doubling up as much as her enormous belly would allow. Yet her eyes remained closed.

"Maria! Maria! ¿Esta bien? ¿Que pasa?" Her guardian said softly to her, not wanting to wake her charge if indeed she was sleeping through the painful contractions. But there was no reply. Only the unborn one heard the words as if through the mists of time and winced at the muscular spasms that gripped at her head and chest forcing her slowly but surely into the birth canal past her mother's cervix. To escape the pain, her mind sunk back again through fuzzy levels of unconsciousness to that faraway beach.

## Seventeen

The appearance of the Phoenician visitors on their village beach was a momentous event for Alda and his family. Yet the old chief could hardly know then just how life-changing the arrival of these strangers would turn out to be.

As evening approached, Alda sat in his hut with a few village elders and his two daughters. They were quietly discussing the day's events.

"The strangers seem to offer no threat" he said. He spoke calmly and was clearly a little relieved.

"But we must still keep up our guard. Careful plans must be made to keep the visitors under a close watch without raising their suspicions or causing any offence. Our people must be told that they are to do this ". The elders knew that they were to carry this task.

"Jaan and I will watch their chief and his son and keep you informed, father" Hannh quickly volunteered.

"Agreed!" Alda said. He could not help but smile proudly at the two young women sitting opposite him. They rose and left the chief's hut.

Not more than thirty paces away, in another hut, Amilca and Daavid sat comfortably, sharing their evening meal. First contact between the villagers and their Phoenician visitors had gone off better than Amilca had expected. After the initial fears and mutual suspicion, the formidable looking villagers had welcomed the gift-bearing strangers into their village. The chief even directed that they share with them a good supply of deer meat as well as plentiful and strangely light bread. The bread had greatly impressed Daavid.

"I must find out more about this bread." Daavid remarked, as he wolfed down another small loaf. "It is far better to eat than our hard flat breads from home."

"Take care not to seem too inquisitive" his father said, smiling at him amiably. Amilca was proud of his son; almost as proud as Alda was of his daughters. But nothing further was said of this. Amilca and Daavid both knew that they should take great pains to ensure that they give no offence nor raise the suspicions of their hosts. Theirs was still a delicate truce.

The father and son were staying in the centre of the village near the long wooden hut of Alda and his sons, while the Phoenician soldiers made camp at the edge of the village closer to the beach and nearer to their longboats. Amilca knew that isolating themselves from their soldiers was necessary to engender trust but it was risky, so they still kept a careful look-out in case any trouble should arise.

Alda had of course already posted villagers in strategic locations to keep the visiting warriors under close but discreet surveillance. He was aware that despite the apparent friendly intentions of their chiefs, some of the men may have different ideas and seek to take the village women by force or steal their possessions. He needn't have worried. Amilca had of course given strict orders to his men to stay away from the village women and issued firm instructions to his troop commander, Tor, a giant eunuch of Egyptian origin, to punish severely any transgressions. The men knew better than to disobey.

§

Several days passed quietly. Hannh found herself rather attracted to the young Phoenician visitor. She had noticed how he carried himself with considerable grace but was clearly also a warrior and seemed to be a hunter of some skill. Daavid and some of his men had already accompanied the villagers on a regular hunting party to seek out wild boar and deer in the nearby forests just inland from their settlement. Hannh did not go. She only occasionally joined the hunt, and usually only if her father and brothers were all going.

On the next occasion, the hunters decided that they were going further afield. They were a little surprised to see Hannh march up to the little group just before their departure. She carried a long and a short spear, her slingshot and had a bag of river stones hanging from the deerskin bag tied around her waist. Daavid smiled admiringly at her and she found herself turning her head to the side as if to avoid his eyes.

"Idiot!" she murmured, clenching her teeth and chastising herself quietly. "I am Hannh, daughter of Alda. I lower my eyes to no man".

Raising her head, she returned his smile with a stony stare and tightened lips. Just then her younger sister Jaan appeared.

"I too come with you on the hunt" she announced to one and all.

Hannh cared greatly for her young sibling and could not prevent showing her pleasure at Jaan's presence and willingness to join the hunt. But Jaan had caught sight of the last instant of the stony stare her older sister had directed at the young Phoenician and was perplexed.

"You do not wish me to accompany you Hannh?" she asked gently.

"Of course I wish your presence." Hannh replied with kindness.

"But you are displeased?" enquired the younger sister.

Hannh felt the blood begin to rise to her face:

"No. Not at all" ...she stammered a little and sensed an unsettling feeling that she had never experienced before. She felt confused and a little embarrassed and more and more uncomfortable for the fact that the real reason for her muddled emotions continued to stand before them, impressive and dressed lightly for the hunt, armed with a long wooden spear tipped with a dully shining metal unknown to Hannh. He was smiling and apparently completely relaxed.

She cursed under her breath.

Daavid gestured towards Jaan, smiling even more broadly, flashing his near-perfect white teeth and gesturing that she should come along with him, though they could not communicate in words. Hannh's temper flared immediately. Grabbing her sister's arm, she pulled her off in the direction the other village huntsmen were now beginning to take.

"Why do you drag me away?" She said to her sister, a little surprised.

She was beginning to suspect that Hannh was not so much upset with her as with herself and that her strange behaviour had something to do with their attractive young Phoenician guest, who now followed along happily just a few paces behind them.

BEGINNINGS　　　　　　　　　　　　　　　　　Gary Heilbronn

When all this happened, a look of surprise had at first crossed Daavid's face, but he sensed that he should nonetheless be a little pleased. He had no great experience of women and had spent much of his young manhood years accompanying his father on distant sea voyages. But sometimes, he had noticed at home and in the lands where he had travelled, that one or another of the young ladies had given him long sideways glances, often coyly, from the safety of their friends company or from a distance while carrying out their chores. Even in those lands where the women's faces were sometimes veiled, he had noticed their keen dark eyes follow his movements. But here was this stunning young woman, with the obvious bearing of a chief's or even a king's daughter and she was clearly attracted to him though confused, perhaps by the opposing claims of her modesty and her strength of character. He was unexpectedly touched deeply by her, but was cautious.

"I must be very careful," he thought sternly to himself. "I must not cause offence; particularly after the orders my own father has given to our men!" He walked on, following the two women at a short distance, though he planned to catch up with them a little further on.

The small group of hunters set off at a pace along one of the several well-worn tracks leading from the village out through the coastal forests toward the open grasslands. These prairies spread out as far as the eye could see until they met the foothills almost half a day's hard trekking from the coast. The coastal forests were home to many smaller beasts like red deer and fallow deer and even wild boar. Large grey rabbits were also plentiful as were wild turkey and smaller birds which were not so fleshy. But the young hunters often brought them home too and they were welcomed by the villagers. They introduced more variety in their diet.

Today the group were seeking larger prey. They were hunting the great bearded buffalo that roamed on the far edge of the grasslands. It was now early autumn and the spring rains were still ahead of them. These magnificent beasts with their giant heads and massive shoulders would likely be grazing closer to the edge of the coastal forest where fresh water was still plentiful and sat in strings of small water holes that only linked up and turned into rivers after the rains had fallen. The grazing was good along the edges of the forest. The grass there was still lush and green.

As the small group of hunters from Alda's village proceeded along the rough trails, Daavid began to try to communicate with Jaan. She liked him and told him the words in her language for the plants and trees they passed and anything else they happened to come across. Daavid learned rapidly. From time to time he responded, telling Jaan the names of such things in his own language.

Hannh listened to all this chatter from a few steps ahead of her companions, focussing more on the gradually thinning forest around them and keeping her senses tuned for the movement of forest animals and any possible dangers. She had easily assumed leadership of the group. All the hunters from Alda's village respected her hunting prowess and after all, she was the chief's older daughter.

The group had walked for some time before they neared the edge of the coastal forest. The coolness of the early morning had succumbed to the warmth of the mid-morning sun. The forest shade was thinning over their heads and the cover it provided was becoming sparser, allowing a patchwork of sun and shade to fall on their bodies and offering some rudimentary form of camouflage. Abruptly, Hannh signalled to stop. Through the trees about three hundred paces out on the plain were a small group of about a dozen buffalo. These animals usually congregated in large herds that moved fast, migrating over vast distances. But for some reason, this small group of animals had wandered off much closer to the edge of the forest and the main herd was nowhere in sight.

"There are waterholes nearby" Jaan confided to Daavid, leaning over almost whispering in his ear and gesturing by bringing her scooped hand to her mouth: "perhaps this is why they are here."

The young man picked up the meaning of a few of the words she spoke and understood the gestures.

Beside them, Hannh replied: "Whatever the reason, the presence of this small group of beasts is a gift from the Gods for which they must be properly thanked on our return home. But for now, extra care must be taken to avoid startling them." Hannh knew that should this occur, they would probably have to trek for hours to find the next herd and it would be unlikely that they would find a small group of animals as easy as these to corner and make a kill.

Unbeknown to Hannh's little troop of hunters who were approaching the small herd from the north-east, another small hunting party of young men had also spied the herd from their position about eight hundred paces off in the opposite direction and they were approaching rapidly. The young men were far from their mountain home and were now entering the open grasslands; but the grass was chest high in many places and they were all downwind of the herd. A gentle breeze was blowing from the north-west. In this hidden hunting party, there were just five young men; they had lived from about seventeen to nineteen summers. They were now near to the age when they would take wives and establish families of their own. Their stomachs were full of courage and their minds dominated by the wilfulness that filled the hearts of most young men.

The proud young hunters came from a village situated further up in the eastern foothills of what would later be known as the Cantabrian Mountains. It was a difficult life these days in the foothills. There were other tribes in the vicinity and fighting often broke out amongst them over access to the water-holes and hunting grounds. Sharing was not even considered when there was often not enough to go around. These tribes had not yet developed a level of agriculture that Alda's people had achieved, living, as they did, nearer to the coast on more fertile soil. The hill peoples' diet was primarily based on the meat that their hunters brought home. It was supplemented by some root vegetables and even oats which had originally grown wild but had for some years been farmed in a rudimentary way by the womenfolk of the hill tribes. With the husks removed, the oat seeds roasted and crushed provided a good source of nutrition.

Amongst this small group from the mountains was Zum, youngest son of Chnnta, chief of his tribe and feared for his strength and violent nature. Zum had lived almost eighteen summers. He was tall and had grown strong. He was also skilled with weapons for the hunt and in battle. But Zum was a headstrong young man who from a young age had often fought with his peers to claim his supremacy. He was a favourite of his father and had already accompanied the older man in raids on neighbouring tribes and the skirmishes which often occurred when the hunters were out on extended forays into the mountains and along the foothills. They showed their enemies no mercy.

## Eighteen

It was unusual for hunting parties from the mountain tribes to be so far from home. The tradition was that these people rarely ventured towards the coast as the holy men from the mountain tribes believed the far off sea to be a bad omen for their people. So when this hunt was undertaken, Zum had led the group off towards the coast over the protestations of the elders and the ominous silence of the chief. But Chnnta had not forbidden the venture. He expected that in due course, his son would succeed him as chief and it was a chief's place to take such risks.

Zum and his companions had travelled some hours and come across no wild game worth bringing back to the tribe. But now that they had seen this herd of bison, he was certain that he, Zum, son of Chnnta, had been right all the time and had known better than all the elders. He would return with the meat of a bison and he would be seen by all as one of the tribe's greatest hunters and fighters.

The small herd of buffalo seemed to consist of an extended family group. There was an enormous male with a flowing mane who grazed more towards the grasslands and appeared to be looking in the direction in which the main herd may well have roamed. His powerful shoulders measured the height of a full-grown man and directly above those shoulders, a disproportionately larger head protruded.

He was an impressive beast whose likeness could be seen carved and painted into the walls of the deep caverns above the riverbeds along whose course the mountain tribes often established their villages. Zum had seen such paintings and swelled with pride at the thought of bringing back the meat from such a beast to his tribe. There were also four or five females of differing sizes and ages; considerably less robust than the older male, though still massive beasts considering the meagre weapons that the hunters planned to use to slay them. Several younger buffalo were nearby; amongst them one or two male calves not far off adulthood. They appeared to spend more time chasing each other and engaging in mock battles than grazing. The smaller female calves seemed to be more docile and trailed around their mothers, apparently fearful of becoming separated from the family by too much distance.

It was the near-adult males that had attracted the attention of Hannh and her hunter companions. Though unpredictable in their behaviour, their constant running about and scrapping had seemed to tire them out and they started to graze more consistently in the shaded areas on the edge of the coastal forest. One had even lowered his great frame and had set himself in a half-lying position, all four legs folded under its huge body, in the shade of a large leafy acacia tree. The reclining beast was now no more than two hundred paces to the west of Hannh and her companions. It was somewhat further from Zum's small group but they too had spied the young buffalo in the distance and also recognized its likely vulnerability. Its companions still stood grazing not far away and slowly but surely they were increasing the distance between them and their now dozing half-brother. The breeze continued to blow from the other side of the buffalo and neither it nor the rest of the herd had any inkling that there were humans in the vicinity or that they offered such an imminent threat.

Hannh gestured to her companions to spread out and approach the beast from three sides using the cover that the forest still offered them. She moved off to the north with two of the group's best hunters. This was the most difficult line of approach with the wind coming from the north-west. So they smeared themselves with a mixture of mud and wild boar faeces to avoid having their scents detected as they swung around partly in the direction of the gradually abating breeze. Daavid and Jaan stayed put temporarily with another two hunters – they would move in closer more slowly and become the central line of attack on the beast as they had the shortest distance to go to reach where it was resting. The other group of three hunters headed off at speed through the more dense vegetation to the south, downwind of the buffalo and unafraid of having their scent detected but knowing that they had to circle around quickly to be able to join the hunt at the same time as the rest of the group. This tactic left the buffalo with only one line of escape: westward out into the long grass of the prairie. Surprise was still essential if they were to slay the resting buffalo before it had time to flee.

# BEGINNINGS  Gary Heilbronn

Zum and his small band had also moved quietly but quickly toward the buffalo's resting place, careful to keep their cover in the long grass. But they were still two hundred paces away through thick grass, when the pincer movement that Hannh had planned was in place and her companions were all within ten to fifteen paces of the buffalo. It was as close as possible to being on three sides of it and still in the cover of the forest or the long grass. Knowing that the beast must not be allowed to recover its strength and that at any moment it may sense their approach, Hannh quickly whistled, signalling for the attack to begin. Within seconds they all emerged from their cover and had silently run several paces into the clearing towards where the young adult buffalo still lay at rest.

Before the poor brute could raise itself on two legs it had two long wooden spears, one thrown by Hannh and the other by one of Jaan's companions, sticking at opposing angles from its shoulders. It struggled to find its hind legs, stumbling. Its companions, off a hundred paces or so, instantly reacted to the commotion and raced off into the grasslands to the west. The wounded buffalo bellowed in pain and anger but by now Daavid had reached the spot where it struggled to stand and had run his steel tipped spear through the side of its neck severing the jugular vein and with a wild spurting of blood from its neck as it swung its large head back and forth, the beast fell to the ground, quivering. At that instant the other hunters from Alda's tribe were upon the dying buffalo and finished it off with their short spears.

Zum and his four companions stopped in their tracks. They stood stunned at the sight before them. By now they were within a hundred paces of the scene of carnage and had seen the mad rush of the dead buffalo's previous companions off into the long grass. The frightened beasts were too far away and moving too fast for a second attack to be launched, even if Zum had had the presence of mind to call it. After a moment, he recovered his senses and realizing that he had lost not just the buffalo's meat but the honour and acclamation of his peers and the elders, a piecing battle-cry escaped from his throat and he charged in the direction of Alda's hunters, throwing, as his ran, his long spear which found its mark in the back upper part of Jaan's left shoulder. She screamed and fell on to one knee and then dropped to the ground. It was Hannh's companions turn to stand, as if rooted to the ground; wide-eyes looking in disbelief in the direction of their attackers.

Emboldened by Zum's violence, his companions had followed his lead and ran throwing their spears at the group of hunters gathered around the fallen buffalo. When Alda's men turned to face their aggressors, Hannh crouched to speak to her sister who, like in a sick parody of the bison's dying convulsions, lay shivering on the ground in a mixture of her own and the beast's blood. Hannh could see that Jaan's wound was not immediately fatal and rose quickly to face their enemies as they charged down upon them with short spears shaking and held above their heads.

Another of Alda's hunters now fell dead with a spear in his chest and a third lay wounded, rapidly reducing the slight advantage in numbers they had previously had over Chnnta's tribesmen. Already the ferocious looking band of aggressors were within several short paces of the buffalo and screaming, ready to pounce on their foes in bloody hand to hand combat.

Alda's hunters were skilful at the hunt but less experienced fighters than these tribesmen from the foothills. Yet they advanced fiercely towards the screaming enemy knowing that their very lives depended upon their courage in this encounter. The few seconds that had passed had allowed Hannh the time to load her slingshot. She released a volley of river stones in the direction on the mountain men, felling a broad shouldered ugly cousin of Zum's. Zum was now close enough to dispatch another of Alda's hunters with a slash across the midsection and he headed towards Hannh and the strangely dressed Daavid. His adrenalin-fuelled brain told him: "There will be little opposition from this woman and her fine-featured companion". Within an instant he realized his error as both sidestepped his charge; Hannh spun around out of Zum's path and dropped down to a crouching position, one knee almost on the ground as Zum lunged by and with an upward motion of her short spear, she pushed its point up through the young mountain man's lower stomach, lacerating his entrails. They immediately began to bubble and leak from the wound.

"Uhhhr" was the only sound that quietly escaped Zum's lips as he drew in a gasping breath. Daavid, spinning around in the opposite direction, drew an iron-bladed dagger from his belt, reached back, and in a flash, his right arm stretched to the full, he planted the dagger firmly in the centre left of Zum's upper back. The mountain man's already agonized eyes widened even further as his gaze went blank.

Seeing their leader so neatly and efficiently skewered before their eyes, Zum's three remaining companions stopped, turned and fled off towards the edge of the forest with three of Alda's remaining hunters in hot pursuit. Hannh whistled a shrieking call bringing the pursuers to a halt.

"Let them go!" She cried. Her immediate concern was to treat Jaan's wound and carry her back as quickly as possible to the village. She knew that the older women, well-skilled in the application of the medicinal plants and herbs that grew in the forest, would be able to nurse her quickly back to health. Luckily, the other wounded hunter from the coastal tribe was already on his feet. He had only been grazed and knocked unconscious.

Hannh crouched down and spoke comfortingly to her sister while attempting to staunch the flow of blood from her shoulder. Luckily the spear had missed any major internal organs and exited through the muscle at the front. She knew it was better not to remove the spear immediately. Leaving it where it was would minimize the loss of blood. So, gripping the spear at its base next to the flesh, she carefully started cutting a notch into the spear to allow it to be broken off more easily.

Daavid saw how slowly and painfully this was occurring and came over.

"Let me help you" he whispered. He began to cut the spear with his own knife. It cut so much more quickly through the wooden stem of the spear. Soon, the wooden spear was weakened enough to be easily snapped off. Jaan groaned, only partly conscious. The most part of the spear was broken off so as to leave only a small part protruding from the front and back of her shoulder.

Daavid rose quickly from Jaan's side and from trees at the edge of the forest, he cut two young branches well over a man's height long and set them down parallel on the ground. He then drew two deer hides, removed from two of the dead men, across the branches. He proceeded to poke holes along the edge of the skins with his dagger and threaded thick vines through the holes attaching the under and over sides of the skins around the branches to make a rudimentary stretcher. Hannh eyes widened and she stood back, impressed by his skill. The other hunters now stood around almost gloating over the inert body of Zum; their faces showing great relief that the battle had been won and they laughed and talked loudly about the fighting skills of Hannh and Daavid.

The Phoenician was tall and slim but showed enormous skill, great speed and accuracy in the melee. The tribesmen had hardly expected that he would prove himself to be such a warrior. It was less of a surprise to them that Hannh, herself, had been such a force in the thick of the battle. They knew already of her skills, and after all she was their chief's first born child.

Showing her impatience, Hannh issued terse commands to the hunters who were standing idly by:

"You men! Butcher the buffalo quickly and prepare the sleds! Wrap our dead in skins and bury them on the edge of the forest. We must leave here quickly".

The remaining hunters set to work immediately; bleeding, skinning and quartering the buffalo so as to minimize the load they had to carry. Within a very short time the work was done and the group were ready to drag the butchered carcass back to the village on a roughly made sled.

Daavid instructed two of the hunters in the art of carrying on their shoulders the stretcher on which the wounded young woman rested. The bodies of Zum and his ugly cousin were left on the ground where they lay.

Silent eyes watched all their preparations from the hiding place in the forest where Zum's ex-companions had retreated to. When they saw they were not being pursued, they quietly sneaked nearer to the scene of the battle and watched and waited. They knew that to return to the village without Zum's body would mean facing the wrath of Chnnta and none of them were prepared for that. Rather take their chances in battle with their enemy from the coast. They overheard the conversations of their enemies and though their language was not the same as that of the tribe of Alda, it was close enough for them to understand where the group came from and who it was that had slain their chief's favourite son.

They waited and watched. When they were sure that Alda's men had departed, they returned to the scene and stood over the body of Zum, now pale, the blood having drained quickly through his wounds. They walked back and forth, almost wailing, whining and shouting at each other. Their agitation was palpable. Finally, they decided to improvise a sled like that used by Alda's men to drag the slaughtered buffalo home, and take Zum and his unfortunate cousin back to the foothills.

The young mountain men accepted the task reluctantly as the trek across the grasslands would be onerous enough: but to drag the sleds up the rough paths into the lower reaches of the mountains would tire them and slow their pace down to a crawl. They shivered with the thought of the coming reception by Chnnta and already began to exaggerate the size of the force they had encountered and develop an elaborate tale of their ambush at the hands of this ferocious group led by a powerful and violent warrior whose attire and bearing stood him apart from the hunters who came from the coast. The truth would be much less palatable to their chief.

## Nineteen

Before Hannh's party reached their village on the coast, they met a few young boys from the tribe and one ran on to tell the older women to prepare their potions and remedies for Jaan. Daavid and Hannh had taken their turns along with the other hunters to carry the wounded girl's stretcher but their pace had been slow and it was approaching evening when the party neared the village. Alda, fearful for his youngest daughter's fate, had come out to meet them as soon as he heard the news from the young messenger. He was joined by Amilca.

Alda looked worried but knew that the older women of the village were skilled at healing the sick and injured; and Jaan was soon delivered into their care. After all the members of the hunting party had returned and the hastily butchered carcass was shared out amongst the villagers, Alda sat in his long hut before the rough wooden planks that served as a table. Hannh was to his right side and Daavid was beside her. The other members of the hunting party were there along with many of the tribal elders. Amilca, too, was invited to be present. Hannh related the events of the day leading up to the slaughter of the buffalo. The assembled villagers were entranced by the tale which she told with fluency and clarity.

After his language lessons of the day, Daavid was able to transmit to his father, some parts of the story Hannh had told and he added his own comments. By now, Amilca had ceased to be amazed at his son's gift for acquiring new languages. It had been the same when they stopped in Gades (Cadiz) on the southern coast of Iberia. There, he had quickly picked up the local language and this had greatly facilitated their trading activities. Amilca's train of thought was abruptly interrupted by Hannh who in an emotional and dramatic voice related the attack culminating in the deaths of their companions and of two leaders of the mountain men followed by the flight of their fellow tribesmen. She spared few details and there was sorrow over the deaths of the two hunters from their village. Her praise and admiration of Daavid's skill as a warrior brought a small smile to her father's face but the worried look returned when Alda heard the description of the mountain-tribe attackers that they had slain.

"Mountain men are fearsome warriors" Alda said. He spoke quietly though there was a group gathered round him.

"They will want revenge for the deaths of their people. We must take great care when venturing past the forest edge and expect an attack at any time."

Several pairs of anxious eyes looked towards him.

Daavid passed on to his father what he understood to be Alda's concerns. Amilca lowered his gaze towards the floor. He was deep in thought. This was indeed an unfortunate development from the older Phoenician's point of view. Establishing enduring trade relations depended very much on maintaining a peaceful environment, or at least giving as little reason as possible for confrontation with the local people. Now there could be inter-tribal warfare and worse, he thought worriedly, his own son had played a role in starting it. But Amilca was a fair man. He knew that Daavid had had little choice.

"This is not a good omen": he said quietly in Daavid's ear; it may well undermine our plans for a permanent trading base on this part of the coast. Perhaps we should leave and go elsewhere."

Daavid said nothing. His heart pounded. He knew that he was not ready to move on. He did not want to just get up and leave this village. He had to admit it; he did not want to leave Hannh. But how could he say this to his father?

Instead he said: "Let us delay a little our departure. There are things we can learn from these villagers and we can share our knowledge and skills so we will be welcomed when next we come to this land."

This seemed to be a sensible approach and Amilca nodded in agreement.

"As you wish, my son," Amilca replied, "just know that the longer we stay here, the more the danger there is of being drawn into a local war that is not our own".

"I understand, father" Daavid replied thoughtfully, "but I fear that the Gods have already decreed that I play a part in this unfortunate affair".

Soon, the meeting was over and they all returned to their huts more than a little concerned for the future.

The following morning Daavid sought out Hannh. She greeted him politely, but with some reserve. Daavid enquired after the progress of her young sister and was told that she had slept well and that the healers were pleased with her condition.

"Hannh," Daavid said gently. He smiled as he spoke and gestured with his hands to clarify what he was trying to communicate.

"Can you help me learn more of your language, like Jaan was doing? So I can speak to her and the others. Then also, I can tell you about my people and perhaps even show you and your people some of my own people's skills."

Hannh was silent for a moment or two as she considered the request. She was drawn to the young stranger with the fine features and admired greatly his skills as a hunter and indeed as a warrior. She had also been impressed by the stretcher he had so efficiently fashioned to carry Jaan on the hunters' shoulders rather than dragging her along the rough ground. And more, she had seen how his hard metal tipped spear penetrated so easily the thick hide of the buffalo and how his dagger found their enemy's heart with so little effort. She wanted to know where to get such weapons. She looked up into Daavid's dark sparkling eyes and knew only that she wanted to talk to him, be with him and learn his secrets. She placed her left hand on his forearm and spoke:

"Yes I will teach you and you will teach me. We will start without delay." She nodded and gestured, pointing first at herself and then at him and then poking the fingers of her right hand quickly up and down several times towards the ground. The message was clear.

Several days passed quickly. Daavid and Hannh spent most of their waking time together walking around the village, into the nearby forest and along the coast, exchanging vocabulary and trying to understand each other's expressions and customs. This activity had not gone unnoticed. Alda had asked Hannh what they were doing and she had replied that she wished to acquire the knowledge that their visitors had; especially she wanted to understand the strength of the spears. Of course Alda saw the benefit of this. He had already tested the ornate bronze dagger that Amilca had presented to him as a gift on the Phoenicians' arrival. He urged her to find out about these secrets as quickly as possible.

The following day, Hannh broached the topic of weapons with Daavid.

"Tell me now, Daavid, of the hard tips of your Phoenician spears and daggers. What are they made from?" she enquired. She was still gesturing with her hands to try to clarify her query – although this activity was becoming increasingly unnecessary.

Hannh knew that it was a delicate question as martial superiority was often based on superior weaponry and such information was not always freely given. To her surprise, Daavid seemed pleased to share this knowledge with her and responded as clearly as he could, also gesturing carefully with his rather delicate hands.

"These spear tips are made from very hard metals. They come from many distant lands," he said, pointing off towards the horizon. "But there are different kinds of metals and some are more precious than others. Most of our men have bronze spearheads and daggers. Only a few of us have weapons made with very strong iron tips. I am told that these iron tips are difficult to make. They are made by heating and hammering a stone which is very rare".

She nodded, showing her understanding of most of what Daavid had said.

He went on. "When I was a boy I was told that the Egyptians, to the south of our land, had such stones as ornaments and that some generations before I was born, the great Hittite warriors from the north and east of my homeland had used weapons made with such metal when they conquered our lands and fought long wars with the Egyptians. Eventually, the Hittite kings became weak and they were overcome by the Philistines and by other warriors from the north-west, all of whom had learned to master the use of iron. These skills are still not widely known. I have heard in my travels that warriors far to the north of our home use this metal too, but it is very difficult to obtain even by trade in foreign lands. All we have been able to get is some small flattened pieces fashioned so as to attach to the tips of our spears and daggers." Hannh understood enough of what was said to know that acquiring the skill to make these weapons was not enough. They needed a source of iron as well.

"Come Hannh, compare the strengths of our spears with iron tips and those with bronze tips", he said. He led Hannh off to where his weapons were standing. Hannh took the iron-tipped spear Daavid handed to her and buried it forcefully into the compacted earth. She was surprised by the ease with which it sliced through the hard ground. She then turned, and with startling speed, threw the spear with considerable force towards a nearby oak tree. It shivered as it pierced the heavy timber and held firmly in place, splitting the wood cleanly. She then took a bronze-tipped spear in her hand and threw it equally forcefully at the tree. The second spear glanced off the wood, failing to penetrate it and bounced onto the ground. Hannh walked over to examine it. The tip had bent a little but it was undamaged. Of course, their wooden spears, even with stone or bone tips bound to the ends, would have fared much worse against a solid oak tree. Daavid aimed another bronze-tipped spear at another younger tree and threw it with all his force. This time, the spear penetrated the young tree and exited on the other side, though passing through the softer surrounds and not through the hardened central core.

Daavid explained: "the softer metal still makes a powerful weapon if you know its limitations," he said. "It is called bronze and it is made by mixing copper and tin after heating them in a very hot fire. I have seen this done. The mixture of metals is more fluid when hot and then becomes much harder when cold. Bronze is also easier to cast in forms and moulds than is copper and it results in much better tools and weapons. This skill has been known to us for centuries." He looked proudly at the spears.

"Rocks containing tin and copper are often easy to obtain. We have traded tin for generations in Baartan; a land to the north of here. And copper is plentiful even in this land, but far to the south near Gades. Our people and those in neighbouring lands use bronze for weapons and cutting tools: things like swords, spears, arrowheads, adzes, and axes. It is even used for shields. Some people also use it for cooking pots and bowls which are stronger than those made from copper alone."

Hannh smiled at the young man, nodding her head. She was greatly impressed by the Phoenician weapons and carefully stored in her mind the information Daavid had provided her with, though she was still doubtful that rocks could be melted in this way in their fires.

Nonetheless she conveyed all the information to her father that same evening. Alda listened carefully and thoughtfully to what she had to say and resolved to ask Amilca to provide him with a demonstration of how these rocks were melted together as soon as possible. He still had in the forefront of his mind the likelihood of an attack by the mountain tribes and wanted the best possible weapons to combat them.

## Twenty

Daavid and Hannh quickly found that they were spending many hours together and they often walked around the village as they talked. After a few more days their comings and goings ceased to be a matter of discussion in the village or amongst the Phoenicians.

Early on the fourth morning, they passed by an open hut where two village women were rolling dough for the preparation of the light brownish bread that Daavid had so enjoyed since his arrival in the village. The young couple stopped and watched. Daavid noticed them kneading into the mixture, some older dough, kept over from the previous day's baking.

"Why do the women add in the old dough? Surely that will lessen the freshness of the bread?" He asked Hannh. She spoke to the women for some minutes. Daavid did not fully follow their discussion but when they had finished talking, Hannh leaned towards him and spoke almost in a confidential tone.

"Ah, you have come upon one of the secrets of the old women of our village. But as you have been so gracious in telling me about your hard metal-tipped weapons, I will share with you what they told me. ... Long ago, baking bread was just one of the many chores women had to do. So sometimes in the warmth and humidity of the early summer, the dough was kneaded and would be left longer than normal before it was baked in the earth ovens. When this occurred, little bubbles of air grew in the dough and the bread that was made was bigger and lighter than the bread that was made when the dough had not been left out for so long. So they began to practice this way of making bread and although the dough sometimes had a different smell before baking, it always tasted good. Then one day, they kept small parts of the old dough and mixed it with the new kneaded dough. They found that if this was done, they did not have to leave it out such a long time before baking. But it is only with wheat from the fields that this light bread can be made. It does not work with bread made from acorns or maize."

"This is indeed interesting," Daavid said, "... I greatly enjoy the bread your village people bake."

He thanked Hannh for this information and said also that he would share it with his ships' cooks, for he had tired of the heavy flat breads they made throughout their long voyages. Daavid was pleased with what he had learned as he also knew that information like this was as valuable as other items to trade.

During their time together, Daavid and Hannh often visited Jaan. They stayed at her side until she needed to rest from the effort of talking. They shared with her their newfound ability to communicate more and more clearly with each other. In this way Jaan also learned the language and ways of the Phoenicians. Jaan's wounds were healing quickly. The potions and herbal remedies rubbed into them were working but her youth and strength were also in no small way responsible for her rapid recovery. But Jaan was becoming bored with her convalescence and on one such occasion, she asked:

"Daavid, can you tell us about your people and your homeland. Is it very far away? Why do you come to our land?"

Daavid thought for a moment for he wished to give the best possible impression of his people.

"Yes, my home is very far away" he said, "but I do not miss it as I have spent much of my life on voyages with my father. Many people from our land voyage the seas both near and far. This is not to wage war or to plunder but to trade goods. It is that for which our people are known. These voyages are often dangerous as the peoples of foreign lands are not always hospitable and the seas, though we love them, can themselves become our enemy. They can be whipped by the Gods into terrible storms. Some great Phoenician ships and sailors have been lost to the turmoil of the seas as well as to the pirates who roam them."

"You see, many of our ships carry very valuable cargo. It is not uncommon to carry as many as 200 copper ingots from Cyprus or Gades or bring ingots of tin, carried to the shores of the Great Sea by caravan from the landlocked lands far to the north or even from Baartan, across the seas to the north and west. Sometimes our ships trade the rare blue glass that the Mycenaeans use to fashion jewellery or terebinth resin used for making wonderful perfumes.

They also carry the rich purple died cloths for which merchants from the city of Tyre and Byblos are famous; and there are clay pots, some delicately designed pots are carried to kings and merchants in faraway lands. We even have ships that take enormous logs of Egyptian ebony and cedar wood from our homeland across the seas to foreign places. There are also many foods traded, such as figs, olives and almonds."

He paused for a moment as clearly the sisters had a lot to take in.

"Even papyrus, which is used for writing, is carried by our ships and traded widely." Hannh and Jaan sat back amazed. There were so many things they did not understand.

"Writing? What is 'writing'?" Jaan said. She spoke excitedly; interrupting with youthful enthusiasm.

Daavid suddenly remembered that he had seen no evidence of writing in this primitive land. There were no stone or wooden tablets used to keep records of village transactions and he had seen no paintings or carvings telling the story of past wars or the greatness of their kings. "Who are these people who keep no records of their past heroes or of their commerce?" he thought to himself. Then he remembered that commerce was virtually absent here and indeed that was precisely what his father and he had come to establish. "Of course", he thought, "we must teach them these skills as well. That will only be to our future benefit." But he stored this idea in the back of his mind to be brought forward and acted upon on another day. He did not explain that the Phoenician's created the first phonetic alphabet which was a vast improvement on Egyptian hieroglyphs and complicated cuneiform script. Nonetheless, he would do his best to answer the question. He contented himself with a brief explanation.

"Writing," he said, "is just making marks that everyone understands upon a piece of material; sometimes, stone or wood or another finer material. The best thing to use is very fine sheets made from the papyrus plant that grows taller than a man in the land of the Egyptians. ... To make papyrus sheets, they lay lengthwise many slices of the leaf of this plant with other layers criss-crossed over it. It is moistened with water, dried and rubbed smooth either with ivory or perhaps by using smooth shells. These sheets are one or two handwidths wide and are made into rolls which can measure as much as the length of one of our ships. We have traded much of this papyrus with the Greeks who live to the north of our homeland."

Jaan looked perplexed.

"But what do these marks do?" she said. Her exasperation showed. "Are they paintings of the great beasts of the plains and of warriors on the hunt? I have heard stories of such paintings in the caverns of the mountains towards the sunset, but I have never seen them."

Hannh nodded in agreement but said nothing.

"I, too, have heard tell of such paintings" Daavid replied, "and I have even seen the ancient paintings of the Egyptians telling of the exploits of their great Pharaoh Kings". He spoke kindly without a hint of pride.

"But no, the markings that I speak of are used in commerce and allow the merchant to recall how much produce he has bought and sold and who he has bought it from or sold it to and for how much. In this way, he can know that his business is successful and how rich or poor he has become. And most important, I forgot to say, is that everyone uses the same marks so that once you learn what each mark means, then you too can know the secrets of the merchant's trade."

"But that is enough for today, Jaan," Hannh interrupted. It was growing dark outside and Hannh felt Jaan needed to rest.

Jaan was unsatisfied. She moved with a little difficulty on her bed finding a more comfortable position.

"Tomorrow, Daavid", she insisted, "you must tell us more about your people and their history. And tell us more about this writing."

"Perhaps I will ask my father to do this Jaan," Daavid said. "He knows so much more than I of our past. But now you must rest and regain your strength. ... Who knows what dangers may confront us in the days to come."

In that instant, Jaan lost her enthusiasm and lay back on her bed. She had all but forgotten about the threat of attack by the mountain tribesmen. She still suffered from their last encounter.

Hannh was annoyed and taking Daavid by the arm, led him quickly from the hut where Jaan was convalescing. Daavid could see that he had upset her and indeed that Jaan looked tired and a bit worried.

"Why must you say such things? We know there may be danger from the mountain tribes but she does not need to think of this now. We do not want Jaan to be worried while she is weak. It will not speed up her healing," she whispered sternly in his ear.

Daavid realized that he should not have spoken like that in front of Jaan but the closeness of Hannh's face to his and the fragrance of her skin excited his senses and raised his blood. In both his hands he took Hannh's angry face and kissed her gently on the lips. Hannh's body responded despite herself, melting the frozen look she had been showing to the young man just a moment before. She had never before felt like this. In truth she had never kissed a man like that before. She moved closer. She felt his arms close around her and his firm embrace. They kissed again this time slowly but with passion. Both knew in their hearts that time was short and the moment must be seized irrevocably.

§

Back in her tidy sunlit apartment in central Bayonne, Maria still slept fitfully but she slept nonetheless. Helena maintained her silent vigil. She began to think that Maria was more than asleep. It seemed that she was unconscious and, in a strange way, absent. Her body registered and reacted to the regular contractions, but somehow it seemed as if the link to her conscious brain had been suspended. It was as if she was under deep hypnosis or in a comatose state. Helena was worried. It had been just six minutes since her unconscious compatriot's last contraction. She had timed it. The previous one had been nine minutes before that, and the one before that eleven minutes and fourteen before that one. The time of birth was rapidly approaching. Maria seemed to have slept through all of these contractions. Helena was amazed but hesitantly pleased.

"I suppose we should be grateful to God that she sleeps through as much of it as possible: she said quietly to herself," just as another fiercer rattling shook the sleeping woman's torso and lower limbs.

Maria now lay on her back with her belly protruding and legs slightly apart. The convulsions rippled through her otherwise prone body almost like a wave. She unconsciously curved her spine and brought both knees up towards her swollen belly. But she slept on as if anaesthetized. The only other visible sign of her pain – and clearly she was suffering considerable pain – being the clenched teeth and grimace on her radiant but pale young face. But precisely when the grimace ended and smile began, Helena was at a loss to decide.

Wildly opposing sensations of pleasure and pain flashed across the unborn one's mind. Her hypothalamus, hidden in its protected place at eye-level, almost in the middle of her brain and just above her tiny pituitary gland, registered all these sensations. Her memories of Daavid's embrace mixed in with the forces slowly rotating her soft skull, seemingly malleable under the pressure of being forced through her mother's pelvis by the increasingly powerful birth contractions.

Maria was not a large woman; some might say that she was of a build unsuited to childbearing but this was her second pregnancy and perhaps because of her relative youth it seemed to be proceeding even more effortlessly than the first. But she must not think of the first time. Thoughts of her first birth could only bring back so much pain; not of the body but of the heart. Memories of her lost young son could not even be permitted to creep into Maria's mind.

Perhaps this was why, in some subtle, subliminal way, the young woman's thoughts and emotions had been infiltrated by those of her tiny unborn child. The child's return to such an intense moment earlier in her own time somehow pervaded both their spirits and contrived to keep her mother in a state of mostly gentle unconsciousness throughout what would otherwise have been a waking ordeal for both of them. But the ordeal was not yet over.

## Twenty-One

It was the morning after Hannh and Daavid's first night together. Alda had not slept well. He knew he could no longer wait. He must act. He called to have a message sent to Amilca. He requested that his visitor join the chief in his hut for important discussions. Hannh and Daavid were sent for as well. Alda knew that with the two young people present to translate, fewer misunderstanding would occur between the two chiefs. Alda awaited the others restlessly. He needed to move matters along quickly.

Hannh normally shared a smaller hut with her younger sister Jaan. It was much simpler than her father's rather regal residence but situated not far from it. Of course, Alda's hut was much grander. It was the home of a chief and it needed to be big enough to host the village councils which were held quite often. The chief and council met to consider matters as innocuous as crop planting schedules and as serious as theft and assault amongst the villagers, though such events were indeed rare.

Since suffering her injury at the hands of the mountain men, Jaan was staying full-time in a larger hut where the village healers tended the sick and wounded. It was located towards the edge of the village, nearer to the sea. It was safer there and not far from where the Phoenicians had made their camp.

But that night Hannh had not slept alone.

It was the custom of the women of her people to decide themselves when they wished to take a husband, and equally when they wished to rid themselves of one. Then, there were no other issues. Caring for children was the responsibility of everyone in the village and there was no question, in such cases, of which parent the children would live with. They lived where-ever they ate and slept. Personal possessions were minimal. All fields and domesticated animals were communally owned, though it was of course the duty of specific villagers to care for them and work the fields, as the case may be. Other villagers were hunters and the spoils of the hunt were shared amongst all. Consequently, on divorce, there was little or no marital property to be divided, equally or otherwise between the ex-spouses. In the event of dispute, the chief's council would make the decision and there could be no thought at all that its decision would not be abided by. In many ways, the village functioned peaceably. Indeed, though Amilca had failed to understand it, the ideas of commerce and trade and personal property that he sought to introduce were, at this time, almost completely alien to these villagers.

After the first embraces Hannh shared with Daavid the evening before, she had made the decision that she wanted him, and as the daughter of the chief, there was no-one but her father who would dare to say a word to the contrary. She had led Daavid to her hut and there they had consummated their bond. It had been a night of sweet passion and tenderness the like of which Hannh had not even dreamed of. Though both were young, it was as if two old souls had rediscovered each other. They were awoken in the morning by Alda's messenger. If he was even a little surprised at Daavid's presence in Hannh's hut, he failed to display the least indication of it.

The two young people went quickly to the chief's long hut in the village centre. Amilca was already there. Alda had been waiting for the arrival of his translators before venturing into any important discussions with the Phoenician chief.

His host had offered, and Amilca had accepted, a large portion of warm goat's milk, drawn from the small herd of mountain goats that the villagers had domesticated generations beforehand and now bred happily in captivity. They also provided the village with an alternative source of meat. Amilca was not unprepared for this meeting with his host. Daavid had told him of the keen interest which the chief had displayed in the Phoenician's bronze and iron weaponry. He was also well aware of the threat of attack from the mountain tribes. He had resolved to assist his hosts in whatever way he could, even if it meant sharing his own knowledge and skills. Better that, than to be physically present when an attack occurred and have to choose whether to withdraw or take sides. Such an attack was a very real possibility; and Daavid would clearly be a target for his part in the death of the mountain men.

Amilca knew he would have to be involved and he would prefer to have the support of a well-armed force rather than an untrained and weakly armed bunch of villagers. Moreover, the old Phoenician knew that amongst his men, there were two who were skilled in the construction of rudimentary kilns and the smelting of copper and tin to make and repair their weapons. From time to time, they had even practised other, newer skills learned from the Mycenaeans who had more recently begun to experiment with the hardening of iron weapons by treating them with heat. For obvious reasons, it was essential to have such men aboard a vessel such as his when embarking on a lengthy voyage to far off lands where hostile receptions were not uncommon.

"Come, come!" Alda shouted to his daughter as she and Daavid arrived at the entrance of the long hut. He was happy to see her.

Alda gestured for his daughter to join him a little apart from the others and he spoke quickly to her, telling her how urgent he thought it was for them to have the metal-tipped spears and daggers like those of their guests and that this was the only way to be assured of a victory in the event of an attack by the men from the mountain tribes.

"Will they help us make these weapons?" he asked. Hannh could almost taste the anxiety in her father's voice. She watched him closely.

"We must be careful how we ask for this assistance" the old chief said, "for they will surely want something in return."

Hannh smiled to herself.

She was confident that their guests would assist them. Indeed, she and Daavid had spoken the previous night of how difficult it might be for Alda to consent to the betrothal of his favourite daughter to a visitor from afar. And what that might mean for both their lives in the future. She knew that her father would never object to her choice of a husband in normal circumstances. But in this case, it could mean that Hannh would leave for foreign lands and never see him again. That would be much to ask of him and he may need some considerable encouragement. The only way was ahead, though very delicately.

Hannh nodded to her father and gestured to him to return with her to where Daavid and Amilca sat deep in conversation. The young Phoenician had already told his father that he wanted Hannh as his wife and that she wished this too; but naturally her father's consent was crucial. Of course he had also sought his own father's blessing.

After taking his seat beside Hannh, Alda began to speak.

Hannh communicated carefully each sentence to Daavid who in turned spoke slowly to his father, also choosing his words carefully. He told him that Alda had said he was very pleased that the Phoenicians had come and although he and his people may have been suspicious at first, they all now regarded their honoured guests as friends and looked forward to future visits and to the establishment of trading relations which would be beneficial to both peoples.

As Daavid spoke these words, Amilca showed his evident pleasure at them by nodding and smiling broadly at his host. Alda returned the visible sentiments and continued. He explained that his people, like the Phoenicians, were not warlike but that they needed to protect themselves from some of their neighbours. At the translation of these words, Amilca regarded his host carefully and nodded in agreement. He told Daavid to relay to his host that over some generations, his people too had been subject to warlike neighbours such as the Philistines, Syrian and Hittites who had coveted their lands and wealth.

Encouraged by the understanding that Amilca displayed, Alda thought he could now hazard his request.

"I see you understand" he said.

"It is for this reason that we ask that you show our people how to make the metal weapons like the dagger you presented to me on your arrival and like those bronze-tipped long and short spears that so easily pierce wooden shields and the thick skins of animals."

Hannh passed on the words to Daavid who then spoke softly to his father. Amilca looked down towards the floor as if thinking, though he had expected the request and planned to agree but he did not wish to seem to give away such an important prize without receiving something in return.

Seconds passed and Amilca remained silent.

Alda was beginning to feel a little uncomfortable. Should he have offered something to the Phoenicians before asking for their help?

# BEGINNINGS  Gary Heilbronn

"Surely I cannot expect this aid to be given freely as a gift" he thought aloud to himself. He was beginning to worry.

Hannh recognized her father's concern and spoke to Daavid:

"It is now time for us to seek my father's approval to our betrothal".

Daavid took her hand which she willingly gave, somewhat to Alda's surprise as he had not perceived the change that had occurred in a relationship that previously seemed only to be amicable and he spoke to his father.

"Perhaps you could now seek Alda's consent to his daughter's marriage." He whispered these words; leaning close to his father's ear. Alda watched these interactions with more and more uncertainty.

"This is a great and important gift you seek from us Alda, Amilca began, and it is a gift worthy of the great chief which you have shown yourself to be. But we have an even greater gift to ask from you."

He hesitated. "My son seeks your daughter's hand in marriage."

Alda, shocked, rose to his feet. He spoke, looking towards Hannh:

"How can this be? What say you Hannh?"

Hannh looked her father straight in the eye.

"It is what I wish with all my heart father" she replied earnestly.

Alda had never seen her take this tone before. She looked in every detail the warrior that he had raised her up to be, but she spoke with a softness and emotion that reminded him of her dear dead mother. He returned her clear direct gaze.

Seconds passed. "Surely she must speak from the heart," he thought. Alda knew his daughter was a headstrong and capable woman and a warrior. It had been a long time since he had seen this softer and more compliant side of her nature and he was touched.

Without further thought, he sat down and looked at his visitors.

"If this is my daughter's wish, then it is also my own. Let the exchange of both of these great gifts take place without delay."

Hannh and Daavid quickly passed on Alda's words to the older Phoenician who upon hearing them stood and advanced towards Alda, smiling and offering his open hand. Alda rose and embraced him heartily. Hannh and Daavid exchanged looks of relief. Neither had expected these matters to be resolved so easily.

That same day, Amilca's armourers began to instruct a chosen group of villagers in the art of making a furnace resembling a closed two-chamber pottery kiln. Until then, the villagers had fired their simple clay utensils in open fires but they quickly grasped the intentions of their visitors and set to work building the kilns. It was a skill they would not forget.

Amilca's ships carried some copper and tin ingots for making and repairing his own men's weapons. He was prepared to allow part of this to be used. He also carried small amounts of the rocks from which these ingots could be smelted and even some samples of iron ore. Many villagers were shown these samples and sent out to search for further supplies. They had roamed the countryside for all their lives and some believed they recognized all of the rocks, especially the greenish one that could be found in mounds not far away. They knew they could return with such rocks without much delay. Amilca was pleased that the villagers knew where to find copper ore, but when even the iron ore sample was recognized by more than one of the villagers he was astounded that the reddish ferrous rocks were also to be found nearby.

"What incredible good fortune, my son!" he said. "We seem to have come upon a source of iron. Our armourers must be set to work. Perhaps we can make our own iron weapons. The Gods have surely smiled upon our voyage to this place."

"Yes, my father. They have surely smiled upon me" Daavid replied cheerfully. "And you should know that Hannh and I plan to exchange our wedding vows on the day of the full moon; just six days away."

## Twenty-Two

The days passed rapidly and busily in the little village on the north coast of Iberia where Alda was chief. All those men that could be spared toiled at the construction of the two chamber kilns and the transport of ores of various kinds from sources near and far, even in the foothills where the mountain tribes sometimes roamed. Alda decided that the risks of venturing so far were justified, especially as Amilca had offered to have a small contingent of his men act as armed escorts. The womenfolk of the village busied themselves with the preparations for the ceremony to celebrate the marriage of their chief's daughter to the impressive young Phoenician. Feasts were prepared and Hannh's wedding robes cut and sewn.

Daavid and Hannh spent every moment together. He looked forward to the wedding and had sought his father's permission for Hannh to have the robes made in part from some of the rich purple-dyed cloth that still remained as part of the cargo stored on board the Phoenician vessels. Amilca was greatly pleased and his happiness for his son was boosted by the hope that much prosperity would come from future trade with this place. At times he even imagined that it may rival their great Mediterranean trading centres in Gades or the Balearic Islands. And of course, he hoped he might make a fortune from it.

Daavid and Hannh had visited her convalescing younger sister a little less frequently during these days of hectic preparation but her wounds were healing well and she gained strength daily. Of course, immediately after the meeting of the chiefs Jaan had been told of what had happened by Hannh. It had serious repercussions for her as now she may one day have to replace her father as chief. But for two long days Jaan had been left very much to her own devices and as she was recovering rapidly, she was becoming bored with being confined to the healing hut.

In the evening, four days after Alda and Amilca had reached their agreement on the marriage and military assistance, Jaan sent one of the old village women to ask her sister to come to see her.

Hannh was a little ashamed that she had neglected her young sister and wanted to make amends.

"Daavid, my dearest" she said, "you know that Jaan would love to learn more about you and your people. Could you continue the story that you began some days ago?"

The young Phoenician was more than little pleased. He replied.

"Of course; but the story of my people and who they are today is in some ways the tale of a force that flows through the lives of generations of my ancestors. I fear I may be unable to tell it as it should be told. But I will ask my father to come and speak to you, as he knows much more than me."

Daavid later conveyed the request to Amilca who agreed but as he was busy with the armourers and experimenting with the smelting of the ore that the villagers had found, he told Daavid to begin and promised he would come later that day to finish the tale.

On arriving at healing hut where Jaan was staying, Daavid looked in through the door. He was amazed at how much her recovery had progressed in the last few days.

"You are almost fully healed already Jaan." he said.

She smiled. Not only was she close to full recovery but she also liked her future brother-in-law and was excited that she would be well enough to attend the wedding ceremony that was soon to take place.

"Come in Daavid, I am so happy to see you and to welcome you into our family," she said. Her eyes sparkled with pleasure.

"I am very pleased to hear these kind words." Daavid replied.

"And I am honoured to become part of your family. But I know too, that you wish to hear more about my people, who will soon be closely linked with your own. It is only right that you be told of our history."

"Yes please Daavid." The younger woman beamed.

"I too have thought of how our peoples' destinies are now to be forever intertwined" she said.

Daavid stopped and for a moment looked quizzically at Jaan. He had not looked at his forthcoming marriage in quite this way, but it struck him that it must be so and that his marriage to Hannh must mean something for the future of them all; and for all those who may come after them.

"There is much wisdom in your words, Jaan," he replied. He looked over towards Hannh who was seated beside the bed where her sister lay resting. She returned Daavid's enquiring look with a confident and loving smile as if she had always known in her heart that this would be so. But she could hardly imagine where the future might lead her.

"I will tell you of my own land and my people," Daavid said, "and those things in our past that I do not know well enough, my father will explain, for though he is very busy, he has agreed to come and tell you more in a little while."

§

Daavid began and as he spoke he used his dagger to scratch out on the smooth earth near to where Jaan was resting, a rough map of the Mediterranean Sea, though he called it the Great Sea, its north and south coastline and the lands on its eastern and western shores. It showed the Iberian Peninsula, including its northern coastline where they now were seated.

"Far towards the sunrise and many days sail across the vastness of the Great Sea, north of the land of the great Egyptian Pharaohs and south of the Greek islands in the Aegean Sea where Knossos and the Mycenaean dynasties had until so recently prospered, lies a fertile and forested land. This is where my homeland is found."

He pointed with his dagger to the coast on the far eastern side of the Mediterranean Sea. It was known as the "Great Sea" in biblical times before the Romans renamed it "Mare Nostrum" or the "Middle Sea"; the origin of "Mediterranean Sea".

"There, near to the coast" he continued "we have built the great and thriving cities of Tyre and Sidon, not far from the ancient cities of Gubla and Berytus". The young women stared at the rudimentary map as he pointed to each place, ending with Berytus, later known as Beirut.

"Our people's faces and lives have been always turned towards the sea and we became famous for our trading and navigational skills. We learned to sail the seas far from land by always watching the brightest of stars in the heavens. We have travelled far and wide and traded with many people." He paused for a moment, letting his words sink in.

"Our land has been spoken of since ancient times and back then, it was mostly inhabited by a Semitic tribe known as the Canaanites, though now we are more often known as Phoenicians, the name that the Mycenaeans and Greeks have given us."

Jaan and Hannh sat wide-eyed and enthralled as Daavid spoke of barely imaginable peoples and places.

"Indeed," Daavid said, pleased to show off a little his skills as a linguist, the name 'Phoenician' comes from the Greek word, 'phoinikies', for the colour of the deep reddish purple dye that our people make from a shellfish found on our coastline and then use to colour our cloth. This cloth is much sought after in foreign lands because it is seen as the colour of kings. But in our own land, which some of us call Lebanon, from the Semitic word 'laban' meaning white and likely referring to the snow on the mountains behind the coast there, we are simply known as 'men of Tyre' or 'men of Sidon' according to the city where we were born; or even 'Sidonites' as we are called in the ancient books of the Israelites."

Daavid smiled at the sisters, pleased to be able to show his knowledge. He waited a moment before continuing.

"Of the other great cities I mentioned, Gubla was sometimes called Byblos or Jubayl by the Greeks. Indeed, it was through Byblos that most trade was carried on with the great Egyptian pharaohs, but that was countless generations ago. Then, the people of Lebanon sent cedar wood, olive oil and wine to Egypt while importing gold for ornaments from the Nile valley. Later, wars around our homeland interrupted this trade until the great Egyptian Pharaoh Thutmose III invaded Lebanon and nearby Syria as well." He paused.

"But in due course, the power of the Pharaohs declined and it was no more than a dozen generations ago that we regained independence from the Egyptians and fully resumed our seafaring and trading activities. This of course brought our people great prosperity. We founded trading centres throughout the lands surrounding the Great Sea from the islands of Cyprus and Malat (Malta), close to our homeland, to Tingis (Tangier) on the edge of the great desert in the land of the Bedouins, and even here in Iberia, there is Gades (Cadiz) which is far away to the south and Malaka (Malaga) over to the east."

Daavid indicated these places on his rough map. His listeners were amazed at the size of the land where they lived and the vast sea towards the rising sun. Daavid continued.

"Some of our seafarers have even voyaged further south along the shores of a great dark continent and far, far to the east." He paused.

"It greatly facilitated our trade and relations that we invented a system of writing. I talked to you about it before. And aside from the purple dye we use for our fabrics which are much sought after by the Mycenaeans and others, we also have men skilled in carving ivory, in working with metal, and even in the making of glass. ... But we do not build edifices like the Egyptians or carve stone statues like the Greeks."

Jaan and Hannh listened quietly and intently to the words that Daavid spoke with obvious pride and some emotion. Their minds were almost visibly expanding from what they heard and they were astonished at the places Daavid described.

Jaan could not help but interrupt.

"What is this 'glass' that you say your people are so skilled in making? You mentioned glass jewellery and beads last time you spoke of your people and their trade with the Egyptians. Do we have this here? How is it made?" she enquired.

"Jaan, glass is indeed a wonderful material." Daavid replied.

"You can use it to store foodstuffs and other things but even better, the things you store can be seen through the glass which can even be made in different colours – not at all like the clay or bronze pots most people use, though they are less fragile. The foods stored in glass containers are not adulterated by the container, as can happen with copper and wood. But glass has other uses. Indeed, you'll recall that we presented your father with some glass jewellery when we first arrived."

"Yes, I remember," Jaan replied. "It is certainly beautiful; but how is it made?"

"You are so curious, Jaan and it is a good thing, but as a child, you must have been a constant irritation to your parents." He replied a little mischievously.

BEGINNINGS  Gary Heilbronn

Jaan's gaze fell towards the floor and she was silent.

Hannh looked annoyed and spoke sternly to the young man. "Our mother died when Jaan was young. Our father is chief and has always been very busy, but he has taught us the things we need to know. We may not have seen the peoples and lands where you have travelled but we too are skilled as warriors and hunters, and we know much about the tilling of the soil and the plants and animals of the forest."

"I am so sorry, Hannh. And Jaan, I apologize to you too" Daavid replied. "I did not mean to suggest.... I did not mean that ...at all. I too barely knew my mother. But let me tell you what I have learned and what I have seen in the city of Tyre where glass workers make the many and various coloured glass flasks and jewels that we trade." He continued eagerly.

"The earliest glass objects made were beads but later, hollow vessels were made from the glass. It is said that travellers from far to the east brought the art of glass-making to Egypt and Mesopotamia. So when Lebanon was invaded by Pharaoh Thutmose III, the art of glassmaking was introduced into our land." He stopped for a moment.

"You know, glass is not like some other precious stones or shells that you can find or polish to make them sparkle and shine. Again it is heating and mixing the materials that is essential. Glass is made mostly from sand – like you have on your beachfront – and from the flint found in white chalk in the cliffs along the coastline. I will tell you how it is made." Daavid paused for a moment; then continued.

"The sand is placed in a large clay pot and heated together with a white or grey powder, called soda-ash, which is nothing more than the ashes remaining after seaweed is burnt, or sometimes it is found inland from the sea, in lakes where the water has disappeared and has left only a white powdery substance on the surface of the ground. I am told that the same powder can be made from the ashes of burned wood but I have not seen this done. It is only by adding this powder that the sand will soften and melt in our kilns. When it does, the glass becomes green or brown but then there are other powders the glassmakers add to make the glass transparent."

"Daavid", Jaan interjected, her green eyes flashing; Daavid could see that she loved these sparkling objects. "Is the flask you gave my father made from this wonderful transparent glass?"

"Yes, indeed." Daavid replied with a knowing smile. He could see that she would soon possess her father's glass flask.

"This unguent flask is made from Phoenician glass. Our glassworkers first make a mixture of clay and dung and attach it to the end of a metal rod – this forms the core of the flask, the part that will later be hollow when the rod is removed. They gradually form the core into the shape that they want the inside of the flask to have. Then, hot threads of glass are wound around and around it. They are then smoothed out, usually on a flat stone, reheated, then more threads wound around until the flask is finished. Then, the rod and the clay core are removed to leave an empty flask. Later, a base and handles can be added and even a pouring lip can be moulded into the top."

Jaan stared at him. She was intently interested in his words.

"As I said before, jewellery can also be made from glass. Clear and coloured molten glass is poured into moulds to produce beads and other objects, some of great beauty. This technique can also be used to make glass jars and bowls. I have even seen rods of glass heated and wound together to make bowls in patterns of great complexity and beauty."

The young women were eager to learn and it was through such conversations in those ancient times that the knowledge of these Middle-Eastern arts and crafts reached the far north of Iberia.

The discussion continued and as the young women sat marvelling over these revelations, Amilca appeared at the entrance of Jaan's hut.

In his own tongue, she bid him to enter and thanked him for coming. Amilca could not believe how quickly both Jaan and Hannh had learned the language of the Phoenicians. Of course, there was much that they did not understand but already they could communicate with Amilca.

"I have come to wish you well in your recovery Jaan," he said. "And I am told that you wish to hear some tales of our people's history." He spoke in a strong and direct tone befitting a wise and able leader of men.

"I thank you," Jaan replied, "and would be greatly pleased to hear more. Daavid has already amazed us with stories of your people's voyages beyond the sunrise and encounters with strange peoples. We have learned much from him. Please, do tell us more of your people's history. Sadly we know little of our own past aside from the stories told by the elders and they say nothing of the lives of peoples beyond the mountains let alone across the seas."

"I will tell you what I have been told" Amilca replied. He chose a seat.

For a moment, the four unlikely companions sat quietly together in the large healing hut, surrounded by the mixed aromas of herbs and plants that the old women of the tribe used for their healing craft.

§

Maria's unborn child once again felt an acute pain in her shoulder and a crushing pressure on the side of her head. She shrugged her body with difficulty to try to find a more comfortable position. She was now in a much more restricted space than she previously had to move around in.

With the movement she found some temporary respite and once again, without warning, her consciousness fell rapidly into a dark abyss until the strange smells of the healing hut surrounded her and the sounds of familiar but unusual voices echoed in her ears.

## Twenty-Three

Amilca sat down on a low wooden bench not far from Jaan's bedside. After making himself comfortable, he began to speak.

"I will tell you what my father told me of our history. It is as near to the truth as I know and will help you understand who we are today." Amilca began to recount to the sisters the history of his own people.

"We are called Phoenicians but we are known as men of the city where we were born. Daavid and I are men of Tyre. Phoenician people and their language are Semitic in origin but we come from many places as there have been many invaders through our lands. Mostly we are from around Canaan and many Canaanites were descendants of people known as Hebrews."

"More than thirty generations ago, to the north of our land, the empire of a people called the Hittites had just collapsed, as had already happened to the empire of our long-time trading partners in the south, the Egyptians. Further to the east, our Assyrian enemies were also weak. At that time, the ancient hapiru or Hebrew tribes were becoming more powerful," Amilca explained, "though for countless generations before then they had lived a semi-nomadic existence, wandering between the shores of the Great Sea – a immense stretch of water that extends all the way from our the land of our birth to our settlements on the east coast of your vast homeland – and the ancient city of Uhrr in Mesopotamia, where in those early times, a great and expansive empire was to be found. It was many days march from our land, in the direction of the rising sun, and its territories also extended far away in all directions. From time to time, the hapiru tribes were forced, by various invaders or famine to leave their land and travel towards the Great Sea."

Hannh and Jaan sat silently trying to take in all this strange talk of the Great Sea and the rise and fall of ancient empires.

"Those tribes all spoke very similar Semitic languages but 'hapiru' was the most important one. It was understood and spoken by most tribes around there; even the Canaanite people then living on the edge of the Great Sea. Some people called the speakers of these tongues 'Hebrews',," he continued, "and these wandering tribes often lived on the outskirts of the Canaanite settlements. Perhaps the most famous of the leaders of the hapiru people was a man called Abrham. He was born in the Mesopotamian city of Uhrr. It was then a large city situated on the edge of the Al-hajar desert and had been made prosperous by the waters of the great Euphrates River. But after marrying his half-sister Sirai, Abrham left Uhrr with her and his nephew Lot. They wandered towards the Great Sea and eventually came to live in Canaan. It is said that Abrham claimed that it was God's Will that he do so."

"But famine also came upon the land of Canaan forcing Abrham and his tribe to leave and eventually they arrived in Egypt where his first son, Ishmael was born, not to his wife, but to a concubine called Hagar, an Egyptian slave woman. Many believe Ishmael to be the ancestor of all the Arab peoples living around our land. As their wanderings continued, Abrham's small tribe moved on to the great but evil cities of Sodom and Gomorrah, which, it is said, God destroyed as punishment for their wickedness. Abrham had been warned by his God to leave that evil place and it was there that he parted company with Lot and continued his nomadic existence."

The young people sat quietly, fascinated by the story. Never before had they heard such things spoken of. Amilca then told how prior to the arrival of Abraham, the Egyptians, Mesopotamians and others had regularly invaded Canaan, causing incessant warring, great suffering, poverty and insecurity.

The older man continued. "Although some generations had passed, Abrham was still alive but very, very old and he had come to possess substantial herds of sheep, goats and cattle. Because he was wealthy, he could maintain a body of armed men to defend his people and, if needed, to attack his enemies. Those were dangerous times and there were many invading tribes to be feared, so the Canaanite chiefs asked Abrham to join them and settle permanently in their land. This he did with considerable conviction, for he had said time and again that God had promised this land to Abrham and his people."

Hannh looked up directly at Amilca, opening her arms in a querying gesture, and spoke:

"But Amilca, how do you know all this? Did they write such stories down in those days?" Hannh demanded of the older man, soon to be her father-in-law. "Daavid has told us about writing."

"Yes," Jaan added, "but I thought writing was not something that the ancients knew of or practised."

"You are both correct," Amilca said, "the ancients wrote down stories, and not as we do today on papyrus, or leather, or strips of copper. In those ancient times, there were only stone tablets with designs of figures and some markings that told tales of the past. We cannot be sure of details as these stories were sometimes embellished by the tellers in tales handed down from father to son. There are so many stories. Some even tell of the creation of mankind but no-one knows when or where the stories came from. What I tell you now is only what has been passed on to me from my ancestors. Listen carefully as now the story becomes even stranger."

Amilca went on to explain to Hannh and her sister that with the appearance of Abrham and his people in Canaan, there was a new idea that began to be spoken of: it was the idea of the existence of a single tribal God, and that over the centuries this idea had been accepted by many of the peoples in Canaan and its neighbouring regions. He continued.

"It is said that the God, who Abrham called Yahweh, made a covenant with him, promising to protect him and his descendants, to wage wars on their behalf, and to obtain for them the land of Canaan. Some say that God pledged to Abrham's descendants the lands all the way from the river Nile, in Egypt, to the great river Euphrates near Mesopotamia. Such a homeland would be vast; much, much larger than the whole of Canaan and to keep it, doubtless many wars would be needed."

In this way did Amilca explain to Hannh and Jaan the part Abraham played in the traditions of the peoples in and around his homeland. And at the same time, he introduced into his listeners' oral history, some of the myths of the ancient world.

"Canaan, the land God had promised to Abrham and his descendants, is but a narrow strip, not more than a few days march across. On one side is the Great Sea and on another lies Egypt and the lifeless desert of the Arab peoples. Across the mountains, towards the rising sun is Mesopotamia. These great and powerful civilizations had been our neighbours and many travellers and caravans passed between the Nile River Valley and the great Euphrates River. So, as long as there was peace and stability, Canaan and surrounding lands were prosperous centres for trade and culture. I believe that it is for this reason that we have always tried to be a peaceful people, trading with our neighbours not fighting except to defend ourselves."

Jaan had been listening but could not help interrupting again.

"But Amilca," she said. "Who were Abrham's descendants? You said that his first son, Ishmael, was not the son of his wife, Sarai, but of a slave woman and that he was the ancestor of all the Arab peoples?"

"Ah, here the tale becomes even more strange" Amilca replied.

"It is said that it was only when Abrham and Sarai were very old, indeed Sarai was well past the normal child-bearing age, that God gave them a son of their own. His name was Isaac, and so the story goes, when Isaac was still just an infant, God sought to test Abrham's obedience to him by commanding him to sacrifice his only son. This, Abrham set about doing. It was only when God was convinced that Abrham would indeed obey him that He relented and allowed instead the sacrifice of a ram and the cutting off of the child's foreskin: a ritual called circumcision. Then, we are told, God renewed his covenant with Abrham to secure a homeland for him and his descendants. But, so the story goes, God wanted something in exchange for this great gift. The hapiru people, each and every one of them, were to follow the laws and rituals laid down by God, including the rite of circumcision of all boy children, just as he had required of Isaac."

The sisters sat back, appalled.

"But Amilca!" cried Hannh, "the hapiru God must be cruel indeed to order the mutilation of infants." Hannh's hand reached towards her own belly, sensing that already there was a life growing there.

Daavid had been quiet for all this time. Now he spoke.

"But father, some say that it was Ishmael, his first-born son, who God commanded Abrham to sacrifice. This is the belief of many of the Arab tribes to the east and to the south, though the peoples to the west, here in Iberia, know nothing of these arguments."

"That may be so, my son," replied the older man, "but if God truly sought to test the faith of Abrham, would He not more likely command the sacrifice of his and Sarai's own, long-awaited son, a mere innocent infant, rather than Ishmael, who by then was already a grown man and a son born of Abrham's relations with an Egyptian slave woman? You must make up your own mind, but if this legend is true and Isaac was indeed their own son, common sense tells me that it is more likely Isaac that it speaks of".

He thought for a moment and continued.

"Perhaps it is of no real importance which son the story refers to, except to those priests and kings who claim to be more favoured by God than others."

Amilca now looked at Hannh and spoke slowly. "Hannh, I have thought much about this ritual of circumcision, and though it seems harsh, it is perhaps just a small sacrifice; just a test of faith that every hapiru male must endure to witness his covenant with his God."

"But father," Daavid interrupted "is it not also a way of preventing disease in young boys. I have heard that it avoids many cases of infection caused by uncleanliness. This must be a good thing".

"That would seem to be true, my son, and it is a ritual that is practiced in other lands by other peoples. I have heard of it amongst the ancient Egyptians and also amongst the Arabs and African tribes far to the south. ... But let me continue with the story of our own people's history," Amilca insisted.

"There was another reason why, for the hapiru people, Isaac was a very important man, as it was through the second son of Isaac and his wife Rebekah that the Hebrew people claim their special relationship with God. That son was called Jacob and later became known as Jacob-Israel for having struggled long and hard with his faith in God. And it was during Jacob-Israel's lifetime that the Hebrews began to think of themselves as permanently linked to the land of Canaan".

"Let me tell you more about Jacob-Israel." Amilca persisted. He was keen to pass on his story to his young listeners.

"His role in our history is of much significance. He had two wives, Leah and Rachel, both the daughters of his uncle, and they had two serving maids, Bilhah and Zilpah. By these four women, Jacob-Israel fathered a daughter and twelve sons and those sons, who were known as the 'children of Israel', would themselves become known as the founders of the twelve tribes of Israel."

"Now, the fourth son of the six sons Jacob had with his wife Leah, was called Judah, and it was his tribe that became the largest and most powerful. Indeed, the term 'Jew' which is used for the peoples of all these tribes derives from the name of the tribe of Judah. More importantly, it was to this tribe that the legendary King David belonged. I will say more of him in a moment."

"But to return to the story ..." he said. Amilca was an animated story-teller and keen to continue the tale.

"To escape the drought and famine which once again raged in Canaan, some fifteen or so generations ago, Jacob-Israel's family migrated to Egypt, like the family of Abrham generations before him. It was a large group of some ten or twelve dozen people and they, like many others, were drawn towards Egypt by the richness of the fertile Nile River Valley. Indeed, many people had gone to Egypt before them, seeking trade or work, or just to escape from hunger, but sometimes they were taken as slaves. Indeed, over time the Egyptian Pharaohs became less accepting of these foreign peoples and within a few generations, most had been taken into bondage or become slaves."

"But what are 'slaves'?" Jaan interrupted abruptly.

Amilca sat back and raised his eyes to the ceiling; then recalling that indeed, he'd seen no slaves around this little village.

"Aha!" he exclaimed. "I see that you do not have slaves here. It has always been the way of victorious armies to seize not only the gold and goods of the people they vanquish, but also to herd off as many of those people as they can to make them work until they die or sell them on to others like animals. It is by using slaves that the Pharaohs built their magnificent pyramids, the Mesopotamians built their vast irrigation systems and other powerful emperors erected edifices and monuments to their own glory. The powerful of the world will always seek to own and exploit those who are weaker. It is how kings become richer. But slavery is not a big part of the Phoenician way of life. We are traders and not a warlike people; different to many of our neighbours. But enough of that. ... Back to our people's history."

"So it came to pass that the oppression of the Israelites in Egypt was so great during the reign of Pharaoh Ramses II and his successor Merneptah that these oppressed people were forced to rebel and escape. This they did under the leadership of a man called Moses."

"I do not myself know this to be true, but it is said that the liberation of a people enslaved by a powerful tyrant was totally unprecedented in history and so it must have come through divine intervention. The same may well be said of how they later survived for more than a generation wandering through the dry and lifeless Sinai desert. But, perhaps understandably, this ordeal only seemed to strengthen the bonds between the Hebrews and their God."

Amilca stopped for a moment to reflect on this.

## Twenty-Four

Amilca was visibly tiring after recounting so much to his eager listeners. Hannh could see this and said.

"You are fatigued Amilca and the daylight is waning. You do not need to continue with the story now. We are very grateful for the tale you have told us."

The older man raised his hand to silence her objections.

"No, Hannh. I must finish this story now, for there is much to do in these days of preparation and I fear that I may not have the time to begin again later." He seemed to have renewed enthusiasm. "I will tell you briefly of the strange and wondrous life of Moses and of my own ancestors' place in this story".

"But father", Daavid again interjected, "is this not the same Moses that the Arab peoples speak of as 'the prophet Moussa'?"

"It would seem so, my son, that it is one and the same. He is revered by many peoples from different lands", Amilca said quietly, and continued.

"It is said that Moses was born in a place called Goshen, in the land of the Egyptians. This was in the times that I already spoke of, when the Israelites there were enslaved and oppressed by a cruel Pharaoh. Just before Moses was born, Pharaoh commanded that all newborn male Hebrews be drowned in the river Nile. Moses' mother heard this command and was able to hide her son for three months, but to try to save him, she put baby Moses into a basket made of woven papyrus and let it drift upon the river Nile. As the story goes, the baby was found by Pharaoh's daughter and Moses was brought up as her own child."

"As fate would have it, when Moses had grown to be a man, he saw an Egyptian murder a Hebrew slave. He could not act to save the slave's life but he killed the Egyptian in revenge. Perhaps this saved the lives of other slaves. We will never know. But it would normally have resulted in his immediate execution; it was only because he was so close to Pharaoh's family that he was spared; though forced to flee from Egypt. This he did and he became a shepherd, staying in exile in the mountains until he was a very old man".

Amilca stopped for a moment, reflecting on what he was about to say.

"The story then goes that Yahweh, the God of the Hebrews appeared to Moses in the midst of a burning bush on the slopes of Mt Sinai and commanded him to return to Egypt and set his people free from their slavery and oppression. He was told to lead the Hebrews out of Egypt and back to Canaan, which Yahweh said again was to be their homeland. Of course, Moses asked how he alone could achieve this great feat and, it is said, Yahweh gave to him the power to perform miracles."

Amilca paused again. "Believe as you will, but this was the story recounted to me and handed down through generations."

"Moses did return to Egypt and implored Pharaoh to free the Hebrew people, saying it was the will of God that this be done. But Pharaoh refused and Moses is said to have changed the water of the Nile to blood and then, when Pharaoh would still not comply, he brought a series of plagues including one of locusts upon the land of the Egyptians, but sparing the Israelites. Finally, Pharaoh relented and allowed Moses to lead his people out of Egypt and towards Canaan. But then, he again changed his mind and sent an army after the Hebrews, who were trapped and set upon from behind as they approached the Red Sea. It would indeed take another miracle for the Hebrews to escape, so Moses called again upon Yahweh for help. Moses stretched out his arm, whereupon it is said that the Red Sea rose up in two great walls, separating and leaving a path of dry land between two walls of water. The Hebrews crossed on the dry sea bed, but then when the Egyptians tried to pursue them, the walls of water fell upon them and many of them drowned".

Daavid had heard much of this tale before and had begun to doubt it, but the two sisters were silent and wide-eyed with amazement. So Amilca paused for a moment to allow the immensity of this image to have its full effect on his awestruck listeners.

"In this way," he continued, "the Hebrews were saved and went again on their way towards Canaan. But time passed and when they reached the Sinai Peninsula, Moses made them stop, for he himself was awaiting guidance from Yahweh. So leaving his people, he again climbed Mount Sinai to speak with God, spending forty days and nights alone on the mountain. He then descended from the mountain saying he had received from Yahweh two tablets of stone on which were inscribed what he called the Ten Commandments which were to become the fundamental laws of the Hebrew people."

"But Moses had been away from his people for some time and they were afraid, having only just escaped from enslavement. He found that while he was on the mountain his people had panicked over their plight and had taken to worshipping an effigy of a golden calf that they had carved from ornaments and jewelry they had managed to bring with them. Appalled by how easily his people had abandoned their faith, he angrily destroyed Yahweh's stone tablets."

Amilca looked directly towards his listeners as he spoke. "A wise man might say that it is with such rage and dramatic gestures that great men assure the obedience of their followers. And it had its desired effect. The people were now terrified of God's wrath and once again sought Moses' leadership. So new tablets were hewn and inscribed according to Yahweh's command. Also a wooden box plated with gold was built to transport them. These stone tablets were then placed in this box, called the 'Ark of the Covenant' and it was faithfully carried by Moses' people during the next forty years of wandering in the wilderness and kept safe despite unimaginable hardships: plagues, fires and earthquakes."

Again Hannh and her young sister stared again in amazement, for they had never heard tell of such wonders and such calamities. As he was a talented story-teller, Amilca waited a moment; then continued.

"At last, Moses and his people arrived on the outskirts of Canaan. Moses was very old now and would die before seeing his people at last in their God-given homeland. He only lived to see the Promised Land in the distance from the top of Mount Pisgah and to hand over the leadership of the Hebrews to Joshua; he was another great leader."

"In their years of wandering, the Hebrews had learned not just of the sacred Ten Commandments but of many other new laws and ideas. One such new notion was that all men were created in the image of God and thus were all equal before God. This idea is not accepted by many, for it would mean an end to all slavery and without it, how would the great works of kings and victorious generals be carried out? Already much of the wealth of kings is taken as tribute from vanquished peoples after conquest. However, the Hebrews believed that their lives were guided by a set of God-given laws; and that these laws were greater than man-made laws."

Once again Amilca paused; perhaps for effect. His audience was speechless. When he continued it was in a less dramatic tone of voice.

"But let me come back to the Hebrews' return to their homeland, for it is there that our own family's history becomes part of the story."

"It was only some eight or perhaps nine generations before our present time," Amilca continued, "that Joshua began the conquest of Canaan and, in particular, he is known for capturing the great walled philistine city of Jericho. He was a great leader and established a loose accord of the tribes of Israel living in the region. At that time, the inhabitants of Canaan had become sedentary and felt secure living in their walled cities. Nonetheless, it took over three or four generations and many great and bloody battles before Canaan was truly conquered."

"For much of this time, the tribes of Israel, often also fighting amongst themselves, controlled only the higher, less desirable lands outside the cities. The Philistines, who then occupied Jericho and much of the surrounding land, had earlier arrived on the coast of Canaan from the sea and by land from the north; then they had fought their way inland. They were a warlike, disciplined and well-organized people who possessed weapons made from iron, making them a much-feared enemy. They quickly exterminated the Canaanites then living on the coast and later sought to conquer the hill country occupied by the Hebrews. For a time they were successful and in due course, the Philistines destroyed the army of Saul, the first King of Israel. But after Saul, leadership of the Israelites passed to David and he was perhaps Israel's greatest king. I must tell you about him."

Amilca then recounted the story of David.

"David had grown up as a shepherd boy, but he became known for his courage after defeating and killing the giant philistine warrior, Goliath. According to legend, he did this with his slingshot, having become an expert with this weapon just as you, Hannh and Jaan have done. He was later appointed armour-bearer for King Saul; but Saul became jealous of David who had become a military hero after battles with the Philistines, and though David was a friend of Saul's son, Jonathon and was married to his daughter Michal, Saul sought to kill David. ... Family ties are often sacrificed by Kings. So David was exiled and survived only by becoming the leader of a group of bandits in the deserts of Judea."

"In a strange twist of fate, David later entered into the service of Achish, then King of the philistine city of Gath, who in return for David's services, made him ruler of the town of Ziklag. Thus, he learned the ways of his Philistine enemy and this would prove to be to his advantage in the future and perhaps a lesson for us all."

"David only returned to his people after King Saul and three of his sons, including his friend Jonathon were killed in a great battle with the Philistines at Mount Gilboa. On his return, he was made King of Judah at Hebron. Over time, he united the Hebrew peoples and later he became King of all the tribes of Israel. King David was indeed a great leader and warrior for he then quickly defeated not just the Philistines, the Moabites, the Aramaeans, the Ammonites, but also the Edomites, the descendants of Jacob-Israel's older twin brother Esau. By this time, he had firmly established Israel as a powerful kingdom and had greatly extended its territories far inland, even to Damascus."

"One of the principal conquests of David was the Jebusite city stronghold of Zion, which he made into his own capital, calling it Jerusalem. It was later called the City of David as King David made this city into both the religious and administrative centre of the kingdom. He built his palace there and beneath a tabernacle, he placed the sacred Ark of the Covenant, the most holy relic that the Israelites possessed and some said, the symbol of the Hebrew peoples' unity."

"There's one thing I don't understand, Amilca" said Jaan.

"What's that, Jaan?"

"Why do these great warriors want to build empires and conquer and kill so many people along the way and steal their land? You tell me that the Phoenicians are not warlike; but some of these people were your ancestors and they sound like warlike and violent people."

"That's an excellent question" Amilca replied.

"It has much troubled me as well and I can only say that if the Hebrew people had not a leader like King David, they would have been crushed and enslaved by one or another tribe led by a power-hungry and covetous king. In a hostile and cruel world, self-preservation demands strength. It is the strong and their offspring who live; the weak who are unable or afraid to act find only death or enslavement."

Amilca now looked squarely at Hannh and Jaan.

"There are lessons" he said gravely, "that you both may wish to learn from the life of the great King David, and they may serve you well here in your own homeland."

He continued, "King David succeeded where others had failed for some very important reasons. Of course he had the qualities and strength of a great leader, but others have possessed such qualities and failed. He came to power at a time when the great empires that previously ruled the region had waned and weakened. He built a powerful professional army that did not tolerate tribal unrest. As long as there is division, there is weakness and there can be no safety from your enemies. He also seized and kept control over the great trading routes in the region. This brought wealth to the kingdom and reduced discontent. Finally, he made sure that Israel had strong ties, both trading and religious with the rich and ancient Phoenician city of Tyre just to the south."

"Indeed, it is for this reason that my son and I come from that city. My grandfather, Aaron, named after the brother of Moses, was born into the family of King David. He was a son of David, but by one of David's wives' handmaids and being well educated, he was then sent as David's emissary to the city of Tyre. It was his task to oversee the delivery of the shipments of cedar wood for the construction of David's palace in Jerusalem and any other goods traded with the Phoenicians. In Tyre, my grandfather married a Phoenician woman named Zelph, who like many Phoenicians, worshipped Astarte, the Goddess of love and fertility. Astarte was the female counterpart of Baal, a more local God who took many forms according to the city where he was worshipped."

"Aaron settled permanently in the city of Tyre. He had little knowledge of the family of his wife and the history of her great city, although it is said that its lineage is as long as that of the Hebrews. Perhaps, Daavid and Hannh, their story is similar to yours. But these matters are far from certain as the Phoenicians kept few records of such things. As time went by, Aaron was happy in Tyre and did not wish to return to Canaan, for Solomon, the successor of King David had failed to follow the practices that Moses had established. Solomon undertook the construction of sumptuous palaces and monuments, and my grandfather and his son after him continued as his emissary in Tyre. Indeed, they feared that in the Kingdom of Israel, discord and disunity would result from the reign of King Solomon, who imposed religious conformity, burdensome taxes, and forced labour – almost slavery – upon the Canaanites and people in the north of the kingdom, while unfairly exempting the people of Judah in the south."

"The death of Solomon in more recent years has shown my grandfather's prediction to be true, for it has come to pass that the ten tribes of Israel in the northern more populous and fertile parts of the land have refused to recognize Solomon's successor Rehoboam. I fear that such disunity and division are a sign of weakness and will show the way to invasion and the deaths of many ….." Amilca spoke slowly, his eyes and voice betraying the seriousness of his concerns.

He sat staring into the fire that burned quietly in the centre of the healing hut where Jaan temporarily resided. His listeners also sat quietly, reflecting on the older man's words and the indefinable thread that linked these Phoenician visitors with their Judean ancestors. That all this would soon become part of their own life story was little more than a glimmer of a thought buried deep in their minds.

## Twenty-Five

Darkness had almost descended on the coastal village where Alda was chief. Amilca had told the tale of his ancestry, bid farewell to the young people and begun the short walk back to his hut. He smiled. He felt satisfied that he had passed on to the young women the story of his and Daavid's ancestors and taught them some lessons from the past. He believed that it was important that those living, especially the women, should understand their links with the spirits of peoples so far in the past.

He had quickly acquired enormous admiration for Hannh and her sister Jaan, and thought with pride of the children that his son would father with his new bride. His bloodline was in good hands. He was also pleased with the progress that had been made by his armourers and the men of Alda's tribe. Together, they had begun to fashion bronze and iron spearheads and daggers, though it would be many days before enough weapons could be made and warriors trained to feel confident of an easy victory over the mountain tribes should they indeed decide to attack. Amilca gave no thought to how his actions might be changing the villagers' lives and perhaps also their futures.

He walked without haste in the gentle early evening light, still concerned but confident that their efforts would soon bear the fruits they deserved. At that moment, his reverie was disturbed by the sounds of shouting and commotion coming from the forest sides of the village. Then a banging of weapons could be heard from where Alda had posted sentries to warn of any impending attack. Amilca ran to his men's encampment and roused them with a shout.

"Warriors! To your weapons!" he cried. "We're under attack."

The Phoenicians leapt to obey.

Just at that time, Daavid and Hannh were preparing to leave Jaan's hut. It, too, was near the Phoenician encampment on the other side of the village to where the attack was now heard to be occurring. As the couple ducked and came out through the low door, the first few advancing mountain tribesmen could already be seen in the precincts of the village, furiously swinging axes, maiming and killing any of the helpless villagers in their paths. Women, children old people, domesticated animals. None were spared. Clubs crashed down on skulls, limbs torn and severed, blood and flesh and entrails splattered on the ground. Wooden spears now flew through the air, some finding their marks. Several villagers were putting up a resistance of sorts, but sporadic and disorganized.

The battle was only into its first few minutes, but the volume of ferocious screaming by the attackers and the pained, agonized, moaning and squealing of the injured and dying was rapidly rising to a frightening level. Fires were now burning, some fiercely and others starting up with smoke rising from several huts. Children and animals ran every which way, seeking escape. The mountain men had taken the village almost completely by surprise despite the lookouts that had been posted by Alda. They were unaccustomed to warfare. There were a large number of attackers. It seemed that a few mountain tribes had joined together with the promise of plunder aplenty and slaves. However, not all seemed to be experienced warriors as many were falling to the clubs and spears wielded by the coastal villagers.

The hunters of Hannh's village now easily turned their spear-throwing skills to warfare. Daavid could see Alda already in the thick of the fighting. His great chief's hut was in the centre of the village and closer to the impact of the initial attack. He had quickly seized his daggers and iron tipped spears; having been the first of the villagers to be presented with them by the armourers, but others had them as well. Alda had already dispatched several attackers, before being joined in the fray by his sons, who were beginning to acquit themselves well enough against the enemy force despite the young men's lack of battle experience.

As the fighting passed through the central part of the village, the attackers still had the upper hand and had cut a path through the defending villagers. Hannh and Daavid hurriedly returned to the fray with their weapons and were quickly engulfed in the hand-to-hand fighting that was erupting all around them. Wounded and maimed villagers and mountain men lay about and pools of blood framed many of the bodies. One of Hannh's brothers had already fallen and even before his attacker's great club could be raised again to strike another blow, the warrior who had slain the boy was almost surgically disembowelled by a sideways slash of Daavid's iron-bladed razor-sharp dagger. He fell with a grunt, intestines spewing from the wound, as two other mountain tribesmen ran to the attack, lunging and poking at Daavid and Hannh with their wooden spears. Alda's club nearly removed the head of the small stocky one while his larger more agile companion sprung backwards avoiding a second, powerful crossways swing of the club and at the same time lashing out with his large stone axe at Alda's forearm. It connected with a sickening crack, just below the elbow flailing off a long filet of flesh and muscle, leaving the older man wounded, bleeding and an easy target.

Jaan had been watching the scene from the door of the healing hut. Though her shoulder was not yet fully recovered, she armed her slingshot, aimed and released a volley of river stones at the head of Alda's adversary, striking him cleanly in the eye and forehead. He wheeled around, dazed and blinded temporarily, but long enough for Alda to run him through with the iron-tipped spear held in his left hand. The momentum of the attack seemed already to be slowing by the time the Phoenician oarsmen-warriors, fully armed and with shields and light armour, surged towards the rougher looking, more crudely armed mountain tribesmen. More trained for battle, the Phoenicians cut easily through the ranks of the attackers and a rout seemed imminent. At that moment, a voice so loud and strong and cruel that it struck fear into the hearts of those villagers who heard it, screamed out in the rude tongue of the mountain tribes:

"Stand and fight, slash and kill these animals of the coast. Their wealth is ours for the taking. Wreak your revenge or die like true warriors."

It was Chnnta, chief of the main mountain tribe. Larger than life, blood-spattered and imposing; he stood now not far from Alda, Daavid and Hannh, eyeing them ominously. Beside him, half hidden, stood one of the young companions of the chief's dead son Zum. He immediately recognized the young woman and her strangely-attired companion who had so easily taken the life of his chief's favourite son.

"Look my chief! It is the leaders of the ambush. They are the murderers of your son Zum". He cried out to Chnnta, with more than a little fear in his voice. Chnnta's eyes narrowed and a great animal roar rose from his stomach and burst from his throat. He knew no fear and surged towards Hannh and her small group, followed closely by yet another of his fiercest warriors with the young man from the bison hunt more reluctantly bringing up the rear.

It was clear to Daavid and Hannh that Alda was in no state to fight. He was on one knee, nursing his right arm trying to stifle the flow of blood. Jaan had come out of her hut to help him despite her own wounds, and was busy wrapping tightly around the old man's wound a kind of stretchy bandage made by the village healers from the gut of pigs and bathed in a solution of medicinal herbs. Within moments, Chnnta had lanced his short spear at Daavid. It struck him in the thigh. It was a crippling wound but Daavid knew he had only one chance. Before Chnnta and his companions were upon them, he quickly tore the short sharpened wood spear from his leg extracting it in precisely the way it had entered. It had not pierced the flesh too deeply and fortunately missed any major arteries and veins and only seeped blood. The excruciating pain that he had felt momentarily had now strangely disappeared as he looked up to face not only the scarred and snarling old chief, but also the young, lithe and equally ferocious-looking mountain warrior who accompanied him.

After taking in the sight of younger warrior, Daavid looked back briefly to the older chief only to find that he seemed to have disappeared. So he focussed his energies on defending himself from the slashing spear tip of the younger warrior. The young mountain tribesman was clearly adept at his task, and was poking the sharpened point at the young Phoenician's midsection, slashing sideways and upward in a semi-circular motion, gaining momentum on the descent and stepping forward as the lunged once again, this time at Daavid's face, forcing him to lean back, almost off balance. He could feel no pain in his thigh, in fact it felt numb and he knew that he was not as agile as he had been several minutes before.

Uninjured he would have ducked and pivoted, lashing out across the legs of his aggressor, bringing him to the ground before delivering a fatal blow from above. But he knew that a split-second's slowness in his reflexes would allow the warrior to bring a gruesome club down on his skull. Instead, he stepped back with his good leg taking all his weight on it, dropping his left shoulder and allowing the backward movement of his torso to continue around, he presented the right side of his body to his aggressor and raised his right elbow in the direction of the warrior's face, as if in defense. But instantaneously he flashed the fist clasping his iron-bladed dagger from near to his chest to a fully outstretched position, planting the dagger into the right side of the mountain man's throat, just under his ear and penetrating through to the grey matter at the base of his skull. The attack crumpled along with the body of the surprised mountain tribesman; his mouth agape and eyes glazing over as his still shivering corpse met the ground.

There was an instant of supreme stillness. It was as if time stopped in its tracks. Only a few brief moments had passed but it seemed like minutes. Now it was Daavid's strength that was wilting as the earlier adrenalin surge subsided and the pain in his thigh returned with a vengeance. His mind flashed back to the ugly chief who had thrown the spear that wounded him. As he looked around two movements caught his eye. Some paces off to the left Hannh was leaping back and forth, defending herself from a vicious attack, calling upon all her speed and agility to avoid the swinging club and thrusting spear of Chnnta. But the older man's frustration at her stealthy avoidance of his blows and lunges was becoming evident from the increasing carelessness and the wildness of his attack.

Just a few moments beforehand, Hannh had leapt forward to confront the old chief. She'd seen him bearing down on Daavid after his spear penetrated the young Phoenician's thigh. She'd acted quickly to distract the old warrior, giving Daavid that moment of grace allowing him to remove the spear before defending himself. Daavid's eye flitted further to the left, just as the young mountain man he recognized as one of the attackers from the bison hunt, raised his club above the crouching forms of Jaan and Alda. Daavid knew he was too far away to be able to save them so cried out:

"Jaan, behind you! Alda!" In the instant that Jaan reacted, diving forward rolling away, the blow from the heavy wooden club fell. Alda, wounded and weakened, had barely the time to look up over his left shoulder when the badly aimed blow made contact, glancing off the side of the old man's leather headgear and crashing onto his left shoulder visibly displacing, down at an obscene angle, the shoulder and arm that he'd lifted in instinctive defence. Daavid tried to sprint towards the old man but his wounded leg dragged. Even before he had taken two steps, the fluid motion of Jaan's rolling body had brought her to a crouched position from which she sprang like a mountain lion onto the hunched back of her father's aggressor, whose club had by now slid off Alda's shoulder and thudded heavily onto the ground. In an instant her left hand was under his chin and with the other hand on the back side of the top of his skull grasping a clump of matted brown hair and still using the momentum of her springing body, she twisted the head until the young man's neck snapped audibly; the sharp crack stifling the cry of pain that had just began to escape from his throat. Her momentum carried her past him and back onto her feet as her enemy fell lifeless to the ground, his torso twisting hideously in a very different direction to his unhappy head. Daavid almost gasped in admiration.

Chnnta was visibly exasperated at being unable to strike Hannh or engage her in hand-to-hand combat. The frustration was almost exploding from his bulging eyes; eyes which failed to register enough of the combat going on around him. Yet, as if he had instinctively felt the approach of Daavid and Jaan and their potential threat, he glanced around almost imperceptibly. But it was long enough for Hannh to notice. It was that brief moment of inattention she'd been waiting for and she grasped it. She knew instinctively that it would have been foolish to try to fight the chief of the mountain tribes in hand-to-hand combat as he was so much stronger than her, and as cunning as a mountain lion. Likewise, to allow him too close could have signalled her death, so she bided her time relying on her agility and defensive tactics until the right moment. And now it was here.

She feinted an upwards strike on the left side to which Chnnta had hazarded a glance. He naturally saw it and lowered his massive wooden club in defence, leaving his right arm raised and clasping his spear, presenting to any attacker a large part of his chest and head. She instantly drove her lengthy bronze-tipped spear up under his ribcage into the upper chest, through both lungs and up into his wildly pumping heart. There was the sound of exploding air as blood gushed from the wound and from his mouth. He coughed out red bubbles and glared wide-eyed at the young woman, perhaps recognizing something familiar in his killer's hidden soul; before collapsing dead at her feet.

The tide of the battle had already turned around for the mountain tribesmen as the Phoenicians decimated the enemy with superior weaponry and armour. The few remaining tribesmen quickly retreated. They were no match for a trained force. Relaxing a little, the two sisters looked around, taking in a sight that brought them no joy; they could imagine how much easier and less costly the battle would have been had they had the time to truly share the weapons and training of the visitors.

Hannh knew that the mountain tribes had to be taught a lesson they would not forget and ordered the villagers to give chase. Daavid understood her thoughts and yelled the same command to the Phoenician oarsmen who also sped after the retreating enemy, cutting down the tribesmen as they found them, often alone and in disarray. Few would escape, but enough there would be, to take back to their mountain tribes the lesson that the coastal people were to be feared and respected.

Hannh turned her attention to her father. Alda lay inert on the bloody ground. Hannh reached down and clasped the bronze-bladed Phoenician dagger gifted to him by Daavid's father. She wiped it clean and returned it to the copper and silver scabbard that she had deftly removed from behind her dead father's belt. It was now hers; rightly inherited as her father's eldest heir. Jaan stood silently looking down at the old man, crumpled sadly on the ground. The battle had permitted her to show how great a warrior she too had become, but at a terrible cost. Aside from the loss of her father and a brother, many villagers lay dead and many were badly wounded. The remnants of the herds of goats had scattered and other animals lay butchered. Huts were burning and grain stores were broken open.

"How bitter is even such a victory," Jaan said quietly almost to herself.

"Spoils of battle there will always be", Daavid replied, "but victory has so often a hollow feel and it brings even less pleasure to the vanquished" he said wryly. "At least this day we have saved the village from destruction and the people from death and slavery. We must content ourselves with such small mercies."

Amilca was now approaching the young people. He had gone with his men in pursuit of the retreating tribesmen and when few could still be found, he sent out well-armed units to scout into the forest and finish the task under torchlight. Night and muffled groans now engulfed the unhappy but relieved little settlement. Fires were extinguished, wounds tended and those who remained alive slept fitfully that night.

§

The days that followed passed slowly and sadly as the villagers buried their dead, including their chief, Alda, and struggled to rebuild their homes and herd together the surviving goats and sheep that had dispersed in the wake of the marauding mountain tribes.

Amilca felt that this was perhaps not the place to found the new outpost he had hoped might someday rival their trading base, Gades, on the southern tip of the Iberian Peninsula. They would return towards the Great Sea to seek another more hospitable place to found a settlement and Daavid would be going with them.

The villagers now looked to Hannh to lead them after the death of her father; but her heart was not in it and this was quickly apparent to her people. They knew she would leave with Daavid and the other Phoenicians and told the villagers that it was her sister who would lead them. Jaan and her two brothers remained and they were now old enough to look after themselves and the village. They had proved themselves in battle and what they still lacked in wisdom could be supplied in abundance by the few remaining elders of the village.

Within a further cycle of the moon, Daavid's wound had healed, the Phoenician visitors were to depart and Hannh had prepared herself to leave with them. She knew not what life lay ahead of her but she knew she had found her soul-mate in the young Phoenician standing close by her side. With tears in their eyes, they looked back towards the villagers once again assembled haphazardly on the beach as the narrow ships were gently but rhythmically rowed out over the low breakers and back around the rocky promontory in the direction from which they had come.

# BIRTH AND THE BEGINNING OF WAR

*Bayonne, South-West France, May 1939*

Historical Note
Although reasonable efforts have been made to ensure historical accuracy in **BEGINNINGS: Where A Life Begins**, it should be noted that all references to a relationship between French WW2 resistance worker Max, or Jean Moulin and a fictional character in this book, Maria Abene or anyone else are entirely fictional.

## Map of France Occupied Zone and Free Zone

## Twenty-Six

The unborn babe twisted and tried to turn her tiny body. Her shoulders and limbs jerked and twitched. Her heart pounded as she struggled, seemingly against the now almost rhythmic contractions of her unconscious mother's pelvic muscles. The contractions came and went every couple of minutes and Helena wished that her patient would wake and put in that last conscious effort to force the baby out through the widening birth canal.

It was time that the ordeal was over. The crown of the baby's head was visible and was already protruding through the opening but not enough for Helena to provide any manual assistance; at least not unless there was an emergency. Maria was still incredibly unconscious.

"How is it possible?" Helena thought aloud, "though she seems well enough; and babies are sometimes born with a mother under a general anaesthetic."

The contractions had for the moment slowed down. But the baby was so close to being born. Helena was unsure of what to do.

"Should I just let nature take its course?" she said quietly to herself. "God has His own way of making things happen."

There was a moment of respite for the unborn one. Her muscles ceased to twitch and her heart began to beat more regularly.

"Was it over yet?" she thought to herself and knew the answer was 'no'. She slowly regained her strength and her mind stayed fixed firmly in the present. Why was it that she had felt held back, fixed to the womb and unable to move freely on her way towards her separation from her mother? Now she remembered. She'd been moving her arms, twisting her body, as if avoiding the blows of the mountain tribesman's great wooden club and the short thrusts of his sharpened spear. And she had managed to lift the tube connecting her with her mother over her little shoulders and now it held back her progress from her mother's swollen womb and her emergence into the world.

She felt a soft touching and wiping of the crown of her head. It was a new and yet totally familiar sensation. She had sensed that there was someone else outside. Her own mother's voice had been absent for some time though she had felt the restfulness of her repose; and the regular rhythmic muscular pressure around the pelvis was comforting, but increasingly uncomfortable.

Her time of rest lasted only a few minutes. All too soon the squeezing of her chest and shoulders resumed. She once again felt herself being pushed and pulled onwards through the birth canal, and yet held back at the same time as the constriction around her throat began to increase with each muscular spasm of her mother's unconscious body.

Feelings of agitation began to creep into the heart of the unborn babe and she willed her arms to move in a vain attempt to remove the increasingly stretched tube from around her head and neck. But she was only a little less than helpless. Using her mind, she fought and fought throughout the duration of the shuddering contraction slowly becoming aware that she was only contributing to her increasing weakness and making it even harder to move further down the birthing canal.

At that moment, the tension was released once again as the contraction subsided. The pressure on her throat diminished a little and she no longer felt pushed and pulled in both directions. But the respite was only for a brief moment and the spasm recommenced, this time more violently than before. Her head began to feel pressure from within as if bloated by blood, and the touch of Helena's fingers circling around the crown of her now bluish skull trying to make space for her head to slip through only worsened the stretching she felt between her head and her still constrained shoulders.

Once more, the convulsing pressure of her mother's muscles subsides.

Helena was becoming increasingly concerned. The baby needed to be born and Maria needed to be awake to help this to occur. Now that the contractions were following very closely upon each other and that they had for the moment subsided, there was no choice. She placed her hand firmly on her patient's shoulder.

"Wake up! *ma chère, réveille toi!*" She spoke soothingly in gentle French rather than the neutral Spanish they usually spoke. Helena shook Maria even more abruptly and she started to stir.

"Wake up. Wake up. It is time for the baby to be born." Maria's eyes opened slowly as if she had been in a deep sleep and far, far away.

"What, what ... is it? Helena, what's wrong?" The barely awake young woman managed to say ... and then felt the wetness around her thighs from the amniotic fluids she had had shed some time before.

"Am I having contractions? I didn't feel anything. Is my baby all right?"

"Your baby is here and it is time for it to be born. You must help now." Helena said quickly.

"Come, sit up and on the next contraction, take some quick deep breaths and push down as hard as you can." She said kindly but firmly, completely unaware of the fatal effect this advice could have on the struggling baby.

"Let me put these pillows behind your back and get ready." She said gently as she helped Maria shuffle backwards to a semi-sitting position.

Now the almost born child felt the empty anguish of fear in her stomach as she recognized her life and death plight and her mind raced and raced.

"How do I escape? Perhaps..." Her strained little body had relaxed a little and slipped backwards within her mother's womb as Maria changed her position on the bed. With it, the circumference of visible head reduced, to the increasing consternation of the midwife waiting for her outside. But for the unborn child, the slight slip backwards and the release of the umbilical cord's pressure round her neck slowed down the blinding pace of her thoughts and as they settled, she became aware of the need somehow, to sever the cord that bound her to her mother. It would have to be done before she would be able to escape.

**BEGINNINGS**  Gary Heilbronn

She had memories, so many memories. Some of the birthing ordeal of animals and others of the birth of human babies and of the connecting cord being cut with a knife. But this was only after the baby had been born as the placenta attached to the cord would not follow through the canal until shortly after the birth. With each of the contractions, she had felt some tearing within the womb as the continual downward pressure on her body stretched the tube that curled around her shoulders and began to rip out the placenta's tiny finger-like connections to the wall of the uterus.

"...But would it all, the tubes, placenta and its contents come with me now and allow me to be born?" she asked herself but she did not know.

Yet something within her told her that she must act. By nodding her head just a little she was able to move her bottom jaw to where she could feel the tube near her little mouth. The already stretched tube was softer and more malleable than she had felt it to be when she had much more space to move around in the womb. With very little effort she managed to nudge the tube so it slipped across her open mouth and sat between her gums at the front. The soft slippery tube lay there for a moment as she rested and waited. She could slowly feel the contraction begin again, and as it strengthened even more than before and she felt her inevitable movement down the birth canal being held back, she closed her jaws tightly on the tube. She had no teeth but just beneath the skin of her gums were the strong sharpish tips of the tiny deciduous teeth that would normally be expected to break through in the third or fourth month after she was born.

Maria was now wide awake, sitting up in her bed; her knees raised and apart as a new and painful force grabbed at her lower abdomen and forced a scream of agony through her clenched teeth. Her stomach muscles tightened and her head moved forward, her eyes squinting and her fist clenching fiercely, her fingernails almost piercing the skin and drawing blood from Helena's left arm just above her wrist.

"Breathe in! Breathe in!" Helena urged, fighting back the pain she herself felt from Maria's penetrating grip. Maria sucked air furiously in short shark gasps into her lungs.

"Now push long and slow." Helena said. The young mother did as she was told. The unborn child was still hidden, but the infant felt as if her body was ripping apart with this latest pressure. Her jaws closed down again and again and again on the increasingly stretched tube of blood vessels which distended and distorted with the pressure, then slowly punctured in one, two and then three places. Then, under the increasing pressure of her mother's flexing pelvic muscles and the downward force being exerted by Maria, the tiny perforations widened, slowly connecting one with the other until they tore apart.

Dark blood began to seep then pump from the severed tube. The sudden release of the tube previously caught around her shoulders catapulted the head of unborn babe like a giant river stone from a slingshot straight out through the orifice at the end of the birth canal; accompanied by tissue, the severed umbilical cord and a copious amount of dark blood.

Helena was already turning the baby's head and helping its shoulder out as more and more blood pumped from the severed ends of the cord.

"There's too much blood." Helena whispered to herself as her body tensed with fear for the mother and baby.

The unborn one was already beginning to lose her own small supply of blood from the ragged-edged tube extending out almost twenty centimetres from the centre of her belly as she slipped fully into the world, gasping for breath and dripping blood from her mouth. The midwife was shocked but only momentarily at the bloody sight. She looked around her and grabbed a clamp from the small collection of instruments she had carefully placed close-by during the hours she had waited at her patient's bedside. She quickly clamped the cord several centimetres from the end and passed the blood and slime caked baby to its mother in a thick towel. Immediately freed of the baby, Helena's concern was only for the mother. She seized the other length of bleeding umbilical cord and expertly tied a knot near its end, just as quickly wiping away as much of the blood and packing the vacant space between her patient' legs with clean towels to await the expulsion of the placenta. Its roots already stretched and loosened from the uterine wall, the placenta took only a few minutes to find its way out through the birth canal. Helena attended to all this.

The young mother was transfixed by the sight of her newborn baby girl.

Maria held her young daughter carefully and snugly in against her breast. "You're so beautiful" she sighed, tears in her eyes, "I shall name you Anna-Maria, after your great grandmother. But I shall call you 'Anna'."

For a few moments, she could not drag her eyes from the little child.

"Helena. Helena." Maria said finally noticing the blood dripping from the infant's mouth, "why is there so much blood in her mouth?"

"Look! Look here", she said more quietly as she placed her skinny little finger delicately and gently into her daughter's tiny mouth, "look, what is this?" She carefully withdrew a small piece of umbilical cord from the baby's mouth.

Helena looked intently at the small piece of tissue. It was clearly a piece of the umbilicus. She said nothing but began to understand. Finally she said softly:

"Never, Maria, have I heard of such a thing before. It is really extraordinary. While I waited throughout your contractions and the baby seemed to be coming but did not, I saw her begin to go blue and I feared that the umbilical cord was wrapped around her neck. Oh, Maria, I was so very afraid and feared for the lives of the both of you".

She paused and looked straight into the young mother's eyes.

"This tiny thing must have understood what was happening and rescued herself from strangulation and the certain death or terrible brain damage that can come from cutting off the blood supply to her brain. Maria, it is almost a miracle. God must be looking out for her. She has bitten through the umbilical cord to release herself from its grip! I had heard that about one in a thousand or so babies are born with natal teeth, but I have never heard of anything like this before."

Helena stood there with a look of disbelief on her face, gazing at the tiny infant with the reddened gums and cheeks and the sparkling eyes. Maria also fixed her gaze on the tiny bundle, still smeared in blood and swathed in a thick cotton towel. In amongst all the vivid colours and the anxiety of the near-fatal birth, neither notice the tiny, roundish stain on the left side of the little girl's throat. Later that day Maria does notice it, and her heart floods with memories of her dear maternal grandmother who'd carried a similar mark. But for now, it's Anna's deep, penetrating eyes that draw them to her like a magnet.

At length, Maria's soft voice breaks the silent tension.

"Helena, I beg of you, please. You must speak of this near-to no-one. We cannot give anyone the slightest reason to take an interest in us or draw attention to us. You know our situation here. We must be very discreet." She was now looking straight into the eyes of the young midwife and Helena knew she was deadly serious and a slight shiver moved across her shoulder-blades.

"A young mother will do anything that it would take to protect her baby." Helena thought to herself. "And that baby! Who knows what she might be capable of?"

In normal times Maria would have nothing to fear from Helena. But these were not normal times and the two of them were compatriots exiled in a foreign land. They were still within the reach of the vicious fascist madmen who had seized such bloody control of their homeland. And in such a world, no-one could be trusted absolutely.

## Twenty-Seven

Maria was young and strong and after the birth, she took only a little time to recover and to be able to nurse baby Anna. Breastfeeding came easily and Anna put on weight quickly. But Maria wanted to take as little time as possible before weaning the infant. She knew that as soon as she was able, she had to work to earn a living. Maria would not allow herself to rely upon the charity of her Basque compatriots for one day longer than was absolutely necessary. She had been told that a post in the Basque Museum and Cultural Centre awaited her on her recovery and she wanted to start work soon.

The museum was in the Maison Dagourette, a small old building in *le Petit Bayonne*, the attractive, old fortified part of the city of Bayonne, and she looked forward with eagerness to a return to some kind of normal life and being able to talk to and socialize with people of similar background and interests and ideas.

In due course, the day came for Maria's new career and her new life to begin. It was early July, 1939 and just a little more than a month had passed since the birth. She settled into a short working day with plenty of time off in order to care for baby Anna. Her main task to begin with was to catalogue parts of the collection and the working hours were conveniently from 10am to noon and then 3pm to 5pm in the afternoon. She easily found an older lady, a Basque exile like herself, to care for Anna in the hours when she could not be there with her. She wanted baby Anna to be always spoken to in euskara so that that would be her mother-tongue and not French or Spanish.

Maria had only been able to breast feed Anna for a little over a month but at least that meant that now, she did not need to be home to feed her at every meal. With surprising speed, the weeks passed by. Maria and Anna settled into a comfortable routine. Maria found her duties at the museum to be enormously to her liking. Indeed she was even learning knew facts about her culture and history to add to the vast body of knowledge she had already acquired. The museum's collection had been expanded; there was a great deal of research to do to verify the authenticity or precise historical and cultural accuracy of not only the new pieces but also many of the older parts of the collection. That, along with continual cataloguing took up many painstaking hours of her time. A smile of contentment returned to her face. Had she found happiness again?

§

With her focus wholly on her homeland and her young baby, Maria barely noticed the increasing political unrest and belligerent German military activities in northern Europe. That was all so far away and she hated even to read in the newspapers about those detested nazi allies of General Franco and the fascists in Spain.

So it was a shock when, one morning in late July 1939, the order came for the Maison Dagourette to be occupied by the *Foyer des Soldats*. It was to provide an area of recreation and reading for serving officers and soldiers. But at least, the museum could still function and receive visitors.

Now Maria felt she had no choice but to follow the course of those worrying events up in the north, though they still seemed so far away. It was only after Germany signed a non-aggression pact with Josef Stalin's Soviet Union on 23 August 1939 and the Nazis marched quickly into Poland that life really changed. That was on 1 September and France and Britain were so surprisingly unprepared for any such military action. They were forced to declare war on Germany just two days later. Anna was a little over three months old when France was officially at war with Germany.

Germany's invasion of Poland was in defiant renunciation of the Munich Agreement that Hitler and Mussolini had signed just a year earlier with the pacifists then controlling the French and British Governments. How the two fascist leaders must have laughed at those weak fools! The antifascist and communist movements in France and Britain had already been openly hostile to their governments since they had earlier failed to assist the republican

BEGINNINGS                                             Gary Heilbronn

cause in Spain. Then came their governments' appeasement of the Nazi annexation of Austria and Czechoslovakia. Maria watched these events with disbelief, knowing as she did that weakness would never be a match for fascist evil.

But the weeks and months passed and strangely, despite the war, nothing much seemed to be happening in France. Some newspapers even called this period "la drôle de guerre", roughly translated as the 'funny sort of war' while the British press called it the "Phoney War". These expressions caught the fancy of the French and British peoples, perhaps because they hid the cruel reality of the war that they all feared would soon be upon them – many still had personal memories of the millions who died in the Great War of 1914-18. Maria's memories of war were much more recent. Anna was now 'of this world' and her memories of the distant past were retreating.

§

From September 1939, French armed divisions moved east and north under the defensive strategy adopted by the country's aging generals, notably General Maurice Gustave Gamelin. He'd been the hero of the 1914 Battle of the Marne and had been responsible for the extension and reinforcement of the old Maginot Line of defensive trenches that had proved so valuable in the Great War. General Gamelin, perhaps still living in the past, believed that the expected German invasion would be from the north and try to pass through central Belgium and Holland.

This ill-informed belief would become an earth-shattering mistake for the whole of France.

At the beginning of the war, the French high command was staffed by such aged veterans of the Great War. The old military men were undoubtedly heroes in their younger days; but their strategic thinking and tactics seemed not to have evolved since then.

Maria read also in 'La Petite Gironde' newspaper of an ex-cavalry Colonel, called De Gaulle, who called for a more mechanized army in France, based around highly mobile armoured tank regiments; like those that had already been established by the German army.

However, the prevailing military view was to have their tanks dispersed in a supportive role throughout the infantry battalions. De Gaulle was much criticized in some sections of the press, especially since the old guard of the French *état-major* under Field Marshall Pétain, and Generals Gamelin and Weygrand strenuously opposed the young colonel's views on the value of tanks in warfare. It was to be another of the many fatal mistakes they made.

De Gaulle did have some political support. It came from the then Finance Minister, Paul Reynaud who had earlier also opposed the September 1938 Munich Agreement when the British and French governments had so naively allowed Czech territorial integrity to be sacrificed; and Reynaud sought to augment defence spending in France. So in January 1940, De Gaulle was named as head of the fourth armoured tank division. But in fact, it barely existed except on paper and was still then being formed and equipped. That was to be a slow process and as time would show; it was too little and much too late.

Maria carefully read the news of these depressing events though they barely touched on her day-to-day existence: looking after a growing toddler and working the remaining hours at the Museum. Her life was busy and she was content. She still felt safe in south-west France; far enough away from the Germans and from her enemies in her unhappy homeland across the mountainous border to the south.

All that was to change on the sunny morning of Monday, the 14th of May 1940. And it all happened so quickly. Maria opened her copy of 'La Petite Gironde' newspaper to discover that the nazi *Wehrmacht* had outflanked and overrun the French and Belgian forces camped on the Maginot Line, taking them completely by surprise. They had advanced rapidly from the east with ten mechanized divisions: seven of them being armoured tanks, through the forested highlands of the southern Ardennes in the south of Belgium and north-east part of France; near where Attila the Hun had been defeated by a coalition of the Romans, Franks and Visigoths just one year less than fifteen hundred years beforehand.

The Nazis then crossed the Meuse River, taking control of the northern part of great champagne regions of France and cutting in two the forces of the French army.

The French people and the elderly Generals of the French *état-major* were in a state of shock.

In the fortnight that followed, only worsening news was to be read in the newspapers. There was the capitulation of Holland on the 15th of May and then, on the 19th, came the order from the new French President of the Council of Deputies, Paul Reynaud, for the replacement of the hapless General Gamelin by his colleague General Weygand. The previous day, Reynaud had also appointed an experienced, but aged Field Marshall Pétain – he was more than eighty-three years old – as vice-president of the Council of Deputies.

These changes brought some hope. Weygand set up a new line of military defence along the river Somme, envisaging that the *Wehrmacht* would head immediately southwest towards Paris. But once again, the old-guard French Generals were out-manoeuvred and the highly mobile Nazi forces headed west and north of the river Somme defences to encircle some forty-five divisions of the allied forces in Flanders, forcing their rapid retreat to Dunkirk and Belgium's capitulation to the Nazis on the 28th of May, 1940.

All of this in a fortnight!

Celebration of Anna's first birthday was the only happy moment at a time when the future looked far from bright.

## Twenty-Eight

Maria and many others followed all these wartime events from a distance. And there *were* some snippets of good news, it seemed. In the first days of June 1940, there was the successful night-time evacuation across the channel to England of one hundred and thirty thousand French soldiers, together with more than two hundred thousand members of the British Expeditionary Forces. But the bad news was that the soldiers were compelled to leave all their equipment on the beaches at Dunkirk. At least these experienced troops were themselves saved.

There had also been the brilliant counter-offensives of De Gaulle's new tank division, resulting in his promotion to temporary General.

But these bits of good news were just a drop in the bucket compared to the ominous advance of the Nazi war machine.

Maria was stunned by the speed of all these disastrous events. As she sat reading her copy of 'La Petite Gironde' newspaper on the comfortable sofa in her sun-drenched living room, she was reminded of how quickly the republican movement in Spain had crumbled before the might of Franco's fascist forces and their Nazi supporters.

"It was just a little over a year and a half ago" she whispered.

She was worried that the same thing would now happen in France, though many of the French people living around her, in their far-flung south-west corner of the Republic, seemed strangely oblivious to the fact that a Nazi invasion was imminent. Maria's neighbours like so many others had hopefully observed that Field Marshall Pétain and the *état-major* were heroes of the Great War and had previously defeated the Germans. Surely they would again prevail. But privately they admitted that the cost in human suffering may once again be unbelievably high.

The uncertainty they all felt had not long to be endured.

On the 5th of June, President Reynaud called General De Gaulle to Paris and named him Under-Secretary of Defence. But it was once again too little and much too late.

Immediately after the Dunkirk evacuation, the German forces attacked General Weygand's line of defences along the Somme and within a week the German tanks had breached the French lines and were heading south for Paris and east towards Lyon. It was all over.

A widespread retreat of French forces was ordered on the 12th of June. This also heralded the massive exodus of ten million civilians towards the south. Some travelled in wagons or on foot, while the more fortunate moved slowly south in their overloaded cars or trucks. Paris was captured by the Nazis relatively quietly on the 14th of June 1940.

The same day the crumbling government of France withdrew and installed itself briefly in the south-west, in that old anglicized city of Bordeaux. The borders of occupied France, to the west and east, would be secured by the Germans within just a few days. It was devastating and once again, it had all occurred so fast.

Maria had barely time to come to grips with what was happening around her, as a trickle of refugees grew to a stream of thousands arriving from the north. The government in Bordeaux was now deeply divided. Marechal Pétain and General Weygand were in favour of capitulation and an armistice with Germany, while President Reynaud, Jean Monnet and De Gaulle were desperately seeking some means of continuing the combat; including even a proposal for a partial political union with Britain! That proposal failed. Reynaud resigned as President of Council of Deputies and was put into detention and replaced by Marechal Pétain.

De Gaulle and Monnet immediately escaped to Britain to join Churchill and to continue the struggle against the Nazis. They were however, not warmly welcomed there and treated with suspicion.

It all happened so quickly. It was Monday, the 17th of June, 1940, less than a month after the Germans had entered French territory, that Field Marshall Pétain called on the French people to cease their combat and proposed an armistice with the Germans. It was set to be signed just a few days later on the 22nd of June.

This was a worrying time for everyone as country after country in Europe had so rapidly fallen to the might of the Nazi forces. The shock and uncertainties of the French people seemed palpable to Maria who could not help sharing in the general malaise. Her submerged feelings of emptiness and fears from the year before came surging back into her heart. More than anyone, she knew what it was to live under the rule of the hated fascists. Things had changed so much since the Great War when there had been, at least for a time, some honour amongst enemies.

These new events had thrown her life once again into turmoil.

The day following the cease fire, here was an enormous thirst for news. Maria read the newspapers avidly. She then sat alone on the historic evening of Tuesday the 18th of June, ears glued to the little radio as General Charles De Gaulle, in London, delivered his famous discourse over the BBC air waves, calling on the people of France and its soldiers in the outposts of her colonial empire and elsewhere, to pursue the resistance against the German invaders. The radio broadcast crackled and faded in and out, but at least it was not as yet being interfered with by the German transmitters. The discourse was solemn and austere.

Only later were the BBC's "Free-French" transmissions softened a little by having the broadcast begin with a theme-song – the playfully rhyming, singsong *Chansonnier* jingle

*Radio Paris-ment, Radio Paris-ment.*
*Radio Paris est allemande.*

It was to remind its listeners of the lies coming from Radio Paris, under the control of the German propaganda machine, although some French intellectuals such as Simone de Beauvoir still worked for the collaborationist Radio-Vichy. It was perhaps a matter of survival.

Maria had been among the very few people in France to listen to the actual BBC broadcast by De Gaulle and hear him movingly proclaim that 'the flame of the resistance must not and will not be extinguished' in France. Yet word of the call to resistance spread quickly and was already widely but discreetly embraced by many French people when on the 28th of June, British Prime Minister

Winston Churchill finally, formally recognized De Gaulle as the leader of *France Libre*, as the Free France government in exile was then called.

There was increasing turmoil in France, a rapid capitulation of French armed forces to the Nazi *Wehrmacht* and a reluctant accession to power of an aged Field Marshall Pétain with a puppet government based at Vichy. Thereafter, the country that French people often refer to as the "hexagone", in view of its six-sided shape, was roughly divided diagonally into an 'occupied zone' in the north and northwest, and a 'free zone' in the south and southeast. Naturally, changes had to occur.

§

Bayonne, where Maria was living, was itself within the south-west extremity of the line of demarcation for the German occupation. The rest of the far south-west corner of the country inland from the coast was still in the 'free zone' but now squeezed between fascist, pro-Nazi Spain and Nazi-occupied France.

For Maria, a flood of desperation was again rushing into her being.

Almost immediately after the occupation had begun, the Basque Museum received a new directive for the building to be taken over by the *Secours Nationale Française*. This was worrying news as that was known to be a controversial and sometimes corrupt organization. It was supposed to provide food and assistance to the aged, the sick, children and others suffering the effects of the war, though it also had a propaganda role and its funding came partly from the liquidation of the property of persons who had lost their citizenship.

At least it would take some time before the Nazi occupation was fully in force.

At the Basque Museum, urgent decisions were being made and it was quickly and secretly agreed that while there was still time, the few most valuable parts of the museum's collection should be moved by truck to safe hiding-places. Utmost secrecy surrounded this activity and the choice of hiding-places.

One of the places chosen was the small village of Saint-Sever, further to the north-east in the heavily wooded Landes region and within the 'free zone'. It lies about forty-five kilometres north of the city of Dax and about a hundred and fifty kilometres south of Bordeaux. But it was only 17 kilometres from Mont-de-Marson, through which the line which separated France into two zones passed on its roughly inverted L-shaped course northwards to the border with Germany. The line proceeded north-easterly up to Tours, then south-eastwards to Chalon-sur-Soane and Dôle in the east.

Maria didn't have the same ties to Bayonne as the others working at the Maison Dagourette but she had a small child to care for. So when she was asked to take on the role of guardian for the small but valuable part of the collection being placed at Saint-Sever, she was at first alarmed. She would still be so close to the occupied zone and the hated Nazis; but she thought that she may well be safer, hidden away there in that little village than in Bayonne, actually in the occupied zone, or even further to the east in Provence, where many of the refugees from the north and from Paris were now headed.

On the other hand, Maria had reasoned, at least she would be further away from the Spanish border and General Franco's secret police who still made regular forays into French territory to eliminate their enemies. So she agreed to the move without further thought. After quickly packing the few scant belongings that she and her daughter had, they left her home in Bayonne with the hope of spending the following months of the war in relatively safe seclusion.

But in wartime, who could know what the future might bring?

## Twenty-Nine

Maria's first year living away from Bayonne passed quickly and quietly. It was sometimes hard to imagine that a war was going on. She had moved into a tiny old house on a backstreet near the outskirts of Saint-Sever, a small town in the countryside about a hundred kilometres north-east of Bayonne. It was almost like a village. The house was considerably less bright and salubrious than her sunny and spacious little apartment in Bayonne, but she hoped to be able to keep a low profile there.

"But I must take care," she continually reminded herself, "in wartime any outward show of affluence only attracts attention and can cause jealousy, especially if you are a stranger."

The facade of the house was very private and there were bushes around the front of the property half hiding the house's entrance from the eyes of any inquisitive neighbours; the sort of people who find enough time on their hands to follow just a little too closely the comings and goings of others. There were always such people in villages.

Several prized items from the Basque collection at the museum, still wrapped carefully in their storage packaging, had been secreted in two hidden caves some way from the outskirts of the town. Their transport had been carried out on different occasions under cover of darkness. Maria was to visit them only occasionally to check that all was untouched and such visits were to occur only at times when she could avoid drawing unwelcome attention to their hiding place. She was not overly concerned.

"After all," she said to herself, "these are not what the Germans really want, like famous works of art and treasures from *le Louvre*. But it's funny how wars are really about stealing other people's wealth." Indeed, these were not the paintings of the great masters and there was little of any great value to anyone other than the Basque people. They were really only there for safe-keeping. Maria might have been a little more concerned had she known that some

Jewish religious artefacts that had been entrusted to the care of the Basque Museum by Bayonne's Jewish community had also been secreted in the packages. But she didn't.

She continued, for the present at least, to receive a small salary from the museum administrators and with careful management was able to live well enough in the countryside. Some local farmers even managed to produce their *foie gras* from the enlarged livers of the mallard ducks and geese. It was not only for their own consumption, but there were always those with money to pay for such delicacies. Otherwise, ordinary farm produce, eggs and chickens were still available if you knew where to look for them. Even seasonal vegetables were cheap enough and they could be conserved for the winter, with some being kept in storage in case times got much worse.

By the autumn of 1941, most people did expect times to get much worse and occasional shortages were beginning to be felt, as farmers and villagers intensified their conserve-making and regular stockpiling activities, though mostly in secret. Of course Anna, at just two-and a half years old, was aware of none of this.

§

Winters are not too harsh in far south-west France and for Maria and little Anna, life continued to go by fairly quietly except for the occasional passage of refugees from the Nazi occupation. Maria often watched them as they arrived, usually from the north, via Brive or Bordeaux. There was often great suffering. She had to hold back her tears as she identified with the plight of these refugees from the fascist terror. They were usually the very young and the old, often Parisians of Jewish origin, though for the most part, no-one could tell them from anyone else. Although some had the word "Juif" stamped on their identity cards following an early directive from the Vichy Government, at least in the "free zone" they were not yet obliged to stitch the Star of David on their coats. That discriminatory labelling was introduced to facilitate recognition and rounding up when the time came for them to be trucked off like animals to no-one really knew what fate across the German border and in Poland.

Maria had heard about this forced transportation to work camps from some of those refugees who had passed through the village; and she'd even heard the whispered rumours of the extermination camps of Hitler's 'final solution to the Jewish problem'. That sounded more familiar to her. The Franco fascists just executed people they disagreed with. They didn't bother about work camps.

After the fall of France, it had even at one time been suggested by the German SS that all four million Jews in the occupied territories should be deported to the French colony of Madagascar or set up in a separate state in Eastern Europe. But neither of those more humane solutions had been put into effect.

The Nazis had other things to think about. Britain had not surrendered quickly, as Hitler had expected, and the Suez Canal was still not under German control. Even worse for the German high command, they began to be pre-occupied with the slowing down of the war against the Soviet Union on the eastern front. Had Hitler studied more deeply the course of the Napoleonic wars, he might have been even more concerned about the future of this campaign.

Maria kept herself busy. She tended a small vegetable garden of her own and gave much time to the upbringing of Anna. Although she spoke only in French when outside in the village, she spoke only euskara in the privacy of their home, She felt instinctively that it was only by strictly separating the contexts in which the two languages were spoken, that Anna would learn both without mixing them up and her efforts were starting to bear fruit. When the old people admired the child and spoke to her in French or even in the local "patois", she smiled hugely, spoke a word or two in the language she had been addressed in, and the old people quickly fell for her charm.

Anna was growing. She had spoken her first words at nine months and three days, and taken her first steps at eleven months. The little girl had become quickly mobile but until she reached two years and several months at the end of 1941, she had still enjoyed outings in the old perambulator that Maria had rescued from an elderly neighbour's barn and carefully cleaned and restored to good working condition.

§

Still the months passed; not so much slowly as uneventfully. In late March 1942 Anna was almost three years old. It was springtime; and days were still short and the nights still cold. One evening just after dark, something happened that would change Maria's life forever.

Maria had already put Anna to bed and was checking that the tomato conserves made the summer before were still edible and that the beeswax seals were still airtight when she was surprised by a soft but urgent tapping on her door.

"Stay calm" she told herself willing away her fear. She carefully returned the glass jars to their hiding place under the kitchen floor.

Though it was not yet fully dark, the villagers were home and closed up behind their wooden shutters. She had been planning to bring her little wireless out from its hiding-place in the wall – radios were illegal and being caught with one meant prison or worse. But she wanted to listen for news of the war on the BBC broadcast from the Free France organization, now well established in London.

"Who could be at the door?" her thoughts screamed at her. It was more than eighteen months since her arrival in Saint-Sever but she had no friends, only a few acquaintances; and none were in the habit of visiting her. People no longer made new friends, especially in rural areas. They were suspicious of each other and even more wary of strangers. Of course, villagers openly socialized with the newcomers on the streets and in the cafés and at the market, but conversations were short: about the weather and the vegetables on sale; and the interaction went no further. Few people spoke about the German occupation as no-one could be trusted. It was a relatively solitary existence Maria led with her happy young daughter.

So when they came, the ten or so rapid knocks on her front door brought a stab of fear to her heart. She stood still and waited. Her mind raced back to her hurried departure from San Sebastian and the cruel death of her baby son. Her thoughts flashed to Anna and the need to protect her. In that moment, the last few years of relative security seemed to melt into nothingness. Her hand trembled almost uncontrollably. She wanted to run away. A few seconds passed and the knocking was repeated. There was no choice but to go to the door.

"Who knows I am here?" She thought anxiously. "Aside from the local village people and just two or three people from the Museum, there is no-one."

Fighting off her fear, she gathered enough strength to pull the door slightly ajar, looking round it into the darkness. Light from her small living room lamp was shining weakly out through the door onto two unknown male faces. One looked rather young, perhaps twenty-five with dark curly hair and a vaguely familiar appearance. The other belonged to a man slightly older, perhaps forty. He was a good-looking man with a broad-brimmed hat turned down a little over his right brow, but with dark intelligent eyes. The image was softened by his broad full mouth ending in boyish slightly upturned dimples, and a strong, slightly cleft chin. Maria was immediately attracted to the man. She tore her eyes from the older man and looked quizzically at the younger, more familiar face. He looked back at her intently.

## Thirty

"Maria? Is it you?" the younger man asked pointedly in euskara. "I am Théo, son of Georges, a colleague of yours from the museum in Bayonne. My father has sent us here" he said expectantly.

Maria immediately saw the resemblance to her close colleague. The one who she had seen soon after her arrival in Bayonne and who had helped her so much since then; making sure that the post at the Museum had been held for her until after the birth of her daughter. He often seemed to be somewhat distant, but had always been in the background and undoubtedly, she believed, he had contacts with the Basque 'government-in-exile'. It had been set up in by the leader of the short-lived Basque Autonomous State, José Antonio Aguirre, after he had been forced to flee to France following the bombing of Guernica by the Nazi Luftwaffe on April 26, 1937. It was a day that the Basque people would never forget, especially as it came just before the fascist takeover of Bilbao.

Maria's face relaxed a little as she began to let down her guard. The younger man sensed this and immediately asked:

"Can we come in, please, rather than stay outside too long, in case someone from the village should see us".

"Yes, come in. Come in quickly." Maria said to both of them in euskara. She knew that their presence would put her and her daughter in danger, but her duty was also to her own people. These were the people who had looked after her throughout her time of need and brought some semblance of safety and normality into her life, back home and here in France. She owed them everything.

"Please sit down. Can I get you something to eat or drink? There's some vegetable soup still warm and I have bread and a little Bordeaux wine," she added eagerly in euskara, wanting to offer a warm welcome to such friends; until she suddenly saw the blank look on the older man's face and his hesitation when she spoke.

The younger man noticed her sudden reticence and the questioning look she gave his companion.

# BEGINNINGS  Gary Heilbronn

"It is all right, Maria", he said in French, "he is not Basque but is a great friend of the republican movement and a hero of the French resistance. He is called 'Max'."

The young man looked towards Max and back to Maria. He was smiling. Then he spoke, solemnly.

"Max once held important posts in the French administration and though many were opposed to his views, he boldly advocated and supported our cause. He was the 'chef de cabinet' of the Air Ministry in 1936 and did all he could to convince the Popular Front government of Léon Blum to help us in our fight against the fascists. They even secretly sent us aircraft."

The young man paused, before continuing.

"It was only the weakness of that government's leaders and the agreement they made to ignore our plight with that coward Chamberlain and the British appeasement movement that left our people isolated and at the mercy of Franco and the Nazis."

He almost spat as he spoke of them, but quickly remembered he was inside her house and apologized. Maria looked back at the older man, peering into his dark friendly eyes. He had a strong, perhaps a little distant look on his face but his eyes seemed kind.

He spoke to her in educated French.

"I have been told of your past, Maria, and I am sorry for your losses. I have been assured by my Basque friends that you are completely trustworthy. So I will tell you that I am only passing through this village. I am in this region on a mission of great importance. It has been conferred upon me by none other than the leader of the French resistance movement, General De Gaulle. And in this mission, I need your help."

His voice was low and soft and smooth like melted butter. He had a way of making his listener feel important. Though his words seemed carefully chosen and hinted at the grandeur of his task, there was only humility in his tone and evident passion for his cause.

Maria's heart pounded. The last thing she wanted was any further involvement in politics and the resistance movement: neither at home nor here in France. "I am not a soldier" she thought to herself. She wanted only to live quietly and nurture her young child and to watch her grow into a young woman. But there was still fascist oppression in Spain and now there was war in Europe against the Nazi occupiers and she could not escape it. At the same time, life here in Saint-Sever offered little else but relative safety and she could hardly deny feeling excited by the arrival of these two strangers and the prospect of working, in whatever way she could, against the hated fascists: they who had taken so much from her. There was, in reality, no choice.

Her face, previously pale, flushed a little. But was it just excitement at the prospect of work with the resistance? Or was it the increasing attraction she felt for the dark-eyed stranger sitting in front of her? He was clearly a man passionate about a cause, as her Alberto had been, though this man was older and more mature than her lost husband. But she was now older too and the laughter lines around the corners of his eyes and the slightly upturned edges of his boyish mouth were deliciously attractive to her. It had been so long since she had felt this kind of physical need for a man and her warm blood began to simmer at the closeness of his presence.

Maria looked his way and her bright green eyes met those of the older man. In that moment something intangible passed between them. Both felt a kind of shared spiritual intimacy and knew that here and now, a moment had arrived for their lives to mesh together, if only they chose to grasp it; to make it happen. She saw the intensity in his dark eyes and knew that he, too, felt their communion. It was as if an electric current flowed between them. The intense feeling of attraction was mutual and only seconds had passed, but the image of this moment and of his face she would carry forever in her memory.

Théo spoke again, unknowingly interrupting the brief moment of closeness that his companions shared.

"Maria, we have little time and as Max said, we are asking for your help. We need to eat something and to rest for a couple of hours. There are things we must do very early tomorrow morning while it is still dark. We cannot tell you as it is better that you do not know. But after that, we need to return here quietly and spend tomorrow resting and out of sight. Perhaps we will have to leave tomorrow night, but there are many things to be done, so we may need to stay another day or so. Is this possible?"

"Of course!" Maria replied almost too eagerly; though she had not really given any thought to how practical it would be to try to hide from the eagle eyes of the villagers, the comings and goings of these two men over the next few days. She only wanted them, or at least the older man, to stay with her for as long as he could; or at least for a short while.

Maria fed her guests. They ate heartily, exchanging few words between themselves while keeping up a polite conversation with Maria. It was in odd contrast to the intense eye-contact between Maria and Max. Eventually, they finished eating and she showed them where they could rest in the spare room where Anna slept. She quickly and quietly picked up the still sleeping young child and carried her into the other bedroom where she was settled down in a corner.

After a short while the house was quiet again and Maria was alone in the comfortable little space that doubled as kitchen and living room. The lamp was doused but a fire burned low in the centre of the uncommonly wide country fireplace. It was set into and occupying almost half the kitchen wall, with its broad stone chimney rising up at the back of the house. A small wooden stool stood on either side of the fire so one could sit, as country people had done for centuries, inside the old fireplace itself, either side of the fire, leaning against its warm walls on cold winter's nights.

Maria cleared away the dishes from her guests' light meal and washed and dried them. When she had finished, she stood in front of the little fire gazing for some time into its depths. No sound came from the rooms where the other occupants of the house were resting.

Minutes had passed before she felt the presence of someone beside her. She was so pre-occupied with her own thoughts that she had not heard his footsteps. Her eyes glanced to her left. Max stood beside her. He no longer wore the high-collared coat and woollen scarf that he had first appeared in at her door and his slightly battered broad-brimmed felt hat had been left, perhaps too carelessly, she had thought at the time, on the kitchen table.

But for the first time she noticed the thin jagged scar just below his jaw line. She had no idea that it was a self-inflicted wound suffered as part of an escape attempt almost two years before when he was 'Préfet de Chartres' – the city's highest administrative officer. He had remained behind when the Germans arrived to formally surrender the city to the Nazi invaders and do what he could for the remaining population. He had soon after been taken prisoner and tortured for failing to collude with the German military authorities' false explanation for the execution of a number of unarmed Senegalese colonial troops. They had stayed behind to fight but the Nazis wanted to blame them for various cases of rape and murder of women and children in nearby villages. Max had narrowly escaped with his life by faking a suicide attempt. Ever since, to hide the scar, he had worn a scarf or silk neckchief, even in summer.

"I came out ... for my hat," Max spoke a little hesitantly, as if he felt he needed an excuse for being there beside her.

"It was left on the table," he elaborated unnecessarily. For once this elegant and seductive man was a little unsure of himself. He was standing close by her now and they both were looking into the fire. Maria raised her eyes, smiling at the man who had already rekindled a glow of passion in her breast and set a sparkle in her eyes. She blushed.

"You know, it has been a long time since I met anyone like you": she said. She spoke softly but with the mature confidence of an attractive and still youthful woman. She touched his arm lightly with her left hand. She stood so close she could smell the slight fragrance of his *eau-de-toilette* – it pleased her though it seemed a somewhat surprising affectation in wartime. Max returned the smile and moved slightly to face her. He looked in her eyes. She was more than a beautiful young woman and the firelight played on her eyes, highlighting her cheekbones and the fine line of her nose. He was a man who was far from immune to feminine charms and was reputed to have had many love affairs. Though none of this was then known to Maria.

"Maria", he said, "these are such perilous times and ...". But she extinguished his words with her lips pressing softly against his. Her hands reached around behind Max's back and his strong arms enclosed her shoulders, gently forcing her breasts up against his chest. They held this embrace and time stopped for them.

Afterwards she could never recall if it was she or Max who had led the way to her bedroom, quietly opening the door, so as not to awaken the sleeping Anna on the couch in the corner.

On the other side of the room on Maria's double bed, they caressed each other in silence as time passed. But a kind of sixth sense had half awoken the small child, who made no sound and still mostly asleep, found the soft sounds of their love-making entering into her child's consciousness, bit by bit infusing her being as her mind opened up to a darkened room in a stone building far away on the opposite side of the Iberian peninsula, and even further away in time.

# SIEGE OF SAGUNTUM

*Middle of the east coast of the Iberian Peninsula, 218 BC*

## Map of Carthaginian Empire 3rd Century BC

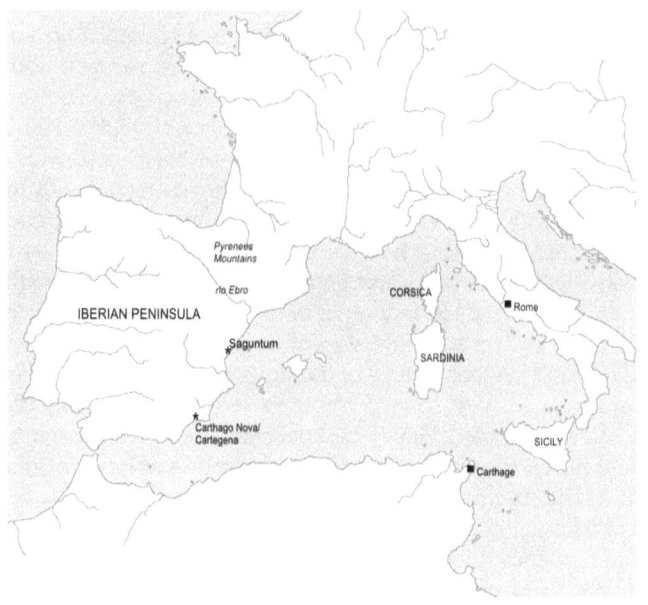

## Thirty-One

*The walled city of Saguntum,
east coast of the Iberian Peninsula, 218 BC*

There was a touch of desperation in the embraces Alia shared with the slim, fair-haired young man who had so recently become her husband. They lay on the large bed in their heavily draped, darkened bedroom. She exuded the radiance of youth. Her long limbs looked strong and the fine features of her cheekbones and nose crowned her generous mouth and almost mischievous smile. Closed lids briefly hid her flashing dark eyes and several strands of her thick gleaming black hair were stuck to her brow by the sweat of their physical exertion. Her fingertips gripped her lover with an intensity that would leave a series of small bruises along his slender upper arm and on the right side of his taut buttocks. The marks stood out as if in silent tribute to the small brownish stain on the left side of his lover's slim tanned throat; it reddened unevenly as her excitement intensified. Slowly and deliberately, she drove her body to an almost silent climax as the other members of her family slept fitfully in the several spacious adjoining bedchambers on the upper floor of a large, finely-built stone building.

The residence resembled two squares, the smaller one inside the other, enclosing an ample, open internal courtyard where fruit-laden bushes and colourful flowering vines grew in beds around a central well that reached deep into the ground. The house itself was old but solid. The original ground floor had been built generations ago in a style reminiscent of dwellings in the late Etruscan era, a popular style of residential architecture in early Roman times. Decorative bricks and tiles were used but the structure was based on stone with powerful wooden beams. At the front, an arched entrance corridor led into the spacious open atrium where, in the middle, a large stone basin was placed for the collection of rainwater with an overflow into the nearby well.

An imposing structure, it stood with a few others of similar opulence on the higher ground in the eastern part of a large

BEGINNINGS                                          Gary Heilbronn

settlement of Phoenician origin, but at that time known to its Roman rulers as 'the Greek free city of Saguntum'. Much later, it would be called by its Spanish name: Sagunto. The city had been built into low foothills close to the coast of the vast Mediterranean Sea, about mid-point along the eastern edge of the Iberian Peninsula, opposite the Balearic Islands.

Over generations, the residence had been rebuilt and added to with elaborate care and with little concern for the cost. For money had most of the time been plentiful in Alia's family. So their stately home, the land it was built on as well as several fields nearby, had been in the peaceful possession of her merchant family for many generations; indeed, longer than she or most of her ancestors could remember.

But what seemed like a perpetual peace had all of a sudden disappeared and perilous times were once again upon them and their fellow inhabitants of Saguntum. They watched over several months, as many legions of soldiers, said to be under the command of a young and ambitious Carthaginian general named Hannibal, had come and gone around the outskirts of the city. Now the soldiers were looking very much more like they intended to stay.

§

Less than three years beforehand, Hannibal had taken command of the Carthaginian army. It was an army that had some time before that, been routed by Roman forces in lands far, far to the east. But surprisingly quickly, the Carthaginians had returned in force to the Iberian Peninsula and by the previous summer, young Hannibal had already subdued most of the tribes throughout nearly the whole of the peninsula south of the mighty Ebro River. Only Saguntum, about one hundred and sixty kilometres to the south of that river's delta, and some of the wild peoples from the mountains in the far north-west remained unconquered.

Alia's mother had once confided to her that her family believed some of her ancestors had come from that distant region, but the young woman felt little affinity with what she had imagined to be barbaric mountain people. After all, she was a cultivated and educated young woman born into a wealthy city family; and anyway, most of the stories the family elders had handed down, spoke of their origins in lands far to the east across the vast Mediterranean Sea. They told of the many voyages of discovery and trade that her ancestors had made throughout the length and breadth of that seemingly interminable stretch of water. It was an occupation her ancestors had pursued for centuries, amassing a considerable fortune, and indeed, an occupation that Alia's family still engaged in.

For several centuries before Alia was born, the Carthaginians had been on the Iberian Peninsula. Traders and warriors from ancient Carthage, situated on the southern shores of the Mediterranean, had then occupied much of the Peninsula. This occurred well after their sea-faring forbears, the Phoenician, had established their early trading settlements at various places along the eastern, southern and western coastline. But after a time, those early Carthaginians settlers, had also left, seemingly having lost interest in Iberia. Their attention was elsewhere and by the end of their twenty-three years long war with the emerging Roman Empire, later known as the First Punic War, and still some two hundred and fifty years before the birth of the Christian prophet, it was the Roman civilization that was in ascendancy.

The Carthaginians had seen their fortunes several times rise and fall over the past handful of centuries. Their ancient Capital, Carthage – whose ruins would litter the hills outside the city of Tunis two millennia later – was said to have been founded in 814 BC by the warrior-Queen Dido, the sister of Pygmalion, a little known King of the Phoenician city of Tyre. She had been forced to flee Tyre after her husband was murdered by her brother, the king. Those were times when power and family bonds rarely sat peaceably at the same table, though perhaps times change very little. However, as the legend goes, her trials and tribulations were not over and to save the city that she founded, Dido committed suicide rather than marry Iarbus, the native ruler of the lands where Carthage was built and who had threatened war if she refused to marry him. Choosing death over an unhappy marriage is a tale that resonates through history, though less so with Kings and Queens who often prefer to arrange the death of their spouse or suitor rather than their own.

The city of Carthage had prospered as it had an important strategic trading position, good harbour, strong defensible position and a fertile hinterland. So, with the decline of the great Phoenician city of Tyre following its subjugation by the Assyrians, the people of Carthage slowly took over much of their Phoenician ancestors' maritime and trading empire. As time went by, the Carthaginian Empire grew wealthy and seemed barely to have noticed the virtual secession, in about 410 BC, of those old colonies of Phoenicians and Celt-Iberians which had so much earlier been established on the Iberian Peninsula.

# Thirty-Two

During several centuries preceding the Christian era, both Carthage and Rome had in turn grown affluent on revenues flowing from the silver and copper resources of the Iberian Peninsula as well as from their overland trade routes for precious tin supplies from the north. A number of the trading families residing in the ports and coastal cities along the western edges of the Mediterranean had likewise accumulated great wealth. Alia's family was one of these.

Alia had questioned her father, Leontius, about the return of the Carthaginians after so many decades' absence. He was an educated man and explained that in the past, both Rome and Carthage seemed much more preoccupied with political and military clashes over territories closer to their homes further to the east. There were alliances with the Persians, Egyptians and Greeks, the North African conquests, and the loss and recapture of Sicily and Sardinia. In due course, a war (that was later called the First Punic War) had erupted between Rome and Carthage and it lasted for a quarter of a century. It was only the defeat of the old Carthaginian leader, Hasdrubal by the Romans outside Panormus and his execution by his own troops in 253 BC that brought a somewhat shaky truce between these two empires.

"Unsurprisingly," Leontius remarked, "dissidence continued and by 247 BC, Hamilcar Barca had reorganized Carthaginian forces on Sicily and was again threatening Rome. But the failure of reinforcements to arrive from North Africa led to his crushing defeat by the Romans in 241 BC. That saw a final end to the war but brought with it the Carthaginian's loss of the whole of Sicily where remnants of the Phoenician civilization had persisted."

"As a result, for many years, Carthage was financially crippled by having to pay heavy post-war reparations and indemnities to Rome. Inevitably, this bred resentment in the vanquished – a lesson that victors seem unable to learn. To make matters worse for the Carthaginians, soon thereafter, their interests in Sardinia and Corsica also had to be handed over to Rome as payment for Rome's non-intervention in rebellions within remaining Carthaginian territories."

Alia had been listening then leaned back, looking a little perplexed.

"But father, the Carthaginians had been crushed. I do not understand why they have become so powerful again."

"Yes, Alia; but they needed to acquire wealth quickly. So, perhaps it was not surprising that the gaze of Hamilcar Barca soon turned westwards and he sought to re-conquer much of the old Carthaginian territories here, on the Iberian Peninsula. But that he managed to do so within four years of the end of the First Punic War was remarkable."

"In this venture, he took with him his nine-year old son, Hannibal. Now Hamilcar Barca's died in 229 BC, and his successor was his son-in-law, also named Hasdrubal. He continued the re-conquest of Iberia and it took only a few years for him to found New Carthage or Carthago Nova on the southeast coast of the Iberian Peninsula, some three days ride to the south of Saguntum."

Cartago Nova was later to be known as Cartegena.

Leontius looked quizzically at his daughter. It was unusual for a girl to be interested in affairs of state, he thought. But he continued.

"Rome still seemed strangely uninterested by the Iberian Peninsula; apparently it was too pre-occupied with the tribal, Celtic peoples they call the Gauls, far to their northwest and the fading Greek civilization to their east. Perhaps they accepted Hamilcar Barca's occupation of Iberia as a means whereby the enormous war debts Carthage owed to Rome could be more rapidly repaid. I can see how this strategy might have made sense at the time. Rome received the profits and all the hard work was done by the Carthaginians."

"And", Alia interrupted, "this is why we find ourselves now under threat. It is in fact in Rome's interests that Hannibal succeeds!"

"What you say may be so, my child, but that threat was supposed to be avoided. This was because in 226 BC, Rome signed an important treaty with Carthage agreeing to Carthaginian expansion on the Peninsula; but only in the areas south of the natural border formed by the Pyrenees Mountains and the Ebro River; it flows east from the Cantabrian Mountains, in the far north-west, and empties into the Mediterranean Sea. That treaty left all territory north of the Ebro – the land of the Gauls – to the Romans.

It also guaranteed the liberty of the Greek free cities such as Saguntum."

Leontius looked pensive and said no more as if he had a premonition of what was to be the fate of his city. This was a treaty that young Hannibal would some years later completely ignore when, in a venture of mythic proportions, he force-marched forty thousand men and many hundreds of elephants north to cross the Pyrenees mountains near the coast, traversed the plains of southern France and pushed across the Italian alps, to challenge Rome at its own backdoor. It was a strategy that would herald in the commencement of the conflict later called the Second Punic War. But that was yet to come.

Leontius did not need to tell Alia the rest of the story as it was well known to all. Hasdrubal had been assassinated by an Iberian tribesman some distance to the south of Saguntum and his brother-in-law, Hannibal, just twenty-six years old and a sworn opponent of Rome, was elected as replacement. The young general then launched a series of successful military campaigns against various tribes between Carthago Nova in the south and the Ebro River far to the north, leaving only Saguntum untouched along the eastern coast.

Alia's family and most of the other residents of Saguntum had for some time been troubled by the presence of Hannibal's army outside their city. Their comfortable world was now threatened by concerns for their security. Had they known of Hannibal's future plans for the conquest of Rome, perhaps they would have acted with greater haste. But perhaps their fate was inevitable.

The Saguntines now felt isolated and vulnerable. Also, there were strange rumours about. Some said that Rome had encouraged the Saguntines to attack its neighbour, the Turbetes tribe. But Alia knew this was untrue, as did everyone in Saguntum, since all their soldiers were kept close to home to assure the defences of the city. Such rumours and lies were certainly worrying. The situation was indeed deteriorating and any remaining optimism in the city was fading.

That night, after the evening meal was done, Alia's father addressed the gathered family. Alia and her husband were present. He told them that the city Senators and Praetor now feared that it had, in fact, been Hannibal himself who had paid the Turbetes people to claim they had been attacked, so as to justify the Carthaginians leading their forces against Saguntum, despite their guarantee of freedom found in the Ebro Treaty with Rome. If they did this, little mercy could be expected from such enemies.

"But father," Alia's young husband replied, "it is well-known to the people of Saguntum that, at the time of making the Ebro Treaty, Rome had established a clear understanding with Carthage that the freedom and independence of Saguntum from Carthaginian control was secured."

The old man looked directly back at him. The young man went on.

"The treaty was said to guarantee the liberty of the Greek free cities, including those south of the Ebro River" said the young man, half pleading.

Relying on this treaty, the people of Saguntum believed that peace would continue as in the past and that there would be no war. Such words echo ominously throughout history. Yet for some time this belief had comforted them in the face of the manifest build-up of Carthaginian forces in the vicinity of the city walls.

"But Quintus Gaius" Alia's father replied calmly, "no-one in Saguntum has even seen the Ebro Treaty, nor can anyone actually point to any specific clauses or terms in it which could be said to make such guarantees."

His listeners' heads were bowed. Their worry was palpable.

"Treaty-making is indeed an obscure art," Leontius said, but the irony was lost on most members of the family. He continued.

"... certain matters may be omitted or purposely left vague so that an accord can be reached on the fundamentals."

His listeners sat solemnly staring down at the top of the long heavy oak table where they still sat in numbed silence.

So it would be with the Ebro Treaty; and though Leontius and his family would never be aware of it, this state of affairs would indirectly give rise to much controversy, not only in the days and weeks that followed and Rome dithered when faced with news of Hannibal's siege of Saguntum, but also much later when those great historians of the Roman era: Polybius, Titus Livius and Appian grappled with the varied and conflicting accounts of the events at

Saguntum and strove to identify the real reasons for the outbreak of the Second Punic War between Rome and Carthage. Perhaps, they ignored the character of Hannibal and the inevitable effect of the humiliation, hatred and economic deprivation which festers in the minds of conquered and over-taxed peoples.

## Thirty-Three

Morning light streamed into the spacious bedroom where Alia still slept. The thick stone walls kept in the coolness during summer, but the wide openings onto the terrace made it difficult to keep the house warm on those occasional winter's evenings when a cold breeze blew in from the sea. But today, the sun was already warm.

Alia had been married for only four months and her husband, Quintus Gaius was beside her. He was of pure Roman descent, son of another well-established trading family living in Saguntum. But his own family's commercial connections were with Rome, unlike Alia's family, whose trading links were solidly forged with the lands along the southern and eastern shores of the Mediterranean.

Their marriage had been seen by both families as a happy commercial liaison with great potential, though Alia, not much more than a teenager herself, had blushed when she looked upon the young man, transported by his great beauty and quickly smitten by his copious charm. He had been raised and educated astutely by his family, who saw his future in high levels of city administration, perhaps even in Rome, but either way, somewhere well-placed where he could foster the family's commercial interests and fortunes, now already massively enhanced by the liaison with Alia.

Her family, unlike that of Quintus which had been on the Iberian Peninsula for only a few generations, seemed always to have been in Saguntum, and was reputed to have been one of the merchant-families that had traded throughout the Mediterranean for centuries. They were also said to be enormously wealthy with many ships and vast stores of gold and other precious jewels and metals. Of course such stories were often exaggerated. But for so many past generations, life had been peaceful and prosperous for everyone in this busy coastal city, especially for the old trading families. It was only now, with Hannibal at their doorstep, that they had begun to realize how precarious their position actually was, here on the east coast of the Iberian Peninsula, so far from the protection of Rome and no longer allied with Carthage.

For months, the presence around the city of vast numbers of Carthaginian troops supported by many Iberian tribesmen from other regions had been a serious concern and the people of the city began to feel, also, that food supplies were arriving less frequently than in the past and in a much diminished state. So envoys had been sent by the city Praetor to Rome to seek military reinforcements and undertake negotiations with Carthage to ensure that Saguntum's alliance with Rome would be respected by Hannibal under the terms of the recent Ebro Treaty. The envoys had been absent for many, many weeks and no firm results had yet been had. They were still in Rome. The townspeople had heard only vague messages of Rome's support but also of endless discussions within the Roman Senate over full meaning of the Ebro Treaty. The Senate in Rome had no powers to make laws, but it was responsible for foreign affairs, public revenue and the administration of religion. So its support should hopefully guarantee the city's freedom from attack.

However, more recently, confusion had increased as the Senators in Rome had taken up the debate of the ridiculous notion, which Hannibal's own envoys to Rome had apparently transmitted, that he and his army were actually there outside Saguntum to assist the Saguntines in their disputes with several of the tribes in the region. The Saguntine envoys fretted over how gullible the Roman Senators seemed to be. When news of these latest debates were received back home, the city elders wrung their hands and became even more worried though they still tried to reassure themselves that Rome would in due course come to their aid.

§

Alia parted the thick crimson curtains of her bedroom and came out onto the wide tiled upstairs terrace of their impressive two-storey family home standing high up on the sloping outskirts of the city of Saguntum. It was set back further than many of the other residences, especially those of the Iberian residents. Their homes were found closer to the city walls. From her vantage point, Alia could see above those walls. She saw that there was considerable activity among the ranks of the troops outside. Past the fortifications that spread out on to less sloping ground, large wooden constructions were being pushed and pulled by hundreds of soldiers towards the outer city walls. She was seriously alarmed.

"Quintus! Father!" She called out loudly. "Come quickly. The troops of Hannibal are approaching the city in force."

By the time the two men had joined Alia at the edge of the balcony, a call to arms could be heard from the several Saguntine lookouts posted at various strategic points around the city walls.

"They seem to be carrying battering rams!" Quintus shouted. "They're going to try to knock down the walls just where they are the highest and strongest ... just where they have been re-inforced the most! This must surely fail!" he cried. He blurted out these words with the confidence of youth.

Alia glanced towards him quizzically. There seemed to be tens of thousands of soldiers amassing outside the city walls and here was Quintus Gaius convinced of their own safety. She wondered if he was just pretending to be confident for her sake. But he stared towards the walls seemingly oblivious even to the presence of his young wife.

The fortifications around Saguntum had been built from stone and added to time and again over the centuries, until they stood, in some parts, almost as high as three fully grown men together. To the south-west, there was relatively flat terrain. It was where an attack was most likely to occur, and the walls had been built even higher there and a stone tower manned with dozens of javelin throwers and archers overlooked the approach. Along the top of the walls, there were wooden and stone walkways to allow movement of lookouts and guards, and there were gaps at regular intervals along the way through which archers could fire arrows or throw javelin. At various positions, wide platforms had been built where fires burned in heavy iron pots to enable the archers to light the tarred ends of their arrows before unleashing them on the enemy below.

Alia's family group watching from high on the hill; all stared, transfixed by the slow inevitable movement of the siege engines being pushed and dragged by hundreds of men. Within a short time, the sounds of the battering rams could be heard against the walls and the flashes of arrows and javelins had begun. Alia and her father and husband had long since been joined by other members of the family. They seemed to be riveted to the ground where they stood, watching the skirmishes at the walls for what seemed like hours. What else could they do? Finally the flash of weapons and cries of battles subsided somewhat and it seemed that the Carthaginians had called off their assault.

Before long, small groups of Saguntine warriors could be seen slipping out from the narrow exits in the walls and attacking the siege engines that had been placed under guard close by the walls. From her vantage point, Alia could see that greater casualties were being suffered by both sides in this hand to hand combat. At least, as dusk enclosed the besieged city, the skirmishes slowly abated.

The following day, all was quiet and both sides tended their wounded. On the third day, the battle began again by mid-morning. It was while Alia was down in the cellars aiding the family servants in taking stock of the food and wines they had stored in great pottery urns. If a siege were to persist, it would be critical to make food and water supplies last as long as possible; hopefully outlasting the enemy's resources. All of a sudden, a great shout of triumph sounded from the walls close to where the siege engines had been positioned. Rushing upstairs, Alia cried out:

"What has happened? Have the enemy retreated?" Her father, who was coming back into the house from the outside, looked at her.

"No, but perhaps something as fortuitous has occurred." He replied. "Hannibal has been wounded by one of our phalaricas thrown from the city walls. May it be the will of the Gods that he dies from his wounds. His men are retreating and leaving the siege engines and battering rams unguarded. Our soldiers are destroying them as we speak."

The phalarica was the Saguntine weapon of choice. It was a javelin with a smooth and round wooden shaft up to its head where there was attached a square section of iron bar the length of four men's hands and tapering down to a point. It could penetrate armour when well thrown. The shaft was often wrapped with leather and smeared with tar, then set alight so that by the time it found its target, the flames would have reached such an intensity, having been fanned by their flight through the air, that even if it

# BEGINNINGS  Gary Heilbronn

merely penetrated a soldier's shield, the heat was so great that his armour had to be discarded, leaving the soldier vulnerable to attack with arrow, sword and club.

That evening, there was much muted jubilation and some relief in the streets and houses of Saguntum.

The calm persisted. But even though the following days were free from the noise of battle, the Saguntines could continually hear in the distance, hammering, sawing and the sounds of the construction of new siege engines and battering rams carrying on unabated. So their spirits had already sunk to a new low when the fighting resumed with what seemed like a new intensity just a short time later.

The noise of battle could be heard at Alia's family home well away from the city walls.

Alia, her husband, Quintus Gaius and her father Leontius were once again at their viewpoint on the upstairs terrace.

'Was it true?" Alia asked of her father. He looked at her quizzically.

"It was rumoured that the Carthaginians had amassed more than 150,000 fighting men to undertake this siege? How can we withstand such a force?" she said.

The older man looked sadly at this beloved daughter.

"Even if it were only 100,000 men, our soldiers would still be outnumbered by twenty to one. Our fates now rest with the Gods, my child, if Rome does not soon intervene," was his only reply.

As he spoke the rumblings of another small section of the city walls being dislodged reached their ears. Then the sound of a tremendous crash shook the air. They watched disbelievingly as two towers and a large section of the city wall crumpled to the ground. The Carthaginians stormed through the breach in the wall and now were confronted by waves of desperate Saguntine soldiers and townsfolk fighting for their own and their families' lives. From their vantage point, Alia and her family could see the ferocity of the fighting and the spilled blood and torn limbs of the many casualties that littered the ground between the outer walls and the houses of the town.

The opposing forces seemed to have reached a stalemate as for some time little ground had been taken or given by either when a great battle-cry arose from the Saguntines. It seemed to endow them with extra strength as they forced their enemies back to the ruins of the wall and into a confused retreat. Again a cheer rose from the throats of the many townspeople who had been involved in the fighting or watching from various vantage points around the town, and the fighting slowed and all but subsided for the day.

Carthaginian wounded still lying on the battlefield within the walls were rapidly dispatched and Saguntine wounded dragged and carried back through the inner walls to houses where their wounds were washed, treated and bandaged. The number of casualties was enormous and the bodies of moaning and broken men and women stretched far over the grounds surrounding many of the buildings near to the inner city walls.

Throughout the hours of fighting, Alia's fury and hatred for the enemy had set a fire in her heart. By its end, her emotions had reached boiling point as she turned to look at the profile of this fine-looking young man, her husband, who stood at her side, arms resting on the low stone wall forming the edge of the upstairs terrace. Alia's face was tormented with the turmoil of her feelings. Here before her was this able-bodied young man she desired and admired, carefully attired and satisfied just to watch his Saguntine brothers give their life's blood to save the city and their families.

"Why was he not amongst them?" she demanded quietly to herself. She knew that if she were a man, it would have been impossible to prevent her from joining the battle. But from an empty place deep in the bottom of her gut, a voice screamed out at her for wanting to risk his safety, and begged her to keep him close by, far from the cruelty of the battle.

"But how could he show no desire to fight for his home and his young wife? Was there no fire in his heart?" she asked herself. "Did he not know what would happen to her should the battle be lost and the Carthaginians take control of the city? Did he not care?" Not all their wealth and position could save her from being ravaged and likely tortured to death. Quintus Gaius was unaware of the confused but cold and distant stare with which his young bride at that instant regarded him.

But Alia's raging thoughts and emotions were curtly interrupted by the entry of a messenger seeking out her father. He had hardly been greeted when he blurted out:

"They have come. A Roman delegation has arrived at the harbour. Your presence is sought by the Praetor. The Senators are now meeting to decide what course of action we should take."

"What wonderful news!" Quintus Gaius shouted. "I knew Rome would come to our aid. Now we shall be saved."

Alia looked at him again and her voice took on a hard edge:

"Let not your hopes and fears cloud your judgement, husband. There are no Roman Legions come to fight with us. You forget too quickly how Rome has left us for so long at the mercy of the Carthaginians though they had been clearly informed of our plight well before the siege began."

The coldness in the young woman's tone seemed to shock all those present, not the least Quintus Gaius, who so far had known only gentle and sweet words from his young wife. Alia's mother turned her face away. Only she, and on rare occasions as her daughter grew into womanhood, had seen the untouchable steely core to Alia's being. And she had heard her husband's own grandmother speak of the thread of ice and steel that ran through the blood of some of the women in the family. Now she began to understand what the old lady had been speaking of.

"Of course they are here to help us!" Quintus replied curtly. "I myself will escape from the city this night, under cover of darkness, and go to speak with them. You will see. Rome will not abandon us to the enemy! ... Father," he spoke to Alia's father, "please inform the City Senate of my plan. It would be well that I go with their blessing. I beg your leave as I must begin my preparations immediately."

## Thirty-Four

The others seemed pleased with the words of Quintus but worried at the danger his expedition would run. Alia, too, was pleased by his words though a nagging seed of doubt nestled in a hidden place in her heart.

"Why do I feel this uncertainty?" she thought to herself. "Is it fear for my husband's safety? I know he runs a great risk in this venture. But is it that which bothers my heart? I tremble not with fear that I may lose him but with fury. But why? I doubted his bravery before and now he undertakes a great challenge that shows us all his mettle. Why does my heart so contradict what my head tells me to be a selfless act of courage?"

Under the cover of darkness late that night, while the Senators of the city still debated the issue, Quintus Gaius slipped out from the eastern side of the city and made his way through hidden paths down towards the coast. Their goodbyes were brief and Alia was never to see nor hear from him again. Nor did anyone in the city hear further news of the envoys from Rome. They soon left for Carthage after Hannibal's messengers told them that it was too dangerous for them to travel to the city under siege and that he was too busy with the battle to receive them. It is said that Hannibal had also immediately sent messengers to Carthage to advise them not to make any concessions to Rome in this matter.

The few days that followed the arrival and departure of the envoys from Rome were again quiet. Hannibal was apparently allowing time for his troops to rest, but he was also taking the time to inspire them with tales of the slaves and the riches they would claim when they took the city. The Saguntines, however, could not rest and worked feverishly to repair the damage to their city walls so that when the fighting resumed on the fourth day after the departure of the envoys from Rome, both sides met and fought with fresh passion and a violence that had so far not been seen.

Multi-storey wooden towers pushed by hundreds of Carthaginian warriors were rolled and dragged up to the walls while catapults and ballista delivered their flaming charges of spears and stones from both sides of the walls. As the battle raged, a contingent of some hundreds of black African soldiers dug into the mud and stone wall base with pickaxes and spades, soon loosening the supports for the wall and rapidly bringing to the ground the newly built sections. They also dragged some of the older parts of the walls down with them.

The battle was now being fought on many fronts and Hannibal's men had seized high ground to the south and amassed their catapults there, enclosing them with makeshift walls built with the stones that had tumbled everywhere around from the broken city walls. The situation was beginning to look desperate for the Saguntine soldiers and people. By this stage, everyone in the town was armed and firing arrows or casting rocks from their vantage points on roofs and balconies near to where the fighting was raging. Alia wielded a bow and arrow like an experienced warrior, though her archery training had thus far been limited to youthful target practice with friends during her early teenage years. Her aim was good and many enemy warriors fell from the strikes of her arrows. Only with nightfall did the fighting subside. Hannibal's men guarded the territory that their forces had seized within the city walls, while considerably diminished areas were left under the control of the weary Saguntines.

§

After retreating to the kitchen and slowly partaking of the meagre meal of soup and bread that had been prepared by the remaining few servants of the household, Alia stumbled towards her chamber and fell exhausted onto the bed she had so recently shared with her now departed young husband. She had thought of him often throughout the day; then drawing her bow and unleashing arrows with a vehemence she could not describe as if in retribution for the violent fate that she sometimes imagined Quintus Gaius had suffered at the hands of the Carthaginian sentries.

Other times, she was convinced that he had not been killed by them but had made his way to the ships of the Roman envoys and joined them in their voyage to Carthage. She was sure he had not perished. He must have left with the envoys so as to strengthen and bear witness to the complaints they would surely be making to the Carthaginian rulers some seven days sailing-time to the southeast.

"It is now too late. Much too late," Alia lamented to herself. "Even if they are successful, no messenger will return to us in time. Our city will be lost even as the Roman Senators once again debate our fate."

She knew the fate that would await a young woman such as herself and the fate of her father, as a wealthy city elder and Senator. It would not just be the loss of generations of the hard earned riches her family had acquired. Not just her home and the peaceful life she had so far led that would be lost, but she had only brutal violation, torture, mutilation and a slow death to expect from the enemy. And even if somehow, she escaped that ordeal with her life, a long and arduous enslavement would be the best future she could hope for.

As exhaustion began to get the better of her and drag her towards unwanted slumber, Alia's consciousness registered a quiet movement coming towards her bed. Her eyes instantly opened, staring into the darkness, her body tensing; then she heard with relief the soft tones of her mother's voice.

"Wait, Alia my sweet child, it is only I, your mother," sighed a low breathy voice emanating from the shadow approaching her in the dark.

"I know you are exhausted, but at a time such as this, a mother must share her most intimate thoughts with her daughter."

"Of course mother. Come; sit by me, here on my bed. The future is so bleak and this may be our last moments together," Alia whispered softly and sadly to the older woman.

Alia's mother was more than twice her age. Not yet old enough to be expected to die of old age but now no longer a woman with a future; except that which can be lived through her children and theirs. Though lines had begun to form under her eyes and around the corners of her mouth, she was still a very attractive woman and her skin glowed, nurtured by the safe and pampered life she had had the good fortune to have led as wife and mother, and then later as the matriarch of a wealthy family.

"My child," she breathed softly, "things look very bad for our city. I pray that although your years are still few, you have known enough of life and a love to carry you through whatever terrible times may be ahead of us ... ."

Alia raised her hand interrupting her: "speak not of my love, as I see now how shallow have been my feelings for Quintus Gaius, my husband; and equally, I have no doubt, his for me. I see as much greater and more profound my real love for my family and my people."

Her mother replied. "But Quintus loved you well enough and has gone to the Gods as a hero, fighting in his own way for your survival, and for the survival of our city. Surely that speaks well of him."

"That may or may not be so, mother ..." Alia said curtly, "for I believe in my heart that he has deserted us all in our hour of need. I believe he lives ... yes, he lives and has fled with the cowardly Roman envoys to a place of safety. My heart is heavy not with his loss, but with humiliation at my own naive heart and my weakness in having bathed in the watered-down wine of his tepid passion." Her eyes blazed with bitterness to echo her words.

"Yesterday, my heart was empty, but today it is filled. It is filled with the fury and passion of battle and our city's hapless plight" she said proudly.

"I have left Quintus Gaius far behind me, with the young girl I was before Hannibal's soldiers smashed through our city walls and lay to waste so many of our young men and women; leaving their blood to soak into that tiny and useless tract of soil we now defend between our city walls and the remaining homes of our people."

Alia's mother winced at the nobility and cruelty and pain in her only daughter's words, but she had seen signs of it before and knew from where it had come and would forever live on. She saw, too, how her daughter had grown in stature. Her presence filled the room she now lay in and the home that would have been hers, for a generation or more had fate dealt her a different hand. These last few months had inexorably changed everyone's lives; forever. No longer could Alia expect a life to be lived like her mother and the others before her, those decades of comfort, peace and tranquillity, modestly married to a sometimes indifferent husband, bearing his children. And to what end? Her fate and her future, if there was to be any, were balanced now on a knife-edge.

# BEGINNINGS                                              Gary Heilbronn

The older woman looked again towards her daughter and gazed into her steely eyes.

"Things may go very badly in the days to come" her mother said quietly. "Should the worst befall you; should you fall into enemy hands and feel there can be no escape from a tortured and dishonourable death, then you may wish to deal yourself the final blow" she said. She spoke softly but with a clear and unquivering voice.

Slowly she withdrew from beneath her cloak an object that, despite the dimness, gleamed and flashed dully with rays of light emanating from the thick candle now burned down low and standing beside them on the large wooden storage trunk near the bed.

It was a bronze bladed dagger. She handed it to her daughter.

The older woman spoke. "This dagger has belonged to your ancestors for centuries and was confided to me by your grandmother to pass on to you when the time was right. She saw in you a spark of life that cannot be easily extinguished; and then there was the stain on your throat. A sure sign, she said. And a rare gift. I believe that the time is now right and pray that you live to hold on to this so that in due course you may pass it on to your own descendants, and not have cause to plunge it cruelly into your own breast."

Alia sat up and reached out with her two open palms to receive the gift of the dagger. Her eyes were transfixed by the weapon. Slowly she removed it from its carved wooden scabbard by its beautifully shaped and gilded wooden handle riveted to its metal core. It had a deceptively short but slightly curved double edged bronze blade, no more than an open hand's-width from its point to a thick base, where on both sides it was inlaid with precious gems. The thick base of the blade was flanked by an ornate protective bar in iron slightly turned upwards at the ends. Below it, was a shiny smooth walnut and gold-plated handle. That it was very old was obvious, as it bore little resemblance to the weapons Alia had seen carried by the men of the family or by the city's soldiers; and lately she had seen more than enough of them to last a lifetime.

As she held the weapon in her two hands, her consciousness dimmed and her mind flashed through images of the faces of many women, beautiful for the most part and young but not young, some illuminated by bright sunlight; others whose faces glistened with sweat and blood splattered from battle; and others in strange attire. Yet all were somehow possessed of the same dark steely expressive eyes and linked, as if by a thread of light connecting the images each with the others. Alia gasped. Only a second or two had passed while she held the dagger, though the faces she saw infused almost a millennium of anger and strength and violence into her heart.

"What is it my child? Why do you shiver? What have you seen?" The older woman enquired quickly, concerned and a little afraid that Alia may have had a premonition of her own death from the blade she now cradled.

"I cannot explain, mother. It was as if I glimpsed the faces of some of my ancestors. It is as if the dagger carries with it, visions of its owners; perhaps those who have used it to shed blood and to take lives, but who have lost a little of their own spirits to the dagger's cold metal core."

Both mother and daughter looked intently into each other's eyes, neither knowing if this may be the last time they would share an intimate moment such as this. The older woman rose from the bed and turned gracefully towards the door. Alia watched her go and settled down slowly to sleep. She knew she would need all her strength for the trials and tribulations of the days to come.

# Thirty-Five

The following morning began quietly. Look-outs had reported seeing a large contingent of Carthaginian soldiers being led off to the west by Hannibal himself. They were headed in the direction of the neighbouring Oretani and Carpetani peoples, some of whom had supplied new conscripts for Hannibal's army, as numbers were being too regularly depleted. There was some hope in the city that troubles with those tribes would allow the Saguntines a respite from attack.

But these hopes were short-lived. Later that morning the battering rams were again brought forward and after fierce but sporadic fighting, more of the walls were brought down and more territorial gains within the city were made by the Carthaginians. On Hannibal's return two days later the attack on the city renewed with even greater intensity and both sides suffered heavy losses, though again, only the Carthaginians won significant territory with a part of the citadel itself being captured.

Early the next morning, the Saguntine look-outs and guards were surprised by the approach of a solitary soldier. He crossed the battle lines and spoke to the guards:

"My name is Alorcus" he said, "and I am an Iberian, like many of the people of Saguntum. I ask to be admitted as a guest of the city, to see the Praetor and Senate and to convey Hannibal's terms for a peace."

This was an unexpected turn of events.

He left his weapons with the guards and as honour demanded, he was admitted to the city. As he walked towards the Praetor's palace, a crowd of the townspeople followed him. Alia had joined the crowd as had her father. There were soldiers and merchants and Saguntine residents from all ranks of society gathered around Alorcus. He told them that the night before a Saguntine had come to Hannibal's camp to seek a peaceful resolution to the siege but upon hearing the terms which Hannibal had laid down, he had decided to remain with the Carthaginians saying that he would

BEGINNINGS  Gary Heilbronn

himself have been killed by the townspeople had he returned to convey such terms.

"Father" Alia said excitedly," this soldier says that one of us went last night to seek peace from Hannibal but has remained with his forces as a deserter. Can this be true?"

Her father looked perplexed and replied:

"This is strange. The Senate has discussed seeking a peace but no emissary was sent; it being believed that there could be no peace without dishonour now that the battle for the city has been all but won by the Carthaginians. Let us see what this Alorcus has to say. But the elders of the city seem resolved to die in the city's defence rather than submit to slavery."

"Father, you speak as if all is lost!" Alia said, trying to hide her astonishment at her father's despair. "It gives me sorrow to tell you this at this time; but I am with child and I will not accept death before my allotted time."

Her father was shocked. Of course, his daughter had been married now for some months but he had been too worried by the siege to think of such things and he had seen her fight like a man in the battles with their aggressors. At that instant, his resolve to fight to the last and die with the city began to waver.

"Alia, you must go, now!" He said quickly. "Pass by the house to take as much gold as you can carry and leave by the secret pathways that Quintus Gaius took when he went to speak with the Roman envoys. All is lost here now. You must save yourself and your unborn child."

Alia stood for a moment looking deeply into her father's eyes. Both knew this would be the last time they would see each other. Then, heeding her father's words, she ran towards the house to carry out her father's instructions and make her escape along the hidden pathways.

Just then, Alorcus stepped up onto a low stone wall near a smouldering fire and addressed the crowd in words that were recorded for posterity.

"I stand before you, people of Saguntum, as your last hope for peace. I am here out of the old ties of hospitality that we have shared in the past and only because your fellow Saguntine, Alco, has deserted you, for fear, be it true or not, that he would be murdered had he returned advocating these terms for peace which the great general Hannibal now offers you. I come here now for your sake alone, as you can no longer hope for rescue by Rome and the battle is all but over; your walls are down and your arms are spent and can no longer protect you. I offer a peace forced on you by the necessity of your circumstances and not by any idea of what is fair and righteous. Now, any hopes of peace must rest upon your accepting, as a conquered people, the terms which a victorious Hannibal sees fit to impose. Since all is at the conqueror's mercy, you must look upon these terms as a free gift that Hannibal makes to you. ..."

The townsfolk who listened moved restlessly looking at each other whispering their fears. Some slipped off towards their homes. Alorcus continued.

"He takes from you the city which he has laid in ruins and all but completely captured. Your fields and lands he leaves to you and will allow you to build another town at a place of his choosing. All your gold and silver must be brought to him and your lives, as those of your wives and children shall be spared if you leave the city with just two garments each and no weapons and nothing more. Bitter as these terms are, you save your lives and in due course, may hope that when the anger of the battlefield has subsided, Hannibal will relax the harshness of these terms."

As the assembled townspeople, guards, senators, soldiers alike, listened in despair to the words of Alorcus, the noise of troop movements outside what was left of the walls could be clearly heard. In the general confusion and alarm, few noticed the elders of the city leave and return with all the gold and silver and precious stones belonging to the city and owned by themselves personally.

From her vantage point in her home above the city centre, Alia glimpsed the tragedy unfolding below. She watched in shock, her heart pounding as the city elders and their families quickly unloaded their gold and treasures into the huge fire which was now raging near the assembly.

But she had no time to lose as she searched for the few items she needed to take with her.

After a few moments, she again glanced out over the terrace. She stopped, transfixed with horror as without even a word, the city elders threw themselves into the flames and were followed in silence by their wives and families. Mothers with babes in arms, young children, their hands held tight by grandmothers and nurses. ... More and more of the wealthy Saguntines quickly followed suit as Hannibal's approaching soldiers burst upon the scene.

Wiping tears from her eyes, Alia ran out the back of the building that had been her home and her world; out towards the forest and the hidden pathways leading out of the city. Tears of pain, grief and horror blinded her eyes as she raced along the narrow paths. Bizarre thoughts flashed into her mind:

"Am I a coward to flee like this? Should I not have joined my people in their fiery sacrifice? How can I go on when all I've known and cherished has been consumed by the flames?"

Her heart was breaking. But with each stride towards freedom, she sensed an increasing awareness of her incontestable commitment to survival; if not for herself but for her unborn child. A fierce resolve grew in her heart as the future of the new life she carried within her became the most vital imperative of her existence.

Soon the stink of burning flesh permeated the city. More townsfolk threw themselves into the flames. Others looked for escape. Old, young, crippled and able-bodied city dwellers ran every which way, only to be cut to pieces amongst the confusion. Alia could still hear their screams as she fled; and all around, the roar of the Carthaginian troops who'd taken advantage of the disappearance of guards from the city walls to crash through the final defences of the city. The people and riches of the city were now laid bare and chaos reigned.

Hannibal's men had been ordered to kill every male in Saguntum and were in haste to carry out this order. The slaughter continued apace and as the news spread amongst the conquerors that a great part of the riches of the city had been destroyed, the soldiers, infuriated by the loss of much of their booty, put to death every living thing that crossed their paths; children, the elderly, animals, none were spared. Bodies and limbs littered the streets and alleyways, scattered on a carpet of red and gore.

But the fiery defiance of the Saguntines had been sadly symbolic, as still considerable treasures and valuables remained in their houses to be shared amongst the victors when the slaughter was complete. Most would be transported back to Carthage, where Hannibal's army would repair to, in order to rest out the winter and gain strength before its historic and much better documented march across the Pyrenees towards Rome.

§

Several miles along the coast, just to the north on a hilly outlook, half hidden by forests, Alia stood. At her left side a woven basket. It was stuffed with food, a few possessions and some gold; its straps were slung over her right shoulder and across her breast; her dagger in its short scabbard slid in behind her braided leather waistband. Her bow and cluster of arrows hung in the same way over her left shoulder. She stared blankly back towards her home. She had no more tears to shed. She took in the vision of the sacked city. It stood before her like a landscape tableau from hell. She watched the smoke rising from so many places in the ravaged city and her stomach churned as she smelt, even from so far away, the still sweet sickly aroma of burning flesh and boiling blood. She saw little movement from that distance and all was silent around her. Not even the squawking of black crows and carrion eaters that she saw circling above the city could be heard. They had all headed for Saguntum to feast on the remains of the dead. But it was not the thought of their feasting on the bodies of the family and friends she had only just left behind that nauseated Alia, but the horror of who had done this to her people.

Aloud to herself, as there was no-one else to hear, she cried:

"These are Carthaginians, the brothers and cousins of my own Phoenician ancestors; though it is true that many Iberian soldiers fought alongside Hannibal, and they too slaughtered their Iberian kinsmen".

Sighing deeply, she thought aloud to herself: "When my Phoenician ancestors came to this new land, it was not slaughter and domination that they wanted. True, they sought riches but their ways were peaceful. They came not with armies and engines of war. Why are the Carthaginians so different?" She paused.

"Is it that the worst atrocities are begot upon a people by their closest kin and not by strangers from afar? Or is it something else? Why does one man seek to take by force or guile that little which others have, while another will work with them to make greater wealth so all may prosper? Is it that greed and envy of the wealth of others is alone their terrible motivation? Is this the essence of the human condition?"

Alia knew what paths she had taken to arrive here. But how she had slipped through the enemy's grasp on leaving the city, she could not say for certain. Perhaps, all the soldiers were so focussed on their pillage and murder that they had not seen her leave by the hidden pathways behind the city. She had taken advantage of the few minutes' grace she had been allowed, before Hannibal's men had burst through the city's inner walls and fallen upon her people.

Of course, only the residents of Saguntum knew of these hidden escape paths. Not the enemy.

She was alive; alive and everyone else from the city was dead or worse. There was no going back.

"But where do I go now?" she wondered. She only knew that some safety lay perhaps in the wild unconquered regions of the far west and north, where her mother had told her some of her ancestors had once lived. It was in that direction that she now resolved to travel.

Little did she then suspect how long and how difficult a journey this would be.

# AN UNCERTAIN PEACE

*Basque country, South-west France, early 1946*

BEGINNINGS                                    Gary Heilbronn

## Thirty-Six

Far away, another war had run its grisly course and was now over. Or was it really? It certainly was not forgotten. In France, even the liberation, in the latter part of 1944, had been frightening and vengeful. A brutal occupation, an undisciplined resistance movement and forced or complicit collaboration by some, had led to suspicion and confusion in the hearts and minds of so many of the war's survivors. The effects would be felt for many years to come. Even by Maria. She saw herself as merely a spectator but still a survivor of yet another war and her heart was heavy and conflicted. It was just that they had lived through so much.

§

By the end of November in 1942, the Nazi occupation of France had engulfed the whole country and what was previously the 'free zone' was overrun with German soldiers. This must surely have been one of the darkest moments of the war, though Maria strangely harboured glimmers of hope for the future. She, at least, had already lived through such times; and just a few years before.

"Why does the light of hope shine eternal in the human soul" she often asked herself. Her all too brief encounter with Max, in late March, 1942 had perhaps reminded her that there was always light at the end of even the darkest tunnel and it kept up her spirits, at least for a time.

Then, coming almost out of the blue in mid-1943, were the victories of the allied forces in North Africa and in the south of Italy. Maria heard the news of them on *Radio France Libre*. For her and others, it marked the beginning of a more widespread hope that the tide of the war might just have begun to turn. Only the south-east corner of France was under Italian administration and that lasted less than a year as Italy capitulated in September 1943. But German forces replaced them. Yet Maria was relieved that at least the focus of the war had shifted eastwards and away from where she was living.

For Maria and Anna, hidden in that quiet little village in the far southwest of occupied France, the closing months of 1943 and the first half of the following year were uneventful. There was hardship, as less and less fresh food could be found and they relied heavily on conserves made from the produce of Maria's little vegetable garden. As summer approached, the long days of June were spent toiling in her garden while four-year old Anna played quietly around her. Little time was left in the evenings to listen to radio reports of the war's progress. But there was progress and Maria could hardly suppress a cry of joy on hearing the news of allied troops having gained a foothold on the northern Normandy beaches. Within days, she watched with barely concealed pleasure as convoys of German soldiers withdrew from southwest France and headed towards the north. Hope of early liberation crept into her heart as it did for others living in the region. The mood of the people lightened and the village seemed to be a friendlier place.

Although it didn't seem so at the time, events were again moving swiftly. By early August 1944, the north, south and east of France had been liberated by American, British and 'Free France' forces. Only tiny pockets of German military resistance remained pinned down. Some were in the nearby Aquitaine region, not far from where Maria lived and others held out in Brittany, even until early 1945. But gradually they were being almost ignored and it was clear to Maria and everyone else that the war in Europe would soon end. She had survived another war and little Anna was now safe.

§

Yet in other ways, things quickly began to change and again Maria saw that the aftermath of war can be as frightening as the war itself. Even before the end of the war, allegations of collaboration and betrayal; recriminations and revenge-taking had begun. Maria lived a solitary life and knew to keep her head down in this poisonous environment. Old scores were being settled around her; the guilty and innocent alike were summarily executed; young women's heads were shaved and men imprisoned for imagined or real fraternization with the enemy. Newspapers were full of such stories with graphic photographs. They brought tears to Maria's eyes. It seemed to her that revenge was an even more powerful human motivation than love.

"What a cruel thought", she sighed. But she was unable to close her mind to the injustices around her; they seemed impossible to prevent and even harder to put right.

Anna was now an active five year old and a joy to her mother. But of an evening, Maria still spent a great deal of time alone, reflecting on the horrors of the liberation. Was it so different to what had happened after the war in Spain? At least this time she was not among the vanquished. Maria knew what war was like; as well as its aftermath. She had lost a husband and a son in Spain's post-war madness.

"The bitterness and hatreds of war don't dissolve in a day; nor do they wash away with the next heavy rains," she said, "especially in countries like France and Spain, so torn apart by extreme factions and bloody political conflict." But her words were heard only by herself.

## Thirty-Seven

With the unconditional surrender of Germany on the 8th of May 1945, the war in Europe was over. But it wasn't until the end of June that Maria could accompany her hidden charge back to its spiritual home in the Basque Museum in Bayonne. There were just a few crates of only relatively valuable artefacts and original manuscripts and paintings. Maria was present as they were unloaded. She visibly paled when she saw Jewish scrolls and other artefacts being removed from the crates and handed back to Jewish community leaders. At the beginning of the war they had been secretly left with the museum for safekeeping and then concealed within her crates.

"Thank God I knew nothing about them during the war!" Maria remarked. It would have been a disaster if they had been discovered by the Nazis. She immediately scolded herself for her ingratitude and lack of courage. Her reaction had come as no surprise to her colleagues, but she couldn't forget it nor even forgive herself for what she saw as weakness.

Quickly, many of the Basque Museum's collections were once again installed and openly exhibited in the Maison Dagourette. Maria smiled with pleasure as she walked in through the museum door each day. She had had so little time there before the war began. She loved the four storey building's high ceilings, enormously thick oak wood beams and bare wooden floorboards, highly polished by the passage of so many feet over the centuries since it was built in the fifteen hundreds. Looking around her, she felt as if she was home again and there were moments when she thought that the war was just a brief interruption to the new life she had begun to rebuild in exile. "Now I'm free again" she sometimes thought and for a moment believed. It was as if a great weight had been lifted from her heart.

But those were only moments.

# BEGINNINGS                                    Gary Heilbronn

The truth was that being there couldn't help take her mind off the loss and years of hardship she had endured; first on the run from Franco's fascists and then hidden away from the Nazis.

She continued her work on the collections, especially those parts exposed in the bright spacious rooms devoted to: 'Les idées et les hommes' – the Basque people and their beliefs. As Maria walked into the first room of the collection, she always stopped to survey the displays. She took her time. Her eyes moved from one section to the next. She enjoyed the way the exhibits illustrated many of the main moments of Basque history and culture over recent centuries. They showed how modern Basque identity was born in the 16th century religious struggles between Catholics and Protestants. That was when the Bible and the Catechisms had been translated into the Basque language. Then, in the 17th and 18th centuries, vexed theological quarrels broke out but this time between the modernist, reformist views of the Jansenites and the traditional Jesuits.

"Religious conflict has been behind so much evil" she thought aloud. It made her sad and challenged her religious upbringing.

Maria found that she often talked to herself as she worked.

She moved on, smiling again as she saw the displays off in the side-rooms that showed the considerable religious tolerance that had always existed in the Basque country. In the Middle Ages, there was an acceptance of Jewish exiles; many had escaped from persecution in nearby Spain. These people had played a significant role in the Bayonne community and many were even granted citizenship, giving them the status of members of the city with all the rights and duties that entailed. "Perhaps little has changed" she thought. Maria knew personally how the museum had so recently helped save the local Jewish community's' sacred scrolls and artefacts from the Nazis.

As she returned towards the main collection, she cast her eyes over the displays showing how the Basques in France had been affected by the French Revolution and the foundations for the concept of human rights; the continual wars of Napoleon's First Empire and the expansionist Second Empire. They highlighted the roles of prominent Basques in French naval and maritime adventures. It reminded her of how the Basque culture and history were indeed part of the history and culture of France itself; and how different it was just across the border in Spain. Maria's thoughts inevitably returned to her own family with its passionate Basque, monarchist and strong Catholic views. Her family had had little time for Spain's nineteenth century Constitutional Monarchs who had tried to import into the country what some saw as a parody of the British parliamentary system. In reality, Spain was then ruled by royal patronage as it had been for centuries.

Perhaps it came from her upbringing, but Maria felt a greater affinity with Spain's earlier medieval kings and queens and she had learned much about them. She also felt that their lives were romantic and that their internecine power struggles reflected the clashes of the great empires and civilizations. It didn't occur to her how romantic and tumultuous her own life might appear to be to an outsider.

She thought again of that great medieval king, Charles I, or Charles V as he was known in Spain. Maria knew a lot about him. He was perhaps the most powerful Christian monarch of all times. He'd been enormously wealthy, having inherited vast European and foreign possessions. His accession to the Spanish throne in 1516 heralded in almost three centuries of royal absolutism that continued unchallenged in Spain until after the bloody revolution in neighbouring France late in the eighteenth century. With his close links to the church, he had himself elected Holy Roman Emperor in 1519. Oddly, he had been raised in Flanders and he was not even able to speak Spanish, let alone euskara, the language of the Basque people. Yet, with time, his popularity had only increased in Spain, even with the Basques.

"It seems strange that he was so popular;" she thought.

"Some said it was because he so staunchly defended Catholicism against Martin Luther's Protestant reformation." she said half aloud "That was in the western part of the empire. Of course, there were also his battles against the expansion of Islam by the Ottoman rulers over in the east."

But there was probably another reason for Charles V's popularity; it was the prosperity that his reign had brought to Spain. And Maria's own ancestors had been among those who had reaped some of its considerable financial benefits.

But that was in a different time if not such a different place.

# Thirty-Eight

Maria sometimes felt that she had rediscovered happiness in those early post-war days back in Bayonne. Her spirits were high even though hers was a relatively simple and solitary existence. She devoted herself to Anna who was now at school and seemed to have settled in; and though the war still cast a long shadow over her thoughts, she took enormous pleasure in her own work.

Above all, her mood brightened whenever she worked in the rooms of the Museum dedicated to the "Redécouverte du Pays Basque" – the rediscovery of the Basque people and countryside. The displays of traditional clothing and household furnishings transported her, if briefly, to another time and place; and the collection displayed other works linked in so many ways to the Basque people. She delighted in the variety of the displays. There were the works of artists and architects who decorated the Basque churches and chapels with their seemingly naïve artwork and designs. In style and form, their works echoed those of the ancient sculptors and painters.

But there was also the collection of texts on philosophy and linguistics from sources as diverse as the Prussian philosopher Guillaume de Humboldt and the Corsican politician Lucien Bonaparte, a younger brother of Napoleon I. There were also literary works from lesser known figures and linguists. Maria was intrigued by the Basque language and its dialects. She knew that they were special, that their origins were a mystery and she had read that euskara was the only pre-Indo-European language still in use.

But as Maria passed through the collections she could not help but shrink from other displays, though she couldn't always find excuses to avoid them. Some focussed too much on the religious history of Bayonne itself and Maria was becoming more and more disappointed with the role of religion as a force for good in the world. Others more darkly represented the peculiar Basque funeral traditions, artefacts and special clothing related to grieving for the dead. After all that had happened in her adult life; almost a decade of war and suffering, these displays touched too closely on her feelings for her lost family, especially her first-born son.

"But I still have so much" she would say; consoling herself. There was her Anna: the brightest light in her life.

And there were the memories of Alberto, now fading somewhat into the past, and of Max, so memorable, even if she knew him so briefly.

"Why is it that I'm allowed so little time with the men in my life?" She sighed as she little more than whispered these words.

Maria's thoughts turned again to Max and 'what could have been' between them. She had shared only two days and three nights with him before his duties led him off to other places and meetings with other branches of the French resistance. He'd never written. How could he? It would've been dangerous for both of them. She'd heard news of him only once or twice during those early years of the war; through occasional visits from colleagues from the Basque museum, but then abruptly, around the middle of 1943, nothing more. On many a night Maria lay in bed thinking about Max until sleep had finally come to her. Sometimes she imagined that he had forgotten her and only much later had she learned the truth. He'd been betrayed and captured. Then there were the rumours of his torture and execution at the hands of the sadistic Gestapo mass murderer Klaus Barbie – the man known as the 'Butcher of Lyon'.

"The war's over. How long will such a man as Barbie evade justice?" she wondered. She feared that it may be forever.

"Was there no justice? The war was lost by the Nazis and Barbie is still free."

She fretted over injustice but it would have been even worse if she had known that at the end of the war Barbie had been immediately recruited by the British and then worked in Germany for American intelligence. Nor could she suspect that the Americans would protect him for decades because of his anti-communism and knowledge of communist underground networks. It would be almost forty years later that an aging Klaus Barbie would be extradited to France from Bolivia, tried as a war criminal, convicted, imprisoned and eventually die in Lyon where most of his atrocities were perpetrated.

For Maria, in the confusion of post-liberation France, the thought that it would be so far in the future before some justice was had, was all but inconceivable. She saw the 'wrongs' that seemed to surround her day-to-day existence and she saw that 'righting' them was altogether another matter. These thoughts often saddened her days.

"Maybe there is really no justice in the world; just survival and revenge," she said.

But such bleak thoughts were reserved for moments of despair. And she did not want to believe this to be true. Did she deserve the life that fate had bestowed on her? Did anyone? Her head told her that there was no justice but her heart was unconvinced.

"And what of Max; or Jean?" Jean Moulin was his name; she had later learned. He had become much more than a legend to the French people. He was now the most well-known member of the *Résistance*. He had fought tirelessly against fascism and for so long. He even held sympathies for the republicans in Spain; something that was well known to the wartime collaborators in Vichy: old *Maréchal* Pétain and his Prime Minister, Pierre Laval.

"Where was the justice in Max's so honourable life and his terrible death?" were her barely spoken thoughts. "And what about the people behind Max's betrayal? Will they remain unknown; never to be identified and punished?"

But she knew that Max had played a dangerous game. He had many enemies and even jealous opponents in the resistance movement itself. And what of the Soviets and the Americans who both had agents and spy networks in occupied France? Both had expansionist ambitions and a deep interest in undermining their opponents. They would have done whatever would maximize their post-war influence over the vulnerable nation. "But was Max's betrayal even more banal than that?" she thought. "After all, at that time there were also thousands of people ready to denounce their neighbours and even their family, for reward or for malice."

"So was Max just another arbitrary victim of the war?" she asked herself. "Some people said that there was no single betrayer of Jean

Moulin and that nazi intelligence had been aware of him and was monitoring his movements for a long time before his capture."

The idea startled her.

"Perhaps the Gestapo had even known of his visit to Saint-Sever" she thought. "Perhaps Anna and I had been in danger and I'd not even been aware of it. Was helping him even more dangerous than having guarded the Jewish scrolls! And I knew nothing of either at the time!"

Maria once again felt a fearful emptiness in the pit of her stomach and began to tremble at what might have been, if these thoughts were true. Yet she despised herself for her fear and cowardice. Nothing had happened to them. But even now, she could not help but heave a sigh of relief as she realized that for such a brief encounter or for something she didn't even know about, things could have been so very different for her and for Anna.

"Is one's fate so arbitrarily determined?" she asked herself. "Is it this way for everyone?"

After all that had happened, Maria still sought answers, though she feared that asking the questions was just a waste of time.

And those were her thoughts and fears as she moved quietly through the rooms of the little Basque Museum in those early post-war days. She had no certainty and no answers, or at least none that she could articulate or that made any sense in her heart.

## Thirty-Nine

Weeks passed. Maria and her colleagues had mostly finished re-instating the displays in the collection rooms of the Museum. Now there were rather tedious tasks she had to perform; checking the collections on display. Only occasionally did they demand her close attention and it was easy for her mind to wander; more often than not returning to the troubling thoughts and questions that pre-occupied so many people after the war and the Nazi occupation. And Maria had a full decade of war and fear behind her.

This morning, she passed again by the displays showing the little known works of Basque literary figures and her mind turned to those members of France's intellectual elite. Many said that they had lived rather too comfortably in Paris throughout the war years, under German occupation. Only Céline who overtly supported the Nazis would pay with exile and imprisonment.

"What a contrast" she said under her breath, "between the lives of those privileged intellectuals sitting out the war and the hardships of the anonymous men and women who worked with the *Résistance*. War is so complicated" she said, enjoying the bitter understatement.

"But there were those who were worse still. Like the so-called *'résistants du mois de septembre'* – those who only joined the resistance after Paris was liberated. Most sought no more than to lay false claim to the honour of the struggle. But some wanted more; to commit vengeful atrocities on whosoever they pleased; and all in the name of the liberation's 'purification' of the French people."

She paused in her thoughts.

"It's enough to make you lose faith in human nature" she said. Sadly, she spoke only to herself. She had no-one to discuss these matters with. And she would never speak of them in front of young Anna. The anger that had swelled so briefly in Maria's breast quickly ran its course and she felt an unwanted seed of cynicism growing within her. "But such are the ironies of war," she reflected; not for the first time.

Only the slightest tinge of bitterness shaded her heart. Anger and hatred had never been a part of Maria's spirit and when she experienced the refreshing harshness of these feelings, they quickly subsided; despite all that had happened. And it wasn't long before those darker thoughts gave way to less harsh memories of the relatively safe but lonely times back in Saint-Sever; especially after Max had gone. She sighed softly.

"In truth, I too, was safe in Saint-Sever and not that uncomfortable. So little happened there compared to the dangers of the occupation and liberation of Paris and other big cities. ... Perhaps," she conceded, "it's too easy to criticize all those people just trying to survive under Nazi occupation in places like that."

Maria always seemed to find excuses for other people.

Yet, Paris and its liberation continued to dominate her thoughts. It was so recent and such an important moment; for all of France.

"It was on the 1st of August 1944," she recalled, "that General De Gaulle arrived back in France. He came with the Free France Forces and the second armoured division under the command of General Leclerc. And after just a few weeks of fighting, they were racing overland to Paris." She paused as her thoughts flowed on.

"Thankfully, they made it there before the Americans or Russians arrived." Like everyone else in the country, Maria was proud that De Gaulle had got to Paris first, to prevent the Americans and the Russians from even symbolically taking control of the city. It was widely believed that both countries had secret imperialist plans for the future of France. Indeed, both had networks of spies operating there throughout the war.

On the 25th of August De Gaulle had accepted the capitulation of the German forces offered by the Commander Dietrich von Choltitz. Maria thought of Von Choltitz and how honourably he had refused to burn Paris to the ground despite Adolf Hitler's direct order to do so.

"How unlike what happened in Guernica!" she reflected sadly.

"Perhaps there is some honour in the German people after all".

Maria's heart was warmed a little by that thought, although in those days, it was rare to think anything good about the German people. Her mind turned back to the liberation of Paris.

"But in reality, it had been the people of Paris themselves who won the liberation of the city, not De Gaulle; though he had so publicly taken charge when it was over. They fought for Paris while the generals sat in their comfortable quarters behind the battle lines." Her thoughts were perhaps a little harsh. "And how many will remember that three thousand Parisian residents died and another seven thousand were wounded in the liberation of their city!"

Maria had read in the newspapers how the lightly armed people of Paris had faced down the well-trained and equipped German soldiers; soldiers who were aided by the armed *Milice* that had so willingly served the Vichy regime. That some French people had collaborated with the Nazis could not so easily be forgotten.

There had been much hardship under nazi occupation and those heroic street battles in distant Paris had provided an enormous psychological and emotional lift for so many in France at that time.

"In some ways, what happened there was almost like a civil war; like we had in Spain," Maria said to herself. "But the fascists had lost. ... Perhaps there are fascists in every country. Yet some of the people of Paris had fought against it. They took to the barricades on the 19th of August, even under confused and chaotic leadership." There were so many disparate partisan groups. She thought of these resistance leaders. What were their motivations?

"But there was much to be proud of", she reminded herself.

Only later would Maria learn how important a role Max had played. He was the founder of the National Council of Resistance and had been sent by De Gaulle to unify the French resistance movements under the leadership of the exiled General. It was a role that led him to his death.

## Forty

It was early spring 1946. Maria was happier than she had been for a long time. The burdens of Nazi occupation and bitter liberation were beginning to loosen their hold on her heart. Even at work, she found moments to stop and just enjoy her new-found freedom. Being back in Bayonne was such a breath of fresh air for her. It was late morning and she stood at the large wood-framed windows on the top floor of the Basque Museum. The sky was blue and the morning sun shone in. She smiled gently and looked out across the narrow river Nive. In early spring, its cold, clear waters flowed fast down from the Pyrenees Mountains and came to a tumultuous confluence with the river Adour which itself was often a raging torrent at that time of year. The two rivers collide in downtown Bayonne, just a few hundred metres away from where she stood.

The scene before Maria had been the same for many centuries and more. It had not been changed by the war or its conclusion. She became pensive, remembering again that despite those dark days of war, there had been Max, even though it was for just a brief time, and there was always Anna. Maria did not know what she had truly felt for Max, but her heart melted at the thought of her young daughter. Yet her mind was unsettled. She still wondered about her seemingly pointless existence.

"Looking back, I still find it all so confusing" she confessed aloud, but just to the clear window pane before her eyes.

"What did I really do during the war?" she asked herself aloud, "aside from submitting to the many hardships that we all suffered, how infinitesimally small a part I played in the war itself" she said, admonishing herself. Though she also knew that survival, especially Anna's survival had been her one true aim and that would only have been put in jeopardy had she been involved in the fighting or the resistance. And it was foolish to compare herself to Max.

"Yes, I helped Max, but only for a brief moment. And I kept watch over some minor historical and religious treasures. That's all."

She turned away from the window and began to study the notices attached to the exhibits on display; making a conscious effort to make a note of any needing rectification.

Compared to her time in Bilbao and her escape from San Sebastian in the spring of 1939, she had not really been in serious danger during the war against Germany – and not even during the liberation; in the confusion, craziness and violent recriminations at the end of the war. She knew that she had a lot to be grateful for.

Of course, her almost safe wartime existence had been far from the fate of so many people elsewhere in the country. Whole villages had been exterminated by the Nazis; sometimes in retribution for some courageous, stupid or wilfully violent act of one or a handful of young members of the resistance. Often, only after the war, did it become known that for little apparent reason, the inhabitants of one French village or another had been herded into churches or town halls and burned alive; women, children and the elderly as well. In other towns and villages even smaller than her own, the men and boys had been lined up and executed at the whim of one nazi officer or another.

She stopped, and looked up towards the dark ceiling as if seeking guidance from some omnipotent being.

"How is it? ..." she asked herself with disbelief, "how is it that some people imagine that their own destinies and beliefs could justify committing such horrors and atrocities?"

She looked down towards the floor.

"But that was war. I know what that means. And in wars, things like that had always happened" she sighed. She spoke wistfully, not with an uncaring cynicism.

"Was that not the truth? Had it not always been so?" she said.

"Was it not continually surprising how vicious and brutal human beings can be? And it's not just the odd individual who acts like that; though often, there is a deranged ringleader who the mob follows mindlessly."

Even during the war Maria, like everyone else, had heard so many stories of random atrocities; and the talk of the rounding up and exterminating of hundreds, and in the larger towns, thousands of

Jews, young and old; people 'in hiding' or discreetly going about the business of trying to survive. But much had passed by almost without comment in the little village where she was living; and probably just about everywhere else as well.

"Did people really not care?" she whispered. "Or was it fear? Or perhaps just self-preservation?"

Maria tried to force herself to stop thinking such thoughts and to return to her note-taking. The effort was unrewarded. Within moments, her mind drifted back to those unanswerable questions raised by the all too recent war. Above all, she was deeply perturbed that 'justice' and 'fairness' seemed to be completely irrelevant to what had happened in most people's lives.

"Did the fate of each of those millions of hapless Jews, whether they were French or emigrant or whatever, differ that much from the fates of so many other young men and women belonging to the various branches of the resistance? They too were captured, tortured and killed by members of the self-styled 'master race'. Did it matter in the long-run that one had submitted to the Nazi occupation and the other struggled against it? Their fates were the same in the end."

But as her mind followed this line of thought, the anguish that was rising in Maria's heart turned into sadness as she continued calmly, almost automatically to perform her everyday tasks at the Museum.

After a time, she stopped again.

"People now say" she reflected to herself, "that as many as two hundred thousand young French men and women belonging to the resistance were either executed or died in concentration camps during this war started by those German and Italian fascists! And what of the many thousands more young people who died in the fight against Franco's fascist forces? No-one remembers their heroism. They fought and lost the battle against fascism in Spain? And no-one has tried to count how many Spaniards, young and old, lost their lives fighting against that repressive militarist regime."

These bitter thoughts came and went in waves. But the hatred they seem to evoke in her heart could not be held for very long before other more compassionate feelings appeared to counter it.

"And, dare I even think it?" she asked herself. "How many young innocent German lives were also sacrificed! And look what is happening right now that the war is over! Does anyone care what the Stalinist governments are doing in the Soviet controlled states of Eastern Europe? The Russian fascists persecute and expel their minorities in horrific conditions; exactly the same way as the Nazis treated the Jews. But no-one sheds a tear for them."

She paused, almost overcome by her emotions.

"Perhaps too many tears have already been shed? And it is the victors who write the history books and the vanquished who are so often forgotten; not just forgotten but so often left without any descendants. It is as if they never existed."

"What can I do? What can anyone do? Even if I knew what to do, would I be able to do it? It's all so confusing," she said softly.

§

In that immediate post-war era in Bayonne, though Maria's heart was troubled, the days passed quietly for her and Anna; but the young girl was growing up fast.

There had been celebrations and from time to time men paid more than a little attention to Maria. She was still a beautiful woman. Couples formed and reformed around her. She was sometimes tempted. But love eluded her and she could not contemplate remarriage in its absence, even if she would have welcomed the intimacy and the male companionship, and yes, a father figure for young Anna. Yet she seemed happy enough.

There were still some shortages in material needs and comforts, but otherwise life was good. At least the city of Bayonne had suffered little damage from the German occupation and its eventual liberation had not involved the battles or bombing that had caused the destruction of so many other European towns and cities. So in Bayonne there was comparatively little in the way of reconstruction to do. Many of the beautiful old buildings remained untouched, as did the sidewalk cafés and sun-drenched parks along the Adour and Nive Rivers that met and joined forces at the centre of the old town before flowing rapidly onwards to empty into the vast Bay of Biscay, just to the north of the glamorous seaside resort of Biarritz.

## Forty-One

The last years of the 1940s passed and a new decade began in Bayonne. Maria proudly watched little Anna grow into a lively and outgoing young girl; pretty, bright, athletic and apparently liked by her school-friends. Mother and daughter were close, but Maria felt that in so many ways she was watching at a distance as her young daughter grew up, not really sharing her life. Before she knew it, Anna was thirteen years old and becoming a young woman.

"Where had young Anna gone?" she would sometimes ask herself.

§

It was 1952; the year that the US government formally recognized the fascist regime of Generalissimo Francisco Franco in Spain. At the same time, US Congress intensified its McCarthyism investigations into what it called 'un-American activities' at home.

Life had almost returned to normal in France, at least on the surface. Maria still worked with the museum and the little family lived quietly but happily. Anna enjoyed school and her friends but she was clearly athletic and spent many hours of her spare time practising gymnastics and playing Pelote with the boys of her neighbourhood.

Not many girls played Pelote. Perhaps it was their parents who discouraged it. It was not 'a girls' game'. For years, even as a young child back in Saint-Sever and then again after returning to Bayonne, Anna had watched intently as the boys and young men played this traditional Basque racquetball game. She soon joined in.

In summer, they played outside on a cleared courtyard with at one end a high cemented wall. Sometimes they used the wall of the village hall or some other community building. Often, a rounded central section had been added to the top of the wall to make it high enough. On snowed-in winter's days beneath the Pyrenees' peaks, Pelote was played in large, high-ceilinged halls set aside for the sport.

Anna admired the energy of the older players and how they caught the ball with precision in the small woven glove-like baskets held in their hands and hurled it, with enormous force against the five-metre-high whitewashed wall at the end of the square concrete playing floor. It was impressive to watch; and noisy. Even Maria was struck by the athleticism of the players. In winter, some boys even played using just a leather glove on their hands. What appealed to Anna was that it was a game that demanded great agility and skill as well as stamina and strength. Not often would another girl try her hand at it. A few did, but it was often half-hearted and just to flirt with the boys. As the years had passed, Anna's interest in the game had grown.

"Do you know much about Pelote?" Anna asked Maria one evening over dinner. Her mother seemed to be a source of so much knowledge about Basque culture.

"Pelote's not a game for girls" Maria said with a smile. She was teasing her daughter, but she loved to talk about anything to do with the Basque way of life. And she did know something of Pelote's history; there was a large display dealing with it in the Museum.

"Pelote didn't start as a Basque game" Maria explained. "Back in the sixteenth century, it had been popular in various parts of France, but during the seventeenth and eighteenth centuries, it was played mainly in the Basque country."

Maria smiled at her daughter who still seemed interested.

"It was only in the late nineteenth century that Pelote was taken up elsewhere in the Spanish-speaking world, especially in Argentina, Cuba and even in the Spanish-speaking parts of North America: in Florida and California. They developed variations of the game and now there are four different versions".

"Either it is played by using small wooden bats called 'pala'; or more commonly each player wears, as a kind of glove, a large woven basket called a 'Chistera': it's just like the oblong vegetable basket with a curved shape you can see in the markets. Or sometimes, the players wear thick leather gloves on both hands. And only rarely now is it played with just bare hands – that must be painful!" Maria smiled. She saw the admiration in her daughter's eyes.

"Of course, in the old days", Maria said carefully, "the ball they used to play with was very hard and really rather heavy; much heavier than it is now and as the players used their bare hands and would often injure themselves. It was only much more recently that the solid ball was replaced by a rubber one, though balls of different sizes and thicknesses are played with depending on the kind of hand equipment or racquet used."

"They must have been tough in those days" Anna replied.

"There is a large collection of Pelote equipment in the Basque Museum, you know. ... It has even been proposed as an Olympic sport." She smiled. Maria was pleased to talk to Anna about these unusual aspects of Basque culture.

Anna looked intently at her mother. After a moment, she said:

"Mother, don't you think that in the old days, games like this would have been good training for soldiers? It would certainly have toughened them up and they could easily use the same skills in battle. Is that what happened? Did soldiers play this game? Was that why it was invented? I wonder if the soldiers who played Pelote back then had to throw stones in battle" she asked with enthusiasm, "... perhaps they had to do this when they ran out of arrows or spears and had no other weapons?"

"I really do not know. ... What a strange questions for a young girl" Maria remarked.

Maria was a little perplexed and looked hard into the depths of her young daughter's dark eyes, thinking that the war, so recently ended, must after all have made a bigger impression than she had thought on her offspring's young mind.

She wanted to change the topic of conversation and said:

"Did you know that it was a Basque boy just a year older than you who improvised the woven glove that many of the players now use to play Pelote? This was back in 1857, and the boy's name was Grantchiki Dithurdibe. So you don't have to be old and wise or spend your life in study to invent or create something new."

BEGINNINGS                                                Gary Heilbronn

"I know what you mean," Anna replied perhaps a little abruptly, "but some people are born to think and talk and do little else, while others are born to do things; to make things happen."

These words cut Maria like a knife. She feared that she would never be anything other than a thinker and talker. Anna continued.

"Sometimes I think that all that the French people do is just talk and talk and nothing seems to happen. At least Basque people really do things. I was told at school that members of the Basque National Party had set off bombs at some of General Franco's buildings in Spain. That's doing something! ... It's doing something important! Not just thinking and talking."

Maria stared at her daughter. She was shocked at this turn in the conversation. Her reply was in a much more serious tone of voice.

"Anna my child, there are all kinds of people in France and of course everywhere else. Don't forget that even if the French army was ordered to surrender in the last war, the French resistance groups did a lot of fighting against the Nazis during the occupation and many of them were executed and some were tortured to death. But even when they set off bombs, destroying equipment and killing German soldiers, the repression that followed was disproportionately horrendous and extreme! Their thoughtless actions resulted in the deaths of many innocent people."

"And look at what madness there was when the Germans retreated! .... The Bolshevik spies and communist supporters in the *maquis* murdered whoever they felt like in many parts of the country.'

Maria paused and looked carefully at her daughter.

You know what the *maquis* was, don't you? It was the name given to those lawless 'liberation' groups that roamed western France during the German occupation. At first they were part of the resistance, but with the liberation, some were more concerned with thieving, torturing and executing whoever they pleased – they were thought to be controlled by the soviet-backed *Front National* and some people say that they wanted to wipe out opposition to a communist takeover in France. We were fortunate to have avoided the worst of their atrocities or a civil war could even have broken out." Maria sighed and raised her head; looking intently at her daughter.

After a moment, she said: "You know, Anna, action without thought can be a dangerous business." She went on. "We Basques are proud of our unique culture and our history, but France has given protection to refugees like us. And you were born here and we live here and you have been brought up here to be a citizen of France as well as to be Basque. You have many freedoms. You speak French at school and you learn Spanish and English. I teach you to speak euskara at home and no-one prevents this; so you can learn about your ancestors' culture. All this is not so easy in Spain, even today."

Anna looked a little bored. She didn't like being lectured.

"Anna, you are fortunate," her mother persisted, "though of course, that doesn't mean that you must forget your Basque origins. We have come here to escape tyranny in our own country and whatever the faults of this place may be, it is possible to live well here and to prosper, even with a somewhat different cultural background."

Seconds passed and no-one spoke. Maria's face had gone pale and now she was silent; lost in her own thoughts

"I'm off to bed." Anna said abruptly and left.

## Forty-Two

Maria had been more than a little taken aback by Anna's cutting words and not just a little hurt by her tone of voice. She had never heard her young daughter speak like this before. There was an unexpected harshness in her words. Maria found it troubling. But it had also touched a raw nerve. She could not help but feel that she herself had really not done anything useful with her own life – except perhaps to help the people who did: Alberto and then Max. "And look what happened to both of them!" she thought to herself sadly; a tear coming to her eye.

"But perhaps it was true" she thought, "that some people's lives were destined to be quiet and uneventful, despite the turmoil that may surround them. While others, inevitably and maybe even without trying, find themselves playing a role, a real role, in the events of their times and maybe even making a mark on history; even if just a small mark."

Maria sat in silence though her mind raced.

"It's all very well to play a role in history or make a 'mark' on life", she thought. "But does this 'mark' that such people make depend on whether they are on the side of 'right' or 'wrong', or is it because they are the victors and not the vanquished? Was not Hannibal a hero to his own people? And what about Franco? While I despise his very name, to many people he is a God and saviour. Some credit him with preventing a Nazi occupation of Spain." She stopped to reflect.

"Maybe Anna is right" she admitted to herself grudgingly, "the more you think about these things, the less clear it is who is right and who is wrong, and the more people like me feel paralysed and are incapable of acting. We never even know what's right or wrong."

These thoughts played on her mind.

That night, Maria was still pensive and pre-occupied. Indeed, she was a little worried by her daughter's newfound self-possession and independence of thought. It took time for her finally to drift off into a troubled sleep.

Anna, on the other hand, fell quickly and deeply asleep. She was happy and relieved.

"This had been the first time", she thought, "that I've shown my mother how I really feel and what I think."

For years, she had felt perhaps even protective of her mother. She'd sheltered the older woman from this part of her personality, though she always knew she had mental strength and independence of thought, even during her early school years. In Saint-Sever when she was still very young, she'd known instinctively that her strong personality had to be repressed as it would only have drawn attention to the two of them; strangers in the village and already viewed with an eye of suspicion.

It was only later, back in Bayonne that things really changed for her. It came with the inevitable interaction she had with other children. They were from families from all walks of life and with origins in various parts of France and even from across the Pyrenees in Spain and Portugal.

Primary school had been a confusing and intimidating place for some children, but Anna had quickly established herself, not only for her physical and mental toughness, but also for the speed with which she acquired knowledge and performed the admittedly rather intellectually undemanding scholastic tasks that the local school teachers set for the children. Her teachers were happy with her and the respect she accorded them in the classroom. The other children had quickly learned to show Anna another kind of respect. The kind usually inspired by those who abide no slight or offence in the school-grounds. Even the boys were reluctant to challenge her, and of course, at that age most of them had no physical or size advantage over the girls in their class at school.

From time to time, there were others who passed through Anna's school; youngsters who were toughened by early years spent under the shadow of the war; often suffering from the deprivation and instability that comes when their parents are forced to move from place to place to eke out or scrounge a living. Some had made the mistake of insulting young Anna in class or in the school-grounds; even making fun of the small, pale brownish stain on the soft skin somewhat below her left earlobe. Few escaped with anything less than bloodied noses, and some even limped home with fractured ribs and broken fingers. But these exactions were never carried out in the view of her teachers or the *surveillantes* who assisted them. Short sharp punishments were administered out of sight, behind the bushes that surrounded the school or around the back of the schoolrooms and rarely was there time for even a small crowd of schoolchildren to gather in audience. Yet most of them knew enough about it all by the following morning; at least before the school bell had rung. Maria knew nothing of this.

That night, Anna fell quickly into a deep sleep. She felt as if she had now truly entered adulthood. She had shown her real self to her mother. She was so happy. She dreamed and found herself far, far away and in a body that was familiar but not her own.

# TROUBLE IN TOLEDO

*Central Spain, 200 km east of Sagunto, early 6th Century AD*

## Map of the Kingdom of Tolosa, 5th Century

# Forty-Three

*Central Spain, about 506 AD*

The room where she slept was dimly lit by a narrow dusty shaft of sunlight streaming silently down on to the sombre tiled floor. It entered the room almost covertly through a narrow gap between two heavy wooden shutters designed only to keep out the full intensity of the early morning sun.

There were few furnishings in the room; just a bed with loose colourful covers thrown over the top and nearby, a low wooden table. On it was a broad-based earthenware pitcher standing in a low, wide bowl. The pitcher had been filled the previous evening with fresh water in preparation for her morning ablutions. In the corner lay two small wooden trunks with thick leather handles fitted on each side. One was home for several skirts, blouses, tunics, undergarments and a few precious trinkets; all that the young woman had to her name. The other held the few remaining items that had belonged to her mother, as well as some extra bedding for the occasional cold winter's night. But it was already hot and she was waking a little uncomfortably.

Through the mist of sleep, she heard her name being called from outside the door.

"Alba! Alba! It's time to rise," was what she heard. She lifted her head; squinting her reluctantly opening eyes as if she expected to see who was there. Eventually, she called back to the older woman on the other side of the door:

"Si, Si, I'm awake. I'm coming. I'm coming now."

"Bueno!" Good! The old woman replied. She was fond of her young colleague. For some years, she had worked closely with Alba in the imposing, two storey residence that stretched along the edge of a high cliff overlooking the sparkling, clear waters of the rio Tajo, or Tagus River in English, in the Roman city of Toletum in central Spain.

The sparse rooms where the two women lived were attached to the offside of the rambling residence at ground-level. Yet through Alba's window, she could see right down to the bottom of the cliff.

## BEGINNINGS                                        Gary Heilbronn

There, the mirror-like waters of the incomparable rio Tajo sat quietly, as if awaiting a signal to set out on their meandering journey westwards for a thousand kilometres or more across the middle of the Iberian Peninsula. But, in Toletum, as Toledo was called in Roman times, the waters of the rio Tajo seemed content to leisurely irrigate the many lush fields and farmlands surrounding the city. To the west, the slow-moving river flowed on and on to pass through open plains and high yellow and brown gorges pursuing its almost endless journey towards the setting sun. It wasn't until just near the coast that it turned southward and gradually widened to become a vast estuary at least twenty kilometres across at the end of its course. There, it emptied its contents into the great Atlantic Ocean so far away at Olisippo, as Lisbon had been called in Roman times.

Alba did not know, but certainly her educated masters in Toletum did, that Olisippo was an ancient city. As legend has it, was visited by Ulysses on his epic voyages late in the 11th century BC. Then, just a few hundred years later, it became a base on the west coast of Iberia for the intrepid sea-faring Phoenicians. Aside from their trading activities, the Phoenicians had introduced wine-making there and in many coastal parts of Western Europe. For centuries afterwards, Olisippo had prospered, before slowly falling on hard times.

The fortunes of the city had been briefly rejuvenated by Roman occupation from about 202 BC after Rome finally defeated Hannibal at the Battle of Zama on his home territory in Carthage, on the North African coast directly south of the island of Malta. This battle brought a troubled end to the Second Punic War that had begun with the siege of Saguntum back in 219 BC. Unlike the Phoenicians, the influence of the Romans had spread across the length and breadth of the Iberian Peninsula, though they again lost interest in Iberia as new unrest erupted closer to home and soon developed into the Third Punic War. That conflict ended in 146 BC when Rome finally crushed the Carthaginians, razed Carthage, sold its people into slavery. Some say the Romans salted the fields around the old capital for miles to ensure that nothing would grow there for generations. But it may be just a legend.

Olisippo's fortunes again revived under a second wave of Roman rule during the first three hundred years of the Christian era, as did Alba's home town, Toletum.

Of course, Toletum was situated at almost the geographical centre of the huge Iberian Peninsula. It was not a coastal town or port like Olisippo and had not been a base for the Phoenician or any other trading empire in the past. However, under the Romans, Toletum had also prospered and became a significant administrative and commercial centre. It even began to find renown for the manufacture of swords and knives. Toledo steel would eventually become a symbol of quality metalwork and that brought much wealth to the city's inhabitants. Of course, wealth always attracts the unscrupulous and others seeking to enrich themselves in whatever manner is possible.

# Forty-Four

The slow decline of the Roman Empire in the early centuries of the first millennium left most of the Iberian Peninsula exposed to the fickle winds of change. During the 4th century AD, Iberia was a low priority for Rome and as a result, the Vandals, Alains and Suevi tribes from central Europe forged westwards to conquer and partly settle in Gaul and Iberia. Under the leadership of King Gaiseric, they swarmed south across into North Africa, circling back eastwards, conquering all the Roman imperial territories there. A century later, these tribes would turn north again to threaten the very existence of the Roman administration itself; then situated in Ravenna.

It was just before the beginning of the 5th century and at near to the end of Rome's pre-eminence, that the Roman Emperor, Theodosius I, sent the warlike Visigoths, Rome's sometime northern enemies and other times vassals, on a mission to re-establish Roman rule in the western part of its empire encompassing Gaul and most of the Iberian Peninsula. In fact, this marked the beginning of the end of Roman rule there.

Although the Visigoth's campaign began successfully, it slowed down when they settled in Aquitaine, the coastal region of south-west France. These conquests were not enough for Emperor Honorius, who by 404 AD had deserted Rome and established his court and administration at Ravenna on the Adriatic coast to the north-east of Rome. Honorius charged the Visigoths to re-conquer Rome's whole western empire and to end the territorial disputes, raids and looting of the Vandals and the other tribes who then occupied the Iberian Peninsula.

The Visigoths complied and on their path southwards, they first conquered the Alains, based in the north, by about 418 AD. Within two more decades; they had also pushed the Vandals, who had settled mainly in Galicia in the extreme north-west of Iberia, southwards where they joined the wholesale migration of these tribes into North Africa. There, they remained for another century, occupying most of the territories on the southern coast of the Mediterranean and being an increasing irritant to Rome.

# BEGINNINGS  Gary Heilbronn

The Visigoths only failed to conquer the north-central mountains and coastal region of Iberia where a small number of the Suevi had retreated to and slowly died out or blended into the sparse local population. So Visigoth influence did not reach the indigenous peoples in those regions closer to the source of the historic rio Ebro – an area later to be known as the Basque country – situated to the south and west of the great Pyrenees Mountains separating the Iberian Peninsula from Aquitaine and the land of the Franks.

§

During the previous few centuries, Roman occupation and civilization had already brought wealth and many advances to much of the Iberian Peninsula. Aside from trade and Rome's administrative, legal and military skills, one highly significant benefit from Roman influence had been the introduction of the Julian calendar, developed at the beginning of the Christian era.

It was a considerable advancement on the previous solar-based Roman calendar that had been much relied upon for the last several centuries of the pre-Christian era. As that era ended, Roman emperor, Julius Caesar, decreed the standard year to be 365 days long, but with a 366 day year every fourth year. The seven days of the week were also fixed. Over a few years that followed, Julius and his successor Augustus also established the order of twelve calendar months, adding two new months: January and February, while renaming the seventh and eighth months as 'Julius' and 'Augustus' respectively. It is impossible to over-estimate the effect of this development on the future.

In those early centuries of the Christian era, the new calendar made a significant impact throughout the Roman Empire and further afield.

It was well accepted by the time Alba was born, towards the end of the fifth century and it would endure well after Alba's comparatively short but eventful life was over. Indeed, over a millennium would pass before the Julian year was seen to exceed the true solar year, and by only 11 minutes and 14 seconds. The correction was made by Pope Gregory XIII dropping ten days from the Julian calendar and declaring that from that time on, only those 'century years' which were divisible by 400, such as 1200 and 1600 would be leap years. This introduced the more enduring Gregorian calendar. Though its creators did not know it then, this lapse of time was probably not caused by inaccuracy in Roman calculations, but was due to the slowing rotation speed of the earth by two-one thousandths of a second per day over the millennium that had passed.

Be that as it may, as far as the Iberians of the early sixth century were concerned, Rome's influence over the administration of secular affairs, even in such a far flung outpost of the empire as Toletum, had been significant and beneficial.

But Rome was far away and the world was changing fast.

# Forty-Five

As fate would have it, Alba was a servant in the home of August Zocodover. He was Toletum's deputy administrator and had been a regional representative first for the old Visigoth King, Euric, the grandson of the Roman Empire's old enemy, Alaric I. It was he who had attacked and sacked Rome back in 410. Then, after Euric's death in about 484, Zocodover performed the same duties for Euric's son and successor, King Alaric II; the great grandson of his namesake.

For the past several decades, the Visigoths had exercised effective control the western part of the Roman Empire and had established what was known as the kingdom of Tolosa. The kingdom of Tolosa then included almost all of the Iberian Peninsula and that part of Gaul (or France) south of the Loire River; the river that divides France roughly in half from west to east. The kingdom also extended westwards from the Rhone valley, near Italy, all the way to the Atlantic coast. The capital was in Tolosa in south-west Gaul; a city that was later known as Toulouse. As the Kingdom of Tolosa covered such a vast territory, there were administrative centres elsewhere, notably in nearby Narbonne; in Barcino (later known as Barcelona) just north of the mouth of the Rio Ebro; and much further south, in Toletum.

In the latter part of the 5th century and after the reign of six Visigoth kings and as many Roman emperors, King Euric declared the kingdom of Tolosa to be independent of the declining Roman Empire. Before that, the Visigoth rulers had been essentially legates of Rome. As such, Euric and his predecessors had introduced many Roman and Germanic legal and administrative principles into the kingdom. Euric's son, Alaric II continued his father's rule for over two decades and when faced with unrest and possible rebellion in 506, he introduced a new and comprehensive collection and interpretation of laws based on several recent Roman Codes and Institutes; these were part of the foundations of modern European civil law codes. It was these laws that August Zocodover was required to implement in his role as Deputy Administrator of the Visigoth kingdom in the central part of the Iberian Peninsula.

This significant collection of laws was known as the 'Breviary of Alaric' and soon after Alaric II introduced them, even Clovis, King of Gaul, applied these laws throughout all of his territories further to the north. However, peace between Clovis and the Goths had been an 'off and on' affair for many years. And barely a year after the introduction of the 'Breviary of Alaric', the Visigoth King Alaric II was back in Tolosa preparing to do battle with the enemy he referred to as that "Frankish upstart King who went by the name of Clovis". This war with the Franks was in a sense a family affair as Clovis was the uncle of Alaric II's own wife. Such marriage ties may have been designed to establish alliances, but they rarely prevented bloody fratricidal wars.

Clovis' own bloodline was as impressive as that of Alaric II. He was the son of Childeric I, grandson of 'Chlodion the Hairy', and great-grandson of Merovech, who was the namesake of the first of the Merovingian kings of France and grandson of Pharamond. Legend has it that the Merovingian Kings claimed a bloodline link direct to Mary Magdalene and the mythical son of Jesus Christ, as well as supernatural powers including that of healing by the laying on of hands. In the business of Kingship, military might and claims to divine or supernatural powers are often contented bedfellows.

Legends aside, 'Chlodion the Hairy' was a great warrior and by the middle of the 5th century he had captured all of northern Gaul. At much the same time, his father Merovech was fighting alongside the Romans and Euric's grandfather Theodoric I, against Attila the Hun who they defeated in 451 in the battle of the Catalaunian Plains. This was situated in the far north of Gaul and a long way from Catalonia, the Mediterranean border province between France and Spain. Time passed, but Chlodion and his son Childeric I had made little progress in extending their influence over southern Gaul which was still under the distant control of the diminishing Roman Empire through their agents, the Visigoth kings. It would be some decades before Clovis united the Frankish people and managed to achieve this end.

§

Such was the complex and violent world into which Alba had been born and was destined to make her way. Anna felt strangely at home in Alba's world; and in her life. Alba was just nineteen and had been lately left alone in the world after her mother had endured and finally succumbed to a lengthy and painful illness. Alba had had the good fortune to find her present situation three years beforehand but as a Catholic she was somewhat out of place in a household so deeply involved in the Arian Visigoth administration. Moreover, there had been concern that the new King, Alaric II might not be as tolerant of Catholics as was his father Euric. But that fear proved to be unfounded.

Yet, Alba had been taken into the Zocodover household and treated well. She had been allowed to have her mother live with her and until the old lady's death some months ago Alba had been able to care for her mother in her little room at the side of the large white house on the edge of the cliff overlooking the sparkling rio Tajo. She would be forever grateful and loyal to the Zocodover family for this.

In her three years at the house, Alba had proved to be an efficient, capable and intelligent servant. She had become accustomed to being around and overhearing the conversations of the powerful administrators of the kingdom. She had even seen the young, long-blonde-haired Visigoth King Alaric II when he had visited Toletum more than a year beforehand and had come to his Deputy's house for an evening meal and entertainment. Her master, Zocodover was more than an able administrator for the King. He had become a regular confidante of King Alaric II since the Deputy's immediate superior, who was the official advisor and representative of the King, was now aging and was often ill or indisposed. It was to the credit of Alaric II that he had sent the old man away to rest and in all but title and emoluments, had replaced him with his somewhat younger deputy.

But August Zocodover was not only a clever administrator, he was a patient man and he knew that in good time, if he was careful, the senior post would be his. Indeed, he was more than patient and careful. He deftly avoided the many intrigues and the scheming that some of his younger colleagues engaged in and that often managed to bring about their own downfalls. At least, until now,

BEGINNINGS                               Gary Heilbronn

murder amongst his colleagues and retinue had not actually occurred.

Administrative service in Toletum was unlike under the Roman emperors in Rome where public office was considered to be a duty that had even to be paid for by the incumbent. Indeed, the administrators for the Visigoth Kings in Toletum, like the army itself, were professionals, salaried from funds obtained by taxes imposed throughout the realm, especially on the commercial and landowning classes. Significantly and no doubt wisely, the moneylenders were even more heavily taxed than other people as they were of little productive benefit to society. The army was of course a central cog in the administration and it was no coincidence that Toletum had a flourishing weapons industry. Yet, it may well have been the failure of Alaric II to make the most of his armies in Toletum and elsewhere that would play a significant part in future events.

With Alaric II now preparing for war, it was a time of great uncertainty in the higher and lower echelons of Toletum administration, as it was within the general populace. There had been many decades of peace and prosperity. But was this now under threat? Times of unrest could also be times of great advancement for those with the audacity to grasp any opportunities that may arise. Even amongst the well-placed officials of the administration, there were those who gave way to their deepest fears and wildest imaginations. There were whispered reports of problems within the military and other preparations for war. Rumours abounded and even legends were revived, none the least of which was the story of the vast 'treasure of Alaric'. Some believed King Alaric 11 had inherited it from his great-grandfather, Alaric I, who had reputedly removed it from Roman coffers when his army had sacked Rome almost a century beforehand.

It was even suggested that amongst the Roman gold that Alaric had removed was Moses' Ark of the Covenant, the most valued relic of the Jewish peoples. That almost mythical object had supposedly been brought to Rome from Jerusalem by Emperor Titus in AD 71 following yet another wave of the repression of dissident Jews in their troubled homeland. Indeed, in 135 AD, the Romans finally tired of their 'Jewish problem'. They razed Jerusalem as they had done with

Carthage two centuries beforehand, and gave the country of Judea a new name, 'Palestina'. This may have been a change in name only; but it was one which would have an exaggerated political effect on the world much in the future.

Back in Toletum, just a little over four centuries later, imaginations were fired by such vast riches and speculation was rife as to where Alaric had secreted all this treasure. Some thought it was stored in hidden tunnels beneath the ancient city of Carcassonne, south of Tolosa, on the road to Narbonne; or somewhere in the high ground called the Mountains of Alaric outside Narbonne itself, in the southern part of Gaul. Others, giving perhaps undue significance to the strange similarity between the name of the city 'Toletum' and the word 'exile' in the language of the Jewish people, asked if perhaps the Ark of the Covenant had even found its way into some hiding-place in or under Toletum itself? In such a climate, anything may seem possible.

## Forty-Six

In the course of her duties in the house of Zocodover, Alba could not help but overhear many of these rumours and the anxious and sometimes whispered discussions. She listened and tried to work them into the tapestry of folklore that she had already learned about her own people; the stories and notions that had been passed down to her through generations.

As a servant, it was not Alba's place to ask questions of her masters and mistresses, nor to seek clarification of such matters. But she was not just discreet; she was also intelligent and could not help but sense the instability of the administration. She knew in her heart that times of instability provided a fertile ground for the plotting and counter-plots that so often surrounded the rich and powerful.

It was also a time to take extreme care.

Her mother had told her stories of their own ancestors who, if the family legends were to be believed, had also been rich and powerful for many centuries in the past, but had lost their wealth at Hannibal's great siege of Saguntum hundreds of years before. But that was so far back in the past.

"Great fortunes, it would seem, come and go." she said wisely to herself, "and there are always people who'll go to any lengths to seize the wealth that others have amassed."

However, she had little time to dwell on such thoughts. After all, she had her work to do. And she was strangely content. Is it not somehow comforting to the poor and dispossessed, like Alba, to believe that sometime in the past they too had been wealthy or prosperous and may yet be again? Inevitably, such stories of better times even so long ago become engraved in their psyches and persistently passed on from one generation to the next.

As the months passed by, Alba began to harbour a growing sense of foreboding but continued to perform her duties, serving meals cooked in the ground floor kitchens and the earthy rich red wines stored in dozens of barrels in the massive but cool cellar that stretched the length and breadth of the extensive stone building. Alba found her work interesting. Over the last three years she had been moved through several posts in the household, each time seeing her humble remuneration increased and finding that her new functions were bringing her closer and closer into contact with her master and more and more in the presence of many of the officials in his entourage.

As a servant, Alba had almost no time of her own. That was especially the case during those long years when she was occupied with nursing her dying mother. Since freed of that task, she did find a little time to follow her own interests. She had few friends and none of them outside the walls of the Zocodover premises, so she often found herself closely watching the guards as they practised their different martial arts in the training grounds not far from the residence. She was particularly attracted to the displays of swordsmanship and hand-to-hand combat. She sometimes thought she could have been a soldier, having herself acquired considerable strength from her work and being graced with natural agility and speed. Even as she went quietly about her work, she would often imagine herself in the place of such warriors, performing their dance-like defensive and attacking moves in slow-motion in her own vivid imagination.

Passing stealthily and unnoticed throughout the busy house, she also heard a great deal of what was going on amongst her betters. She was well aware that the rumours and speculation as to what the future may hold had much intensified as the springtime of 507 saw the plants and blossoms indigenous to the central part of the Iberian Peninsula burst into full bloom. It was then that the depressing news of the outcome of the great battle of Vouillé reached Toletum.

Deputy Administrator Zocodover's residence was the site of his official administration as well as his place of business. It had dozens of rooms and several grand and more modest offices, along with a large high-ceilinged hall with vast tapestries strung across the whitewashed walls. The residence was almost continuously used for meetings and audiences. It was in the building's Great Hall that Zocodover and many of his official's and guests dined while the business of the kingdom was being arranged. It was just such a day in late springtime when news was brought to the Deputy Administrator of King Alaric II's death in hand-to-hand combat with that redoubtable warrior who he had much underestimated, King Clovis of the Gauls. It had occurred on the battlefield at the plains of Vouillé far to the north and it was even suggested by some that the battle was already lost and that Alaric II had taken flight when he was overtaken and killed by Clovis. But these details were only whispered amongst a few higher-ranking officials who had personally spoken to the messenger after his audience was over. It was not the administration's official story.

The loss of this battle and the death of the king meant the rout of his forces and the rapid withdrawal of his remaining troops to Barcino, later known as Barcelona. The troops were accompanied by young Amalaric, the dead king's son and his heir-apparent. The defeat also meant the loss of almost all their territory in Gaul north of the majestic Pyrenees Mountains. Only Narbonne, in the far south of Gaul near to the great Mediterranean Sea and less than a day's ride from Barcino, was still held, but by the forces of the Ostrogoths or the eastern Goths. They had recently come to Iberia to help support their distant cousins, the Visigoths or western Goths.

The Goth peoples had split into two tribes in the 3rd century but intermarriage still occurred. Indeed, Amalaric's own mother was Theodegotha of the Ostrogoths. Alaric II's young heir had been born at the end of the 5th century and although he was a Visigoth, he would also be able to call on Ostrogoth loyalty through his mother and grandfather, the powerful Theodoric, then King of Italy. However, after the defeat of Alaric II, it was the dead king's older natural son, Gesalic, who was elected King by the army and charged with pursuing the war against old Clovis.

The Deputy Administrator and his retinue were dining in the great hall when the messenger with all this unsettling news was brought before him. By chance, Alba found herself posted behind Zocodover when the messenger was called upon to speak and the few words he spoke caused an immediate uproar around the table of officials.

The Deputy stood and called his entourage to order in a powerful resonant voice.

"My friends, my colleagues ..." he paused. "This is not the time for debate or confusion. It is the time for hard work to consolidate our institutions and administration. No opposition to this effort will be countenanced. Anyone transgressing will suffer swift and severe sanctions. They will forfeit their lands and all that is of value. Each of you will now retire to your respective offices, call together your junior officials and pass on the terms of this edict."

The wisdom of the new edict was apparent to all.

As the assembled officials began to disperse, Alba stayed where she was, in the shadows and backed closely to the inner wall of the great hall, nearest the corridor communicating to the anterooms and the kitchens. Even if noticed, she would be expected to stay there to clear away the remaining food and drink and to ensure the cleanliness of the tables. The floors were someone-else's duty. Most officials moved quickly towards the wide arched exits that sat between the several tall portals each standing some four metres apart along the outer side of the hall.

These arched exits opened out onto a wide sun-drenched terrace decorated with large earthenware pots exuding cascades of almond blossoms and colourful orchids. At its edge, the terrace was bordered by three long, low stone steps all stretching the full length of its magnificent tiled surface. Some officials strode quickly across the terrace and out towards the road through the surrounding grove of aged olive trees whose branches were almost hidden by dusty, light greenish leaves and stacked with tiny young fruit. Others trod well-worn paths around the building to their official rooms, hurrying to send out messengers to call in their underlings for urgent meetings. Here and there, two or three small groups of robed officials dallied in animated conversation, whispering fervently amongst themselves. Alba heeded their presence while appearing as unobtrusive as possible.

One small group standing several metres away from Alba was being harangued by a tall dark official. It was not the first time she had noticed his face with its dark malevolent eyes. Usually he hung around the outside of these gatherings, saying little but watching, always watching, especially those officials whose body-language and facial expressions betrayed dismay or disagreement with the orders and edicts of the Deputy Administrator. But there were others he closely scrutinized as well. Officials upon whose support the Deputy could always rely were also subjected to the piercing interrogation of his dark eyes. Alba knew in her heart that he sought to distinguish those who would weakly follow whoever gave the orders, from those who were true and loyal supporters of Zocodover himself. Others, still, he took very careful note of; especially those with ambition, those whose plans and projects had been blocked or delayed by the Deputy or his loyal supporters. The tall official usually said little, seemingly biding his time but he could sometimes be seen walking in the olive groves with one or another of his more under-appreciated colleagues, often smiling and laughing.

Alba believed that the tall, dark-eyed official had a responsibility for agricultural taxes and his name was Zigora, Eneco Zigora. It was a name that strangely filled her heart with disquiet. She had overheard rumours that his official tax collectors were thuggish and often arbitrary in the prosecution of their duties, targeting the weak but allowing the wealthier landholders to escape with little or no payments in return for personal favours. There would always be such people in the administration of the realm.

Alba was circumspect. She knew that life was not fair and that the rich and powerful often exploited and stole from the poor.

"It had always been so and would never be different, even under the rule of a fair and wise king" she said; speaking aloud to herself.

"Wealth and power often corrupt those who have it and almost always attract others with a baser nature." She paused. "Yet some kings and officials are fairer than others. King Alaric II and Zocodover are not without faults," she thought, "but there's some good in them as well."

Then, recalling the news that had just arrived, she said quietly:

"Ah, but now that King Alaric is dead and his successor so far away, we can only hope that the Deputy has strength enough to resist those for whom greed is their God."

Alba could not hear the conversations Zigora was carrying on in the gardens, but she watched intently and from his mannerisms and fierce eyes, she sensed that he was a dangerous and doubtless, violent man.

# Forty-Seven

Zocodover was indeed a fair administrator but also a strong one, unafraid to enforce strict adherence to his edicts. He was convinced that the circumstances he now found himself in were perilous not only to himself and his position, but also to the stable administration of the region. All he had worked for could so easily be lost by a careless move. His patron, Alaric II, was now dead and although his older natural son, Gesalic, was King in title, the balance of military power resided with the boy Amalaric and the relatively newly arrived Ostrogoth forces, especially, the rarely seen and little-known Theodoric the Great; the young boy's maternal grandfather.

Fortunately, Zocodover had made it his business to learn a little more about Theodoric than did most others in Toletum. What he had been able to discover was that in the mid-5th century, some five decades beforehand, Theodoric had been sent as a child of just seven years of age to Constantinople, the old Roman capital in the east. He was there as a hostage to ensure Ostrogoth compliance with a treaty they had made with the Byzantines. This was not an unusual practice. But he stayed there many years and was much favoured by the Byzantine rulers, learning a great deal about Roman government and military tactics. The Byzantines even appointed him consul before he eventually returned to his people and became their king in 488.

Theodoric had a reputation as a man who honoured his treaties, both with the Byzantines and with the Romans; and by arranging to marry off his daughter, sister and other female relatives to various Germanic and Frankish rulers, he had consolidated important political alliances throughout Europe. Indeed, one sister was married to Clovis of the Franks and his daughter was married to Alaric II of the Visigoths. So it had been his brother-in-law, Clovis, who had killed and defeated the forces of his son-in-law, Alaric II. Family affairs are sometimes complicated.

But Theodoric was more than an able diplomat. He was also a ruthless and ambitious man who, just a few years before, at the turn of the 5th century, stole the Kingship of Italy by killing his rival with his bare hands at a celebratory banquet. Theodoric was also of the Arian faith which some saw as an heretical branch of Christianity opposed to the Roman Catholic and Christian Orthodox faiths. But he was reputed to be tolerant of others beliefs.

"That is a good thing," Zocodover reflected quietly to himself. "Toletum is also known for its religious tolerance".

Zocodover felt that this was perhaps a man that he could work with. But Theodoric the Great was not present in Toletum as he then resided in Italy and now his forces were based far to the north around Barcino. In the meantime, there were few options open to Zocodover. The affairs of the kingdom must and would continue as usual while Gesalic pursues the war against Clovis in the north with the support, for the moment at least, of Theodoric's emissary forces.

"But in all the circumstances," Zocodover thought aloud to himself, "Theodoric's loyalties could well change at any time."

Following the edict handed down by the Deputy Administrator, the rumours and disquiet in the ranks of the officials in Toletum had subsided and almost ceased; at least in public. This lull continued throughout the remainder of the year 507 on the Julian calendar. It was business as usual or so it seemed. Taxes were increased to support the war – an unpopular measure – and some armed forces were sent north as reinforcements for the northern troops of Gesalic who was then seeking to retake Tolosa and Narbonne with the aid of the Ostrogoth forces.

The exodus of troops from Toletum was of mixed portent for the Deputy Administrator. It weakened his position there, but at least he had a considerable personal guard under his direct command.

However, quietly and behind the scenes, sides were being taken around Zocodover. Although he followed the orders of young King Gesalic, many suspected that he nurtured his relations with Theodoric and his daughter Theodegotha, young Amalaric's mother. On the other hand, some trumpeted their loyalties to King Gesalic at every possible moment. The latter camp seemed to include Zigora and his followers. Zigora knew that this would be likely to be his only chance to oust the Deputy and take his place. But to do it he would need the support of Gesalic and he was prepared to wait for the right moment.

Meanwhile Alba knew that she too must be prepared for all eventualities. The little safety and security that she had in the world depended on Deputy Zocodover and she began to steel herself mentally for the time when she, too, may be called upon, to choose sides or make a stand. The wrong decision would mean being cast out or far worse.

As the months passed and the summer of the year 508 on the Julian calendar approached, good news had still not come from the fields of battle. Gesalic had failed to retake Tolosa and the city had been burned by the Franks, although with the help of the Ostrogoth forces Gesalic had temporarily retaken Narbonne. But then the Germanic burgundy forces allied to Clovis had taken it back again. At least the Ostrogoth army had held back the Germanic troops' advance to the Mediterranean. Thus, faith in Gesalic's rule was wavering as he was now forced to take refuge further south in Barcino. This meant that for all intents and purposes, the vast kingdom of Tolosa was now lost and the Visigoth kingdom would be forever limited to the Iberian Peninsula itself.

It was clear from the faces of Zocodover and the Visigoth administrators in Toletum that they were worried, but others there were in a state of near agitation. It was just only a matter of time before Gesalic's position would become untenable. Amalaric, under the care and tutelage of his grandfather Theodoric, would soon be old enough to take the throne, and Theodoric was a formidable figure. Zigora and his associates had put their faith in Gesalic but now it looked as though that had been a mistake. There were now few courses open to Zigora. He knew that he must act while Gesalic is still King.

"Surely", he thought, "Gesalic must know where Zocodover's loyalties lie and the young King would be pleased to be rid of him."

Alba was now approaching her twenty-first birthday. She was a clear-skinned, attractive, dark-haired young woman with an athletic, almost elegant demeanour. Her face and bearing showed a calm and obedient disposition which lightly camouflaged a strong character and unflinching self-belief. These qualities were rather uncommon in women of the day. Hers was a male-dominated society. Also unusual for a woman was that in the privacy of her quarters, she filled what spare time she had by practicing the arts of close-quarters combat, often using the old dagger that her mother had stored at the bottom of her trunk and had been passed on to Alba on the old lady's death. She had studied the guards in training and copied the lunging, slashing and thrusting movements of attack as well as defensive blocks, retreats; falling to one knee and counter-attacking with an upward thrust to the lower abdomen. She practiced alone and revelled in her own skill, agility and athletic prowess. She had never pitted herself against a true adversary, nor for that matter, any adversary at all, not even in her practice sessions. However, she had taken the habit of tucking the dagger that she'd cleaned and sharpened assiduously, in its leather sheath behind the sash she wore around her waist. The sash kept in her tunic and held up the light ankle-length skirts she wore while working. Indeed, such modest clothes helped discourage undue attention from the men of the household. And the weapon was hidden but positioned for easy access should the need arise. In those days, it was not unusual for women to carry a weapon for self-defence. The weak were often preyed upon.

Alba's Catholic faith was also strong and despite the ongoing hostilities with Clovis, King of the Catholic Franks, she suffered no discrimination in the Zocodover household and retained a somewhat favoured position amongst the servants. On the rare occasions her master spoke to her it was with relative kindness as she was a loyal and obedient servant, careful to avoid displeasing her master. Her duties had not changed over this period of disquiet in Toletum's Visigoth administration. "It was not a time for change but for consolidation" her thoughts echoed the words of Zocodover.

The Deputy Administrator continued to manage the affairs of the kingdom in Toletum although communications from Gesalic were rare, apart from the regular demands for further financial and military resources. Audiences, meetings and even the occasional feasts – though they were somewhat subdued affairs – continued to be held in the Great Hall of the Zocodover residence on the cliff top above the sparkling rio Tajo, not far from the centre of the old town in Toletum.

## Forty-Eight

In the middle of the ninth month in the year of 508, the intense heat of summer in Toletum was only just beginning to wane. It had been a particularly uncomfortable and humid summer although the Great Hall in the Deputy Administrator's residence was blessed by cool breezes. They seemed to flow along the rio Tajo and work their way up the mostly rocky cliff faces, across the orchards and in through the wide portals of the Great Hall.

Alba was happiest when her duties allowed her to remain in that part of the building during the hottest part of the day, serving at the long heavy wooden tables where were seated the guests and the dozen or so officials who worked full-time on the premises. The Deputy also ate at these tables as did his wife and eldest son, Armando, who was now a young man of about 23 years. "He is quite like his father" Alba had thought. He seemed honourable and could show compassion. He had been educated in all aspects of history, languages and law by private tutors and was destined for a high post in the administration, but had not yet been granted a position nor given any duties to perform. The Deputy intended to find a suitable post for his eldest son, but the time was not yet right.

For some weeks now and with increasing regularity over the summer, Eneco Zigora had been meeting furiously and plotting secretly with several other officials in the Toletum administration. These were all individuals who had reason to be dissatisfied with the Deputy Administrator or who had much to gain from his removal. Zigora had also recruited Antonius, a disenchanted army captain – a rank roughly equivalent to a Roman army centurion – from the Toletum Administrator's personal guard. Zigora knew he would be a critical figure whose authority over a hundred soldiers could be essential in assuring that the personal guard did not react in the event of an attempt to oust the Deputy Administrator.

Zigora had siphoned off considerable funds from the agricultural taxes that his minions had been collecting over the past year and had freely spread much of this around amongst his co-conspirators. He was aware that sooner or later he would be called upon to

BEGINNINGS  Gary Heilbronn

account for the missing amounts and he was also increasingly concerned that the future of King Gesalic would be troubled. Despite his clearly calculating and cold-blooded nature, a seed of quiet desperation was growing in Zigora's entrails. He had long-since hardened his resolve for the task ahead and he yearned to take that irretrievable step. All that had delayed him had been the need to bring the others to his level of readiness and to assure himself of the guard Captain's loyalty – much of which was bought with stolen funds. When the soldier was finally told the truth about the money's origin, he was silent and glared at Zigora. The truth allowed him no option but to commit himself to his corruptor. From that time onwards, there was nothing further to do but to finalize the plans for the coup and allocate the parts to be played by the various conspirators.

So it was that on a day which was ominously and unusually overcast, Zigora was once again present when Zocodover and his entourage dined in the Great Hall. Zigora had amongst his guests an impressive captain of the guards in dress uniform. Other conspirators were scattered round the long heavy wooden tables. At the end of the meal, two of the conspirators rose from their seats and approached Zocodover, who also left his prominent place at the table to meet them. He was smiling agreeably.

"Greetings, colleagues, would you speak with me now or does your business require a private audience?"

It was common that many matters of administration were discussed and dealt with around the table or in short relatively informal meetings a little apart from the others.

"No, not at all Deputy. Perhaps if we just move a little away from the table" the older man replied. They both stepped a pace or two towards the left, imperceptibly forcing the Deputy to move slightly backwards and towards the inside wall of the hall. Meanwhile, Zigora had quietly risen and moved around to the rear of the Deputy from the other direction, passing by Alba who stood virtually unseen, as servants often do, pressed with her back against the wall. She was beside the heavy dark red curtains that hung from the ceiling almost to the ground and concealed a narrow corridor leading to the rear and the Deputy's private offices. The captain of the guards had discreetly posted himself on the opposite side of the hall near the portals leading on to the terrace in order to head off any guardsmen who might enter on hearing a commotion within.

Timing was going to be everything in the plan that Zigora had impressed upon his co-conspirators and so far everything was going like clockwork. Zigora was elated or was it just the adrenalin rush he was experiencing as he glided silently along the inner wall of the hall, towards the Deputy's back. The two co-conspirators meeting with the Deputy were to create a disturbance that would attract attention and provoke the Deputy to anger. Within seconds, the tone and volume of the officials remonstrating with the Deputy was significantly raised and was beginning to attract the attention of the many officials finishing their meals, about to leave or moving towards the terrace. Several glanced in the direction of the argument.

"What's going on? Why are you so upset?" Zocodover remarked trying to calm the situation? He had been taken by surprise when his interlocutors began to accost him angrily and in an agitated aggressive manner. His eldest son, Armando, had half-risen from the table opposite and was looking with some concern to where his father was being confronted, a dozen or more paces away. He was unsure of what, if anything, he should do. He watched as Zigora approached behind his father and on seeing him surreptitiously draw a gleaming double edged dagger from behind his long cloak, the young man cried out:

"Father! Father, take care! Behind you!" But Zocodover was boxed in by his adversaries. It looked as though the whole grisly episode would be over in less than a second or two. Zigora's right hand began to rise above his head but before he could complete the downward strike, a fearful, half-swallowed scream leapt from his opening mouth and a spurt of dark red blood shot out all over the Deputy's back and down the left side of his loose robes. Zigora trembled momentarily and crumbled towards the ground holding with his left hand the almost severed right arm that still gripped the dagger that he had aimed at the back of Zocodover's exposed neck.

As if in direct reaction to the would-be assassin's descent, a dark-haired scowling female form rose as in apparent slow motion from a crouched position behind him; the flashing blade of a slightly curved short dagger dripping blood was gripped tightly in her right hand. It had sliced upwards and across Zigora's under arm through his bicep to the upper humerus leaving a long, neat, gaping wound extending to the underside of the bone as the blade slashed forwards, over the underarm and then turned sideways into his chest. But the bone of the upper arm was not severed; only the flesh and arteries. The victim had not even seen a hint of his assailant's silent approach low and close along the wall behind him. So intensely committed had he been to his murderous purpose.

The officials in the hall were in an uproar. Some of the conspirators who were not immediately involved had slipped out through the portals onto the terrace and had quickly disappeared into the olive grove, praying for anonymity. Alba retreated back against the wall away from the scene. Half of Zigora's blood had now pumped out of the brachial artery. The red puddle grew quickly around him on the tiled floor. He was near dead and no-one was making the slightest effort to save him; not that they could have.

Armando had risen from his seat, knocking over the bench he'd been sitting on. He started running around the long table heading towards where the dying man lay almost at his father's feet. Captain of the Guard, Antonius took in the scene rapidly. Now that Zigora was gone, he knew that the co-conspirators would disappear into the shadows or seek to save their own lives and that he, as the guest of Zigora that day, would be immediately suspect. His options were non-existent.

He knew that only from a position of strength and with an important bargaining chip, could he hope to escape the consequences of this most miserable episode of his life. He reacted immediately and instinctively, chasing after Armando, catching him in full flight as he rounded the end of the table and stopping him dead, grabbing him roughly from behind, his powerful arm locked around the young man's throat. A slight twist and Armando's neck could be broken. Antonius backed away from the table pulling the young man with him.

# Forty-Nine

"Deputy Zocodover!" he yelled fiercely. The Captain of the Guard was desperate. "Deputy Zocodover, guarantee my safe passage out of here or your son will join his ancestors!" Everything had happened so quickly. Zocodover had not even seen his son approaching and it was only on hearing these words that he looked in his direction, with horror. Was it not enough that he had somehow miraculously been spared assassination, but now his son's life hung in the balance?

"Agreed!" The Deputy replied quickly. "You have my guarantee, but you must release my son immediately."

Captain of the Guard, Antonius knew that it was a dangerous gamble to trust the word a man who he had just conspired to murder. There was no time to consider.

"No," he replied abruptly. "He comes with me until I am safely out of the city." These words were ominous.

Zocodover's mind worked feverishly. How could he allow his son to be taken by this assassin's accomplice? How likely was it that the hostage would be released alive?

"What guarantee do I have that my son will be released unharmed?" asked the Deputy.

"You have my word," was the reply.

"But, you do not accept my word as a guarantee of your safe conduct out of the city. Why should I accept your word that you'll release him unharmed?" retorted the Deputy. It was a desperate gamble.

There began a dangerous stand-off as neither side spoke for seconds, their minds racing, trying to find a solution. All of a sudden the captain spoke:

"Then I must kill him and take my chances on an escape!" As he spoke these words, a flash of light burst behind his eyes. He could not understand what was happening as the strength ebbed from his limbs and he felt his grip slacken on young Armando's neck. The young man reacted quickly to the changed pressure and pushed away the centurion's arm, slipping out of his previously powerful grip. For several seconds, Antonius tottered on his feet, swaying slightly back and forward, barely, almost imperceptibly, before collapsing heavily to the ground.

Alba had just retracted the pointed dagger's blade from the back of the soldier's bare neck where she had thrust it up under the base of his skull from behind.

As a lunch guest, Antonius was lightly dressed and wore no armour or other body protection. He had neither heard nor seen the young woman slip behind his large frame. Nor had anyone else! Now she stood over his body breathing heavily with the dagger in her right hand at her side. The blade dripped no blood though there was a slight greyish, watery smear along it. Armando stood a few steps away to her right side. His eyes were wide and his bottom lip trembled. He knew how close he had come to death.

"By the Gods," he said slowly addressing the young woman, "you have saved both my father's life and mine in the space of a few seconds!" Armando had been one of the few to see who it was that had so deftly stopped Zigora in his tracks just a minute or so earlier.

Zocodover, the elder, stood pale, staring at the scene and breathing deeply. He looked towards the young woman with evident astonishment. Seconds passed as he stood there, regaining some self-control. Eventually he spoke.

"What can I do to repay you?" the relieved Deputy said, staring intently at Alba. What had happened and what he now saw had lifted a veil from his eyes. It was as if he laid eyes on her for the first time. Indeed, he had rarely looked so closely and directly at the young woman before this moment. After all, she was just a loyal servant. Now he saw her in a very different light.

"You have saved both our lives. I am an old man. For my life I can only offer you a share of my wealth. You shall have ten bags of gold. You are no longer my servant. If anything I am yours. My son is a young man. He is good and strong and has a future. As from today he has a post in the administration and is responsible for the collection of agricultural taxes. His life also is now owed to you and it would be an honour for my family if he might take you as his wife and you take him as your husband."

Seconds passed. At first Alba stared wide-eyed, at the Deputy. She was astonished by the proposal; then slowly, she reflected on what had just been said.

This was a turn of events that Alba had not expected. Indeed she had had no expectations at all. She had been called upon to act, in many ways to protect herself and her future, and she did so without hesitation. That was her nature. Moreover, she had never really contemplated marriage and such an offer of marriage into a level of wealth and social status that she could only dream of was unthinkable; but it was impossible to refuse. It was true that she found Armando pleasing but had never allowed herself to think of him in such a light. Now things were different. After all she had earned her elevation in society just as any soldier or knight who serves his king well in battle might expect to be granted lands and even be made a nobleman. But could she contemplate marriage to a man who did not care for her?

She looked directly at the Deputy: "My lord, you honour me beyond that which I deserve and were it within my power alone, I would willingly accept such a proposal. But I must first know that my future husband desires also that I be his wife. For, there are still difficult times ahead and a union tainted by an unwilling participant is no true union at all."

"Well said and with much wisdom," replied the Deputy. "I see that you are an intelligent woman as well as a warrior. How say you, my first born son?"

Armando was now calmer. He had been incredibly impressed by the young woman standing in front of him. Not just impressed. He was a little in awe as well, and touched by more than a tinge of sexual excitement. He had not really looked closely at her before. She was clearly attractive, with glowing skin and sparkling but fierce eyes. He barely noticed the small round stain on the side of her throat. It seemed like just another spot of dark red blood that had been splattered across her tunic. A finer woman would be hard to find in all Toletum, he thought to himself. She has manners and good sense. And now she is even wealthy.

Just as it seemed that Armando was taking too long to decide and Alba was sensing hesitation on his part, he spoke up:

"My father, I know of no better woman in Toletum or in the whole of the kingdom to take as my wife. She is a prize beyond any other. I willingly offer her my hand in marriage. May the ceremony be had with as much haste as propriety allows. I would that she not have time to reconsider."

"All is then decided," decreed the Deputy as the last drops of the ex-collector of agricultural taxes' dark red blood drained from his inert body and spread across the floor. With that, servants and underlings rushed to clear away the bodies and blood and plates that had fallen from the tables. Alba, a little dazed, stood her ground and it took all her reserves of strength to refrain from helping the servants with their tasks. But in her heart, she knew that this part of her life had changed forever. She relaxed a little and smiled at Armando.

Arranged marriages were very much the norm in 6th century Iberia, especially amongst the wealthier classes. Alba and Armando's union was of little special significance other than the circumstances of the decision for it to occur. Little attention was paid to the fact that Alba was Catholic and Armando was of the Arian faith although he was far from committed to those beliefs. After all, was not Clotilde, the sister of King Theodoric the Great an Arian and yet married to the Catholic Clovis of the Franks?

§

The marriage took place with as much ceremony as was proper and Alba still lived in the Zocodover residence with her husband and his family, except that now she had moved into much more splendid rooms on the top floor. There, she was surrounded by tapestry-covered walls, beautifully tiled floors and heavily curtained windows looking out over the glittering waters of the rio Tajo. Armando's mother was a good woman. She immediately took a liking to Alba and accepted responsibility for her careful education to the role she would now play.

She treated Alba as her own daughter, being endlessly grateful that the young woman had saved her son from almost certain death, not to mention saving her husband from assassination — which for her would have also meant being thrown out of her home and on the street; a stark end to the cultivated and comfortable life to which she had become well accustomed.

§

Months passed by and merged into years as Anna's passing awareness of Alba's life and times became more fleeting and increasingly receded into dimness.

King Gesalic's unsuccessful rule became ever more unpopular and rumours increased that Theodoric was keen to dispose of him to make way for Amalaric, who would of course rule under the old man's tutelage. Meanwhile, Gesalic secretly sought alliances with the Vandals of North Africa, previously sworn enemies of the Visigoths, and whoever else he could use to bolster his power. But he was continually frustrated in his attempts to keep the kingship.

Alba adapted easily to her new circumstances and had given birth to a son and a daughter by the time Gesalic was chased from the throne and killed by Ibbas, an emissary of old Theodoric. The reign of the Visigoth Kings in Iberia was transforming into Ostrogoth rule though the difference between the two branches of Goths was far from clear.

While regime change through assassination and violence was not unusual, the more peaceful pattern of political alliances through marriage also continued. By 511 the young Amalaric had married Clothilda, daughter of Clovis and Clotilde of the Franks and that year King Clovis died. Thus, an aging Theodoric ruled a vast territory personally and through his grandson until the old man's death in 526.

In theory, all this should have continued to consolidate the Franco-Goth line of rulers. But events have a life of their own and a way of changing the course of history.

Armando Zocodover eventually took over his father's role as chief administrator and served King Amalaric well until the latter's untimely death. Visigoth-Ostrogoth rule over the Iberian Peninsula was already declining under Amalaric who was less tolerant of his Catholic wife than Armando was of Alba and her faith. They lived happily together producing seven other sons and two daughters, and the Zocodover administration persisted, even after Amalaric's bad treatment of his wife, Clothilda, caused a new war with her brother, Childebert I, King of Paris and Amalaric's eventual assassination on the orders of his brother-in-law, in Barcino, in 531.

The ebb and flow of Roman, Vandal, Visigoth and Ostrogoth power in the Iberian Peninsula during the early centuries of the Christian era and the power vacuum that resulted paved the way for the coming of the Moors and Saracen military, political and cultural influence. Over the next several centuries, their Islamic rule would extend over almost the whole of the Iberian Peninsula and at its zenith, push briefly north into the heartland of Gaul, before Christian fanaticism forced the Moors' retreat and their gradual expulsion from Spain between the 11th and 13th centuries.

# DISSENT AT HOME

*Bayonne, Basque Country, South-West France,
mid-1950s.*

# Fifty

The first half of the 1950s had passed quietly enough in the Basque region of far south-west France. Yet an undercurrent of political turmoil fostered feelings of insecurity that had little to do with fascism in Spain or dreams of Basque independence. After all, Basque influence in south-west France had always been more cultural than political. But there was some overt social unrest just across the border in northern Spain. Significant changes were occurring there, in an unsettling era of gradual and inevitable reconstruction. Many non-Basques were moving to the Basque region of the country to take advantage of jobs brought by increasing industrialization.

Maria kept informed about her homeland and was concerned at the changing demographics. She thought the changes seemed destined to dilute Basque culture and the strength of traditional separatist feelings there. This may indeed have been the intention of the central government of Spain. But it also increasingly marginalized those with strong separatist sentiments, intensifying their convictions and their anger.

That Basque separatist sentiment had, in the mid-1930s, culminated in the creation of the short-lived Basque Autonomous State, but this had little to do with the causes for the conflict between the nationalists and republicans in the 1936-1939 Spanish Civil War. Neither side of that conflict was tolerant of dissent or of the ideas of the Basque or any other regional secessionist movement. Indeed, Basque and other regional separatist sentiments existed independent of and were far from extinguished by the Spanish Civil War or the Second World War. If anything, such sentiments were only temporarily repressed.

§

Maria was now approaching her fortieth birthday though she showed few signs of aging apart from the tiny almost imperceptible crows-feet at the outer corners of her bright green eyes. Her hair had darkened a little but had retained its gloss and her skin was perfect, if not a little pale considering the climate and the amount of sunshine Bayonne received. She was relieved that her soul no longer weighed as heavily as it had a few years ago, or maybe she had learned how to bear its weight a little more skilfully. She still loved her homeland across the border, but she had lost so much that was dear to her in the civil war and its aftermath that she would never be able to empty her heart of a hatred for the fascists in power there.

Of course, intellectually, she knew that nothing was ever quite so clear-cut, not even love and hate – the complexity of the history of the Basque people's yearning for independence was itself an example of that.

As before, Maria's life continued to revolve around her daughter. Young Anna had lived her whole life in the south-west corner of France, so it could only be expected that her links with the culture of her ancestors in Spain would be less intimate than her mother's. Anna had inherited her mother's good looks and was growing into a fine young woman though she still harboured the tempestuous nature and judgemental notions so common in teenagers of both sexes. She was a headstrong girl, unafraid to say what she thought. But she was also fair-minded, self-possessed, astutely intelligent and willing to take risks and experiment with life. She was in many ways her mother's daughter, but much more so and it was that extra streak of conviction and independence that inspired both pride and a little anxiety in her mother's heart.

Many of Anna's young friends were, like her, exiles of sorts and she had gravitated, both in school and outside it, towards those young people who felt strongly about the plight of the weak, the poor, the repressed and the under-represented. Perhaps unsurprisingly, they identified the neighbouring Franco regime with the hypocrisy of the church and with all the evils of capitalism and corporate greed; evils that were then coming to be intellectually associated with what many of young people called the 'military-industrial complex'.

Few of these youngsters could bring themselves to overlook the fact that not only had the governments of supposedly civilized Europe, especially the British and French, studiously ignored the plight of the Republican supporters in the Spanish Civil War, but so had the self-styled 'home of democracy': the USA. Worse still, some of that complex country's major corporations were said to have provided considerable assistance during the civil war to Franco's Nationalist army. Dictators are usually a safe bet in civil wars. On the other hand, the Republicans seemed always to be hindered in obtaining supplies, forcing them to rely more on the dubious goodwill of Stalin's socialist Soviet Union. This did little to endear the Spanish Republicans to the American capitalists and the British imperialists. Both those nations harboured a visceral fear and a doubtlessly warranted distrust of post-revolutionary Russia: something which seemed to undermine any moral perspectives which might otherwise have applied.

Anna and her friends at the *Lycée Jean Jaurès* all seemed to enjoy studying Modern and Contemporary European history, especially the French revolution and the causes of the first and second world wars, the effects of which were still very freshly-felt by many in Europe.

In the newspapers, meanwhile, the young people read much about France's failed eight-year struggle to regain control of its colonial territories in Vietnam, Cambodia and Laos. Colonialism was far from unpopular at the time and France's rights to its old colonies had been agreed after World War 2 amongst the allied forces at the Potsdam Conference in July 1945. Yet, as the Americans delayed and delayed in providing the expected support, French forces suffered a final humiliating defeat in south-east Asia, forcing them to withdraw from their ex-colonies with enormous loss of life and pride. This only reinforced the festering distrust of the US government that resides deep in the psyche of many French people and perhaps especially the young. Reliance on Americans is undoubtedly a tricky business.

With all this going on, the 1950s was a somewhat solemn time in France and it was perhaps unsurprising that little reference was made in the newspapers or elsewhere to the aftermath of the Spanish Civil War. It was 'old news' and since it had all occurred, too much else had happened and too many lives had been lost.

Nor did the Spanish conflict receive much mention in the school curriculum that Anna and her friends followed – but neither, for that matter, was anything taught about the American War of Independence or of that country's subsequent civil war and what it had meant for slavery there and elsewhere.

But such omissions in the school curriculum only seemed to excite the interest of young Anna and her pro-Basque friends. After all, a number of them still had relatives in Spain and many had lost family members during those turbulent civil war years.

By the same token, they knew all about American music, with its roots in black culture; they loved and copied this new thing taking over the radio waves.

Maria was certainly aware of her daughter's increasing interest in her Basque origins as well as the politics and history of her people, and though pleased that Anna should take such an interest in her background, she'd always tried to encourage Anna to see herself as culturally Basque, but a French citizen first of all. However, many young French people like Anna didn't feel the same gratitude that Maria felt to her adopted homeland. And many were less than happy with the role that 'la belle France' had been playing in European, colonial and international affairs in a decade when many social ills were being swept under the carpet.

## Fifty-One

It was a balmy summer evening in August, 1956, at nearly the end of Anna's school's summer vacation. The day had been hot and in the afternoon, Anna had taken her second-hand *Solex* 'moped' – barely more than a bicycle minimally assisted by a tiny motor – to go swimming with some friends. Maria was not expecting her to come back early. She knew that Anna and her friends were in the habit of stopping off at one or the other of the local cafés for a *diabolo menthe* – a refreshing combination of lemonade and mint syrup so much appreciated by young people – and discussing life, school and social issues. And of course, they'd be listening to the new rock'n'roll music that some parents thought was driving many young people crazy.

Maria was happy. She felt that her daughter's life was so open and carefree compared to her more cloistered teenage years. Most of her own social contacts had been made at church after the services on Sundays. Social life had been pretty bleak for her as a teenager, but you took what you could get then, and waiting a week to talk to a boy you secretly liked only intensified the *frisson* in the relationship, even if it never went past holding hands.

Maria was musing on memories of those more gentle times when she looked up, hearing through the open window the soft purr of the *Solex* engine as it came to an abrupt stop outside their little apartment building. Within a minute or two, she beamed with pleasure as Anna burst so full of life through the kitchen door.

"Bonjour *Maman*!" she cried out. There was a slightly vexed tone in her voice as she greeted her mother.

"Bonjour, ma Chérie", Maria replied sweetly, "how was your afternoon?"

"You know, mother, my friends and I are so angry" she said. Exasperation was evident in her voice, though it was hard to see any anger in her fresh young face.

"But what could possibly make such happy young people so angry? Are your school friends being nasty to you? What could possibly be the problem on such as glorious day?" Maria asked. Her tone was loving; as usual.

"It's just that we don't understand why the world deserted us," Anna said stridently.

"But it didn't, my darling. Britain and America and many other countries helped the French Resistance chase the Nazis from our doorstep and many of the worst of those Nazis have now been tried as war criminals and executed" Maria sought to explain.

"I don't mean then. I mean before that. In Spain when the fascists were murdering people, like my own father and my baby brother." Anna replied rapidly. A slight tremor had come into her voice. She had never known her father or brother. She knew from what Maria had told her, only the briefest of details of the deaths of the man who had been her mother's first love and the baby whose life had so tragically been stolen from them. Anna was nonetheless, clearly unusually emotional. Maria was a little taken aback. She had not realized that her daughter felt so deeply about these matters.

"But Anna," Maria explained, "you must understand. At that time, no-one but us knew how bad the fascists were. The other countries all just feared Stalin and the Bolshevist revolution. They still do! Though we have an official communist party in France, the western world does not trust them; sometimes I don't either. The Americans have even outlawed the communists. Writers and film stars have been persecuted there for having communist sympathies. Even Charlie Chaplin had to flee the insanity of Senator McCarthy and their Committee on Un-American Activities. He had to come to live in Europe." Maria paused for a moment, and then she went on.

"Back in the 'thirties, many young people like you were also idealists and thought that communism was the best way ahead for the world and many of them joined the communist party or came and fought in the International Brigade alongside the Spanish Republicans. And many lost their lives as well. We must not forget these people; even if they were mistaken about communism; their hearts were in the right place."

BEGINNINGS                              Gary Heilbronn

"But the Republicans just wanted democracy in Spain." Anna complained. "And they lost the war, just as the Allies almost lost to the Nazis until the Americans took our side; though they only did that because Germany's ally, Japan attacked Hawaii. Before that, they didn't care about us at all. And the fascists still rule Spain! It's a dictatorship! And look what happened in Indo-china because the Americans didn't come to our aid as they promised. Why can't 'good' prevail without the help of a country like the America?"

"What happened in Indo-china was surely a disaster, my child; and for everyone. But how can we say that one side was good or right and that the other was not. For that matter, things were not all that clear in our civil war, either. So many different beliefs are mixed up but you must understand that the cause of the Basque people and the cause of the Republicans were not really one and the same! And there were good Catholics on both sides."

"What do you mean?" Anna exclaimed.

Her mother continued.

"Indeed, the Republicans comprised of a range of political factions from liberal democrats to revolutionary anarchists and anti-clericals, even to staunch Catholics and the urban poor as well as landless peasants. The nationalists were composed of anti-communists, some defenders of the Catholic Church, wealthy landowners and monarchist sympathizers, who even included some 'Carlists'! Do you know who they were?"

Anna nodded that she did not.

"The Carlists had been fighting for Basque autonomy for two centuries already. Indeed, the Basques and the Catalans, who both have strong separatist movements, were very much divided on who they supported in the civil war. And perhaps to our shame, after the republican surrender in the west at Santander in August 1937, many Basque troops changed sides and fought for the Nationalists." Maria said with a sigh. She saw how her daughter's eyes lowered, showing, was it... disbelief.

"How could this be?" Anna thought aloud. It was not something the young woman had wanted to hear. It was so confusing.

"Indeed," Maria continued, "it could well be that the religious, economic and political interests of the Basque people coincided more with the philosophy and interests of the conservative alliance of Nationalists under Franco, than with the more liberal Republicans! But in the end and though its people were divided, the region was more identified with the Republicans. And as a result, it suffered terribly from the bombs and the destruction wrought by the Nationalists and their fascist German and Italian and Portuguese allies." Maria paused again, she then spoke thoughtfully.

"You see, my child, I think that the true nature of the Basque independence movement is confusing and somewhat contradictory. Perhaps it would be clearer if you understood its origins. Just listen for a moment. Please."

Maria took a second to think; then, with some authority, she spoke:

"While the Basque country had been isolated and unconquered by foreign invaders almost forever and certainly during the six hundred years occupation of Spain by the Moors, the restoration of Christian rule and Catholic monarchs at the end of the twelfth century brought the beginning of an end to this happy isolation."

She went on:

"Because of political alliances that were made soon after the restoration of the monarchy, independent legal, economic and administrative structures were retained in the Basque region and in some other provinces – though then, they were sometimes called kingdoms." She hesitated again.

"In some ways, the struggle for Basque autonomy can be traced back to those times, and, perhaps incredibly, it depended upon which branch of the then monarchy – the House of Bourbon, it was – the Basque people supported in the various struggles for succession to the Spanish throne." She looked at her daughter. Maria could see she was a little confused.

"You see, throughout most of Spain's history, accession to the throne was traditionally passed down through either the male or the female line. But it may surprise you to know that when Felipe V, who was really a French prince known also as *Philippe de France*, became the first Bourbon King of Spain – he took the throne upon the death of his childless uncle Charles II – he brought with him what is known as the 'semi-salic' system of succession which existed in France at that time."

She took a moment to order her thoughts.

"That 'semi-salic' system meant that the female line could only succeed to the throne if there was no male issue at all from any of the royal lines. This made it exceedingly difficult for the female line to succeed to the throne. Of course some European kingdoms followed the 'full salic' system which meant that only male heirs could ever succeed to the throne and it just shows how much of a male-dominated society Europe then was. ... Of course, the church fully supported this. It has never been kind to women."

# Fifty-Two

"How ridiculous!" Anna exclaimed, "Spain has always had Queens as well as Kings. How could we tolerate this?"

"Let me finish" Maria replied.

"At that time, another claimant to the throne in Spain was a Hapsburg; the Archduke Charles of Austria. His claim to become king was supported by the principality of Aragon – though it was also often referred to as a 'Kingdom'. On the other hand, Felipe, of the House of Bourbon, was supported by the principalities of Castile and Navarre as well as by the Basque Provinces. As he had more support, Felipe became King. To complicate matters further, many countries in Europe were concerned that the monarchy of France and Spain were now too close and too powerful and posed a threat to the others. So, it was easy for this dispute to escalate – mixing politics and religion – and it resulted in the War of Spanish Succession, which raged from 1701 until 1714."

Maria continued confidently as she had been well educated in this part of Spanish history and it had always interested her.

"This war involved not only most of the countries of Europe but even their colonies, especially in North America. In the course of the war, Spain lost many territories, including losing the island of Gibraltar to Britain. However, within Spain itself, Felipe V took revenge on his opponents and revoked their autonomy. These were the principality of Aragon – which included Catalonia, the Balearic Islands and Valencia – and those territories that had supported the Hapsburgs. So they all came under the more centralized Castile administration. However, the Basque Provinces and Navarre who had supported Felipe and the Bourbons retained their autonomy, institutions, taxes and laws, called *fueros*, under the King Felipe's *Nueva Planta Decrees* which were made between 1707 and 1716."

Again Anna interjected: "But mother, what does this have to do with the repression of the Basque people today?"

"I am sorry, Anna, if you think I am going too far back in history, but as you will soon see, religion, politics, money and greed for power are at the centre of everything and it is really the positions taken by the Basque provinces over both the succession to the throne and the primacy of the Catholic Church that were the basis for the Basques peoples maintaining what autonomy and independence they previously had. It was nothing to do with our support of the liberal democratic views of the Republicans in the most recent Spanish civil war." Maria replied passionately.

"Just let me finish."

Anna's shoulders sagged a little, making the effort to tolerate what she perceived as her mother's 'lecture', as she sat herself down at the kitchen table a little to her mother's left.

"All right. But don't go on forever!" she sighed, partly to humour the mother who she cared for very much.

Maria looked towards her and spoke again.

"Unfortunately, the question of succession to the throne of Spain arose again a little more than a century later; at the end of the reign on Ferdinand VII. He wanted to ensure that his unborn child, whether it was male or female, took the throne after his death; and so he re-instated the old equal system of succession by decreeing the *Pragmatic Sanction of 1830*. So the 'semi-salic' rule introduced by Felipe V was abolished. Of course, people who agreed with it thought that Ferdinand's brother, who was known as the *Infante Carlos*, should take the throne if Ferdinand's child turned out to be a girl. Indeed, it was a girl and in 1832, she became Queen Isabella II and reigned with her mother as regent. Carlos then fled to Portugal."

"However, the Basque Provinces had supported Carlos and as they feared that the Queen would take away their autonomy and the special privileges the Basques provinces previously had, the supporters of Carlos formed the 'Carlist' Party which from then on fought a losing battle against the inevitable abolition of the special tax privileges and autonomy that the Basque provinces had previously benefitted from."

Maria paused for a moment, then spoke.

"Now we come to more recent history," Maria said with a kind smile.

"The Basque Nationalist Party (PVN) was formed at the end of the nineteenth century by Sabino Arana, who had himself been a Carlist and in favour of 'semi-salic' succession. The party also rather worryingly asserted Basque racial purity and superiority."

"That sounds like the Nazis" Anna interjected.

"Maybe" Maria replied, "But Carlism also embraced the view that the Catholic Church and God should be the foundation of Spanish society and not any of the new ideas of the enlightenment concerning the 'rights of man' and democracy and all that sort of thing, which were being espoused by the liberals."

"So the Carlists were against democracy!" Anna exclaimed.

"Yes, but these controversies between traditionalist and modern thinking had already been going on much earlier in the eighteen hundreds; even during the reign of Ferdinand VII, but he had been unable to resolve the differences between these two forces during his reign. He unsuccessfully sought compromises, but at least he was firm in rejecting the calls of the extreme absolutist or royalist parties for a revival of the Inquisition!"

Maria did not see the effect that these words had on her daughter. Her face paled visibly.

"The Inquisition had not really been active since the fifteenth and sixteenth centuries, though remnants of it persisted into the seventeenth century and even later when some people were pre-occupied with 'witch-hunting'. Indeed, the Inquisition was only finally formally abandoned in 1834 by Ferdinand VII's widow, acting as regent for young Queen Isabella II, who was then an infant. But it has been said that the 'Carlists' partly re-instated the Inquisition in areas under their control during the First Carlist War, from 1833 to 1839. So they were not the most pleasant of people."

"What! You say that the original Basque autonomists wanted a return to the Inquisition? I can't believe this!" Anna shouted in dismay, a look of horror on her face unlike anything that Maria had seen before. The blood had drained from Anna's face though the small brown birthmark on the left side of her throat had reddened noticeably and her usually sparkling eyes seemed to glaze over. She seemed to become distant.

"Are you all right my dear?" Maria inquired caringly.

But there was no response. Anna seemed to have fainted. Maria took Anna's arm and led her stumbling towards the couch into which she slumped heavily. She seemed to be in shock and looking as if she was unconscious or had fallen asleep. This was so unlike her. Maria's face was strained. She was very worried.

# DEATH COMES TO TOWN

*Zaragoza, Kingdom of Aragon, North-Central Spain, 1498*

## Map of Spain and Zaragoza, 15th Century

# Fifty-Three

*Zaragoza, North-Central Spain, 1498*

At her mother's mention of a return to the Inquisition, Anna had felt a sudden chill piercing down into her soul. She could not help feeling faint as if overcome by the effects of sleepless nights, deprivation, malnutrition and physical abuse. She feels strange. It is dark all around her and smells foul. She is lying on a hard cold stone floor. The stone is not smooth to the touch, but uneven and rough with some sharp edges.

Covering her back is a coarse but worn piece of cloth; something a peasant might wear. Her clothes are soiled. She is in pain, with aches that reverberate deep into her joints and bones. Her body feels tender and aching; she remembers now, it was after having being stretched on the rack. She suffered terribly but she had not confessed to anything.

"What was there to confess to? I don't even know what I'm accused of" she whimpers.

Nor for that matter, is she sure how long she has been in this place; perhaps weeks.

She thinks of her extremities. Her toes are swollen and bleeding after the slow and excruciatingly painful removal of all her toenails; and not all at the same time. The torture was carried out over several hours. The big ones were left for last. She had never felt such pain and had fainted many times before being brought back to consciousness when foul water from a large wooden bucket was thrown into her face.

And the undersides of her hands and fingers hurt abominably, having been beaten with ribbed sticks made from stiff bamboo shoots. Her fingernails, that had always been a source of pride and had, throughout her adult life, been kept long and strong, still remained roughly intact; and although there are some bruises under the nails, there was not much damage to them. Not yet at least.

"Doubtless they will be the next to go", she thought half aloud, "when those toads of gaolers come again to blindfold me and drag me to the torture chamber". She sighed, brooding on her suffering.

**BEGINNINGS**  Gary Heilbronn

---

These particularly barbarous measures – the removal of fingernails and toenails – were usually not inflicted by the inquisitors. They were generally not needed. But she had been an unusually recalcitrant subject and penitence did not come easily to everyone, the inquisitors had learned in their wisdom. It had to be dragged, kicking and screaming from some sinners on whom the Devil had an especially strong grasp. Harsh measures were needed to save some souls, so they had reasoned and so they slept soundly in their beds.

But now, the woman lying on the stone floor in the darkness seeks some rest but the pain prevents it, reminding her of her hopeless plight; and only the force of her mind focussing on the outside world allows her some relief, although it is momentary.

"How did this happen? How in the name of God did I end up here?" She asks herself for not the first time during the long weeks of her imprisonment.

"What have I done to deserve this? What sins have I committed that were so grave? ... Or is it my fate to serve God in this way?"

She'd been like anyone else living comfortably in Zaragoza in the northern Kingdom of Aragon in the year of Our Lord, 1498.

Zaragoza itself had been built on the site of a minor Roman outpost established way back in 25 BC on the banks of Spain's second longest river, the rio Ebro. It flows over nine hundred kilometres in an easterly direction from the Cantabrian Mountains in the Basque country near the far north coast of Iberia, across to the vast Mediterranean Sea. It has always been part of the northern boundary of the Iberian Peninsula, even in Roman times, though in the east, it turns off southwards, away from the Pyrenees Mountains. The old Roman outpost was situated some two-thirds of the way along the course of that great and historic river, near where it meets one of its main tributaries, the rio Gallego, which carries fresh waters down from the snow-capped Pyrenees Mountains not far off to the north.

Azena de Valdés was her name and she was married to Rodrigo de Carvajal who was a descendant of an old Zaragozan family and held a senior post in the Aragon administration. She had never really asked her husband exactly what he did – nor would he expect her to do so; but she thought it was something to do with commerce and merchants in the city, for his family seemed to have many contacts with *comerciantes* and *mercantes*. She had no idea if he too was in prison or if his connexions in the administration had somehow saved him; or even if his post and connexions had somehow been responsible for where she now found herself.

Azena and Rodrigo had four sons and a daughter, and Azena was thirty-seven years old that year. She had grown up knowing of the Inquisitorial Tribunals that had first been set up in the Kingdom of Aragon in 1232 on the order of Pope Gregory IX. They were principally to deal with any of the hapless 'Cathars' who had escaped the Albigensian Crusade that persisted over the previous two decades. The Cathars were followers of what was sometimes called the 'Albigensian heresy' although that old religious centre, Albi to the east of Toulouse, was only one of the many Cathar strongholds. Their main offence had been a rejection of the wealth and idolatry of the Church of Rome of that time. However, these inquisitorial tribunals had fallen into disuse after Rome's terrible crusade against the simple and pious Cathar people had all but wiped them out, not only in southern Gaul but also in the northern part of Spain.

So the Kingdom of Aragon had nurtured traditional Christianity for almost four centuries by now; well after control of the region had been wrested from the Almoravidian Moors around 1118. Of course, it was not until the thirteenth century that the Moors had been finally defeated and almost completely forced southwards and out of the Iberian Peninsula.

To the relief of many, complete Christian control of Spain had now been re-established except in Granada in the far south, although the continued presence of many Moslems and Jews was tolerated, especially in the south. But could this transitional era of tolerance last for long? After a time, some church leaders began to stir up hatred against the Jews and at the end of the fourteenth century and in the early fifteenth century, many Jews were slaughtered in Seville, Cordoba and even in Barcelona, somewhat closer to Azena's home.

Not surprisingly during this time, the Christian Church had encouraged significant numbers of forced and voluntary conversions of Jews and Moslems, mostly on a massive level, pursuant to Royal Decrees. Azena's own husband's grandparents had voluntarily converted and had maintained their considerable influence and wealth as well as retaining various posts in the high administration of Aragon. But many people were jealous of their wealth and position and to some, they were still 'conversos' or newly converted Christians and therefore suspect. Of course, Jews who did not convert were expelled, forced to leave the country without property or valuables, on the reasoning that their continued presence would tempt the 'conversos' back into their old religious ways.

It was only in the late fourteen hundreds, at the urging of Dominican clergymen in Seville and Segovia, that Isabella I, Queen of Castile and Ferdinand II, King of Aragon prevailed on the Papacy to replace the earlier papal inquisitorial tribunals with new Royal Inquisitions. It was argued that they were needed to deal with what was perceived as the problem of 'crypto-Jews'. These were people who had formally converted to Christianity but whose orthodoxy and real faith was still in doubt. Non-Christians were not subject to the jurisdiction of the Inquisition, but conveniently, most had been exiled. Under the Papal Bull creating the new tribunals, the monarch was given the power to name inquisitors and the tribunals were self-funded by liquidating the property of those who had been denounced and punished.

Whether the real motive for these measures was to ensure Catholic orthodoxy or to purge the administrations of such persons or to benefit from the forced acquisition of their property by the monarch — or perhaps all these things — was far from clear to anyone, let alone Azena and others like her. But all of these possible motivations were certainly among the results that Royal Inquisition tribunals actually managed to achieve.

Azena knew all this. After all, it was common knowledge but public dissent was severely discouraged. What people thought in private was another matter.

"How could the same queen and king who financed the discoveries of Cristoforo Columbo and who brought new affluence to the people of Spain also do this to them," Azena thought to herself? She was almost in tears as she lay in the darkness of her cell.

"You must quieten your mind. You need to rest." she said. She spoke forcefully to herself, as if the somewhat ragged person lying restlessly on the rough stone was not her but someone else. Her mind had been furiously trying to come to grips with her situation. She shifted her body a little on the cold hard floor, trying to find a moment of comfort for her tired bones to recuperate; even a little. It didn't help.

## Fifty-Four

"Perhaps the people around me know what they are here for" Azena sighed, thinking of the other prisoners, some of whom she could hear moaning or moving about in their cells. But the thought only increased her sense of isolation. She hoped that even a few hours of fitful sleep would help her. God willing, it would lift just a little of the desperation that she felt, as finally, she began to accept that she would very likely never leave this place alive.

"Or worse still," she thought, "perhaps my dead body will just be left here to rot or disposed of in the trenches with dead animals and other waste and my dear family will never know of my fate."

"But how can I confess?" she asked herself. "I have nothing to confess to. I know of no crypto-Jews, heretics, witches, sodomites or bigamists that I can denounce. And I will not lie before God and name persons who I do not know in my heart to be sinners. ... There is no way out for me."

She was half-sobbing as she spoke these words to herself.

It was not that Azena was surprised when the envoys of the 'alguaçil' – the gaolers and torturers of the Royal Inquisition tribunal – appeared at her door. At that time, everyone half-expected the officials of the dreaded Inquisition, especially in Zaragoza. But she knew that people of Jewish origin, like her husband, were most likely to be visited.

Already, back in 1250, the Jews in Zaragoza had been blamed for other horrors. There was the ritual murder of a choir boy called Dominquito de Var. The story had been spread that there had been a plot by the Jews of Zaragoza to kill every Christian in the city by performing a magic ritual on Good Friday. It was said that they were to use the heart of an innocent Christian and re-enact the trial and crucifixion of Jesus Christ. It was claimed that young Dominquito was captured for this purpose, but the murderer, who had been charged with the task of completing the ritual had first decided to visit a church, for reasons which were not altogether clear, and he was found there with the choirboy's heart in his possession. He had confessed to the whole plot, though perhaps he'd merely agreed with what his interrogators had put to him and he had denounced all the Jews of Zaragoza many of whom were quickly executed for their roles in the alleged crime. Of course their wealth was also forfeited. Who would complain?

Then, more recently, just thirteen years ago when Azena was a young wife and mother of just twenty-four years, the 'conversos' were blamed for the murder of Pedro de Arbués, the first-ever Inquisitor of Aragon to be named by the monarch. This had resulted in much anti-'converso' sentiment and some twenty-five members of mainly prominent 'converso' families had paid with their lives and their fortunes for this alleged crime.

But Azena's own family's reputation as church-going Christians was beyond reproach; at least this is what she had truly believed. And to avoid any suggestion to the contrary, they were always careful to ensure that there was smoke rising from their chimneys on Saturdays so they could not be accused of honouring the Jewish Sabbath. They also kept no Jewish worshipping paraphernalia. None of this had been difficult as Judaism had never been a part of her or her own ancestor's lives and even her husband's family had ceased to regard themselves as practising Jews some generations ago.

"Perhaps I am accused of witchcraft or I have unknowingly blasphemed?" she wondered aloud to herself. "At least if this were so, my husband and children would be safe."

She consoled herself with this thought.

"And I have little property of my own to lose. Or perhaps," she thought with a shiver of real fear, "they want me to denounce my husband as a crypto-Jew? Then they could confiscate all his and his family's possessions, leaving me and my children destitute! ... What am I to do?" she cried in anguish.

Azena now felt very troubled and seriously began to wonder if in reality her imprisonment was not in some way an attempt to incriminate her husband and his family. They had escaped any involvement in the punishment meted out to those who were allegedly involved in Pedro de Arbués murder, while several other innocent 'converso' families had not been so fortunate.

"Was this not perhaps an elaborate plot by the feared Toma de Torquemada, Inquisitor-General of all Spain and the mentor of the young Pedro de Arbués, to again use his protégé's death to eliminate the 'conversos' — people he seemed to hate with such vehemence?"

In that terrifying moment, Azena's relief was palpable though bitter. She was sure that this thought was true and that she had now seen through the Inquisitor General's vicious little intrigue. What hope she might have to counter it, she did not know. But counter it she must, even if her life is to be forfeit in the process. With that conviction in her pounding heart, she now steeled herself for the task ahead and drifted off into a troubled sleep.

Night passed into day, which could be sensed only by the slightly increased light in the dungeon where Azena was locked away and by the more noisy movement up and down the corridors. There was banging and clanging, and from time to time dragging sounds. Late in what appeared to be the afternoon, the heavy wooden door of her cell opened and a scruffy, fat, half-toothless gaoler entered, throwing some bread towards her and half-dropping a bowl with a greasy looking fluid in it onto the ground near the door, spilling some carelessly on the cell floor.

"You are one of the fortunate ones, sen-jor-ah," he said, stressing every syllable of the title with heavy irony.

"You have prison food to eat, though your family's paid a pretty penny for this slop." The fat gaoler gloated unpleasantly revelling in the power he now wielded over those who outside the prison walls were immeasurably his betters.

"And soon you'll have an audience with the Inquisitor General hisself" he hissed. "Then, it won't just be the 'fiscal' to interrogate you and the 'calificador' to decide on your heresy." The 'fiscal' she knew was the prosecutor and the 'calificador' was the theological consultant to the tribunal.

"The great Don Tomas will soon be there to make sure you tell the truth. He'll make you squeal and spill your guts to uz" he taunted, laughing as he spoke and closing the cell door with a vicious slam.

Azena was famished. She had to steel herself against the putrid smell coming from the slops, and could not prevent herself from wolfing it down with the stale bread thrown on the floor. It was food almost good enough for wild pigs, but she had to keep up her strength. She knew that many trials and tribulations lay ahead and that there may come a time when she would need all her physical and mental resources if she had any hope of being able to prevail over her enemies.

She knew too, that had her family been able to provide better nourishment for her during her time in prison – assuming they even knew where she was – they would have certainly done so to the best of their abilities. All she could think was that either they could not do so, or, they didn't even know where she was. Or perhaps the 'alcaide' – the gaoler in charge of feeding the tribunal's prisoners – had taken for his own use, whatever funds or other resources her family had provided for her keep?

No answer that she could think of to any of these questions could assuage her fears and uncertainties.

## Fifty-Five

For some time, Azena had been expecting to be called before the Inquisitor-General, but this did not occur. Each day passed like the one before it except that every other day she was briefly allowed out of her cell to carry the low wooden pail used for her bodily wastes and empty it into a hole in a stinking cubicle at the end of the corridor of cells. Then, as she moved quietly towards the cubicle, she could hear the groans and prayers and even occasionally almost catch a glimpse of the other inmates housed in the cells on both sides of the corridor.

"Take heart," she said silently to herself, "though this is an unpleasant chore, at least it leads me in the opposite direction to the interrogation rooms and the terrible torture chambers at the other end of the corridor."

It was on such an occasion that the gaoler escorting her was called away as Azena was being allowed out of her cell to empty her waste pail.

"You know what to do, sen-jor-ah," he said gruffly and with malice. "Make sure you are back in your cell when I come back. Or you'll live to regret it." He hurried off.

She moved slowly towards the end of the corridor where the waste disposal cubicle was to be found, enjoying a brief moment of what seemed like freedom. She emptied her pail and when she was sure that the gaoler had gone, Azena's voice shattered the silence of that ghostly place. She spoke out loud hoping to communicate quickly with others in the cells.

"Who else is locked up in here? I am Azena de Valdés y Carvajal. I have been here for weeks it would seem and I do not know why or what I am accused of. Who else is here?" There was no response, just an eerie silence and Azena was afraid. She knew she had so little time to make contact.

"Who is here?" She cried out a little more loudly, almost pleading. "I must soon return to my cell. Please, please speak to me.

She heard a shuffling towards the door of the cell near her and an educated but soft voice spoke from close behind the thick wooden planks.

"I am called Alfonso Montesa" the voice replied.

The name brought a feeling of dread to Azena's heart. Some members of the Montesa family had been tortured and burned alive in retribution for the murder of Pedro de Arbués. But this was already over a decade ago. And yet here was another Montesa imprisoned in this place right beside her. It fanned the flames of her worst fears. "It cannot be a coincidence then that I am here too." She whispered to herself.

The voice of what she now thought she recognized to be an old man spoke to her once again.

"I have been here now for many weeks, perhaps months and have not yet succumbed to their torture. They want me to admit that I still perform the Jewish rituals and to denounce my family as 'crypto-jews'. I have refused, but I fear that eventually the torture will be too much for me. The torturers say I was denounced by one of my family who was burned at the stake for the murder of that sodomite de Arbués. But I do not believe them. They want me to think that my family would betray me; but it is not true. This is just the kind of mental torture and blackmail they use." He whispered these words or was it just that he had little strength left to speak.

"I did not know de Arbués was a sodomite." Azena replied shocked.

"Why else do they hate and want to punish adulterers, sodomites and child abusers. Because that is what they are themselves! Even de Torquemada who hates Jews so much; he is one himself. He comes from a family of 'conversos'. And de Arbués and de Torquemada were very, very close. Some say that as a boy, de Arbués was de Torquemada's catamite and shared his bed. Men like that must be sick or evil. And methinks that they love their ungodly work much too much." Montesa's voice trailed off.

These words were all too much for Azena. She had never heard such claims before and to criticize the Inquisition as Montesa had just done was itself a crime for which the Inquisition could punish you. How could she stand here and listen to this? But yet she knew; she knew in her heart what people did to others through hatred.

"Are you here, Señor Montesa, because you have criticized the Inquisition?" Azena asked meekly. She knew many people had been tried for such offences against the Holy Office of the Inquisition itself.

"No Señora, I am here because they want to punish all 'conversos' and want their wealth" Montesa replied.

"They want to confiscate all our property and chase us from all posts in the administration. Look what they have already done to the Jews and next it will be the Moslems. The Jews have all been expelled and all their property taken by the King under the royal Alhambra Decrees of January 1492. Do not be fooled, Señora de Valdés y Carvajal, I know of your family just as you no doubt know of mine, and I know that the Inquisitor-General will not stop until he has disposed of you and all your family and taken everything that your family has worked for, now and for generations before you. Much of the wealth will go to the King but the Inquisitor will take his share."

Azena was aghast at such words. They were almost treason.

"No wonder Montesa is here," she thought to herself aloud. Then she was startled by another voice from a cell on the opposite side of the corridor:

"He speaks the truth, Señora. ... Though he is old and bitter." murmured the other muffled voice from behind the opposite cell door.

"I know not if Pedro de Arbués and de Torquemada are sodomites but the rest of what the old man says, I too believe. De Torquemada is from a family of 'conversos' but he hates us even more because of that. Expect neither honesty nor mercy from the Inquisitor-General. He would not know the truth if God himself spoke to him. More likely it would be the Devil. But go quickly now. I hear the gaoler returning. He must not find you outside your cell."

Azena hurried back to her cell.

She was shaken, but at least she had had some human contact, even if it was only with the other hapless inmates; and she guessed that her plight was no worse than theirs. Yet in her heart she was surer than ever that she was there for a reason. Not because she had sinned or committed any crime but because she was being used by the inquisitors for their own purposes and possibly even by the Inquisitor-General himself. But what could she do?

Two more days passed. They were endured in much the same way as many had before them. Such days slowly drifted by during the incarceration of Azena de Valdés y Carvajal. She thanked God that there had been no more torture and no interrogations. Not yet, at least. Her feet and fingers began to heal and her spirits had improved. This was not just because of the respite from torture but perhaps ironically from the fact that she thought that she now had a better understanding of why she was incarcerated there. And now, stoically, she began to accept the truth that she would be unlikely ever to escape these walls with her life, and that there would be no return to her family. It would not matter whether she admitted to any crimes or denounced anyone or not.

Of course, she knew or had heard that some people had been released by the inquisition's tribunals, although very few had actually been acquitted. Indeed, those had been cases where the family of the accused had managed to bring many witnesses not only to dispute the testimony of accusers but to aver to the good character of the prisoner accused. One way or the other, considerable amounts of money had been spent. But more to the point, she had never heard of any 'conversos' who had been spared in this way.

"It was true", Azena reflected bitterly to herself, "that not only were the 'conversos' almost always found guilty, but they were also burned at the stake or sentenced to do penance in the galleys as slaves. Either way, all their worldly goods were forfeited to the king. Some said that it was only the rich who were burned".

Although to many people it might seem that these rumours were true, no-one really knew for certain, as the inquisitorial tribunals operated in secret.

"People also said that the inquisitors received only some five percent commission on the wealth of those convicted, while the king took the rest" she said quietly. And she reflected briefly on this.

"And of course there were all the bribes and money spent trying to obtain the prisoners' release" she thought bitterly.

Confiscation of property only occurred after the execution or the prisoner's death – indeed, death while awaiting trial was as good as a confession of guilt and many died before their formal trials were over. The inquisitors would anyway have already taken what they needed of the wealth of the accused for the proper functioning of the tribunal and supposedly to pay for the prisoner's upkeep.

Such were the depressing thoughts that preoccupied her mind and allowed the hours to pass by, sometimes unnoticed.

During the days that followed, Azena tried to keep herself busy deciding on the answers she would give to the inquisitors questions; not that it would make much difference what she said. But for her, it was important not to incriminate anyone, even unknowingly. It would break her heart to think that she was unwittingly responsible for another innocent undergoing what she had now being forced to bear.

Her moods swung dangerously from depression to elation and there were times when she almost looked forward to her next meeting with the Inquisitor. Yet she knew in her mind and heart that in reality, whatever she said, it would not convince him of her innocence; nor would he be satisfied unless she denounced someone else, and probably not even then.

They would surely lie and say that on her deathbed, she had denounced whoever they wanted to incriminate. With such thoughts in her head, she spent more and more time exercising her body. It kept her busy and helped her avoid self-pity and feelings of hopelessness. There was not much exercise she could do inside her small cell, but she had the time and did what she could. She knew that to confront the interrogation ahead of her, she must try to keep up her morale and also her strength — and she had always been a strong and agile woman.

As the days passed, her strength returned and her mind became sharpened by a growing hatred of her inquisitors. Indeed, it began to take on the character of an obsession.

## Fifty-Six

What seemed like weeks were passing by, though in truth it may have been much less than that. From time to time, Azena heard movement coming from some of the other cells and sometimes even moaning and groaning as a muffled witness to the suffering of her fellow inmates. On one occasion, very early in the morning, there was a rowdy exchange outside her cell door and the trembling, but piercing voice of old Alfonso Montesa was heard to call out.

"Pray for me today, my friends," he said, "for I go to meet my maker. Pray for my soul", though the voice was stifled by the sounds of the beating he was receiving for his efforts. His short guttural, pained cries were heard less and less as he was dragged away until all that was left was a deathly silence.

After a few moments, the quiet prayer: "May God have mercy on his soul" echoed two or three times around the empty corridor of cells. It came from different directions and from different voices, even one female. The female voice sounded close by. Azena then repeated the words softly to herself – she had been greatly impressed by old señor Montesa and was in no doubt that he, like his family before him, would go their fiery fates with honour intact and without the stain of having denounced another human being to their torturers.

"His suffering will be immense" she whispered. And she thought to herself: "... it was only if condemned persons repented their sins that they were garrotted – strangled to death – before going to the stake. If not they were truly burnt alive. And who could imagine what that might feel like?"

But there was something else. Azena had also been greatly surprised to hear another woman's voice coming from the cells. She had thought she was a woman alone among other male inmates.

"When had this woman been brought here? Had she been here all this time?" she thought aloud but to herself. She yearned for contact with the female voice.

Perhaps her fellow female inmate would understand just how much she missed her children and agonized continually over the things she had not yet said and now, would likely never be able to say, especially to her daughter.

"My only daughter..." she thought, "just fourteen years old. I am not even able to say good-bye, let alone talk to her about so many of the things that a mother should say to her daughter, as has always been done in my family."

Sons were different, she felt, and thought of her own sons whom she loved, but it was as if they would forever be naive little boys. "They lived for the day and fought and laughed and loved and when their lives were over, that would be the end of it for them," she whispered. She did not think it was the same for women.

It had for generations been the tradition in her family for mothers to speak to daughters of their heritage. To help each of them become aware somehow of the sacred spark that each carried within and would in turn pass on to their own daughters and they to theirs. How they bore what might perhaps be called an eternal seed in their bloodline; and how, from time to time, it would bring forth a woman even more special and more redoubtable than any that had come before; and how, from this seed, every female in the bloodline could draw enormous strength and fortitude should ever the need arise.

"While not everyone is called upon to play a role of some significance in life", she reflected, "many have heard and risen to the call and so it would always be. Even those to whom God had allotted a simple, peaceful existence, such as I have led, still harbour an inner core of strength that may always be relied upon should the arbitrary finger of fate demand it."

For a moment she was ... not content, but at rest. Then her thoughts moved on.

"There were also those more exceptional ones amongst the women of my bloodline; those with special parts to play in the history of their times — and a mother would always see this in a daughter so chosen — these ones needed even more care. They needed help to understand how they must prepare themselves to stand alone. And that they may be one day called upon to act with great courage, even for a brief moment. They are persons who are capable of changing the course of history in their times, no matter what sacrifices they may be called upon to make". This was the message that had been passed on to her by her mother. It was her greatest regret that in this regard, she may not have done or said enough to prepare her own daughter. And now it seemed as though the chance to do so was gone forever.

That evening, after the gaolers had made what was usually their final rounds — you could always hear them snoring contentedly in the guardroom soon after they had passed by and rattled the cell-door handles; generally making a needless raucous racket — Azena resolved to try to speak with the woman who was also in the cells.

It should not have been so surprising that there was another woman incarcerated there as both sexes were subject to the Inquisitor's jurisdiction as indeed were all boys older than 14 years and girls older than 12 years. There had been cases of even younger children being accused — often when merely an innocent party to child abuse, but at least, the very young were usually treated more leniently than adult sinners.

After a time, Azena spoke clearly but not too loudly in the direction of the cell where she thought the other woman was being kept:

"It is I, Azena de Valdés y Carvajal. If another woman be incarcerated in these cells, I would speak with you ... Por favor."

There was no reply but Azena could hear vaguely what sounded like movement in a nearby cell. She repeated her plea:

"For the love of God, if there is another woman here, please speak with me.

She heard a tapping from what must have been the cell adjacent to her own.

"Could it be," she thought, "that for all this time there has been another woman right here beside me and I never knew."

She moved to the wall where the tapping was coming from, looking around for some object to use to tap out a reply. There was none. So she brought her face as close as possible to the lower part of the stone wall and called through loudly enough to be heard by someone with their ear to the wall on the other side, but not by the other inmates in nearby cells; nor, she hoped, by the gaolers in their chamber at the end of the corridor nearer to the interrogation room.

"Will you speak with me Señora?" Azena's slight voice drifted through the stone walls. Both knew that the rules of the inquisition tribunal cell block demanded absolute silence. Silence was said to encourage penitence, though it also multiplied the sense of isolation felt by prisoners; and infringement was punished severely.

The voice in the next cell replied: "I know well enough of you, Señora Carvajal. My husband also works in the Zaragoza administration but not in as illustrious a post as your husband. Yet my family is also targeted by the inquisition. I have only been here for a week. I swear that it is not I who denounced you. Still, I will not tell you my name for fear that it escapes your lips under the strain of the rack. I trust that I may be able to do as much for you, but no person knows how much torture they can bear and these are times when no one may be trusted, not even one's own family.

The Inquisitor 'fiscal' told me that one of my husband's cousins had denounced me. ... Could that be true? I do not know what I have done but it must be because my grandparents were 'conversos' just like the grandparents of your husband. I swear that I am a good and honest Christian, and can only pray that I will be believed by the inquisitors when the time comes."

Her voice trailed off into what seemed like sobbing.

All was quiet. Azena took in her words with sympathy verging on pity; pity because this woman still harboured hope that she would one day be freed. "The poor fool", she thought to herself. "Indeed, a poor dangerous fool;" she said almost aloud, "for in her foolish hopes lie the seed of treachery and the risk that she will do anything to be released; denounce anyone, to give the inquisitors what they want."

Clearly, Azena's time spent in the cells had matured her thinking.

With this conversation, Azena realized just how alone, how terribly alone she now was and rather than finding some strength and support in sharing her burden with another accused woman suffering the same fate as she, she found only that the presence of such a person was a drain on her strength and an added reason to fear betrayal or denunciation from someone who she did not even know, but yet seemed to know her.

She thought with conviction: "I now know what I must do."

Azena spoke to her co-inmate with particular clarity and force: "Keep your strength and spirits up" she said.

"They may torture you, but your best chance of release is if you always insist on your innocence and that you know of no crypto-Jews, heretics or other sinners. And keep your faith in God. We will speak again. But be assured that if you denounce another as a heretic or crypto-Jew, it is as good as saying that you are one yourself or in danger of becoming one. That will sign your death warrant. Take great care, Señora. *Vaya con Dios.*" The hope that God be with this terrified woman was the best that Azena could wish for her.

A few moments later the conversation was over and Azena was back lying uncomfortably on the worn old cloth. It was spread over the smoothest part of the rough stone floor; the part that she had come to think of as her bed and perhaps her final resting place. A silent tear rolls down her cheek and she knows she must gather her strength for the ordeals that are to come and her commitment to what she is beginning to see as her destiny. She knows not when or how, but with fearful certainty she does know that she is on an inexorable path towards a confrontation with the devil or at least his emissary here on earth.

"May I not be vanquished, dear God!" she prays under her breath. "Too much will depend upon it."

## Fifty-Seven

It is morning. Azena de Valdés y Carvajal lies in a fitful aching slumber on her cell's hard stone floor; anxiously dreaming of her family's well-being. She awakens with a start. In the semi-darkness she hears the sound of the clanging of the chains on the old metal rings attached to the heavy wooden cell door, followed soon after by the creaking of its rusty hinges. The door opens.

"Get up and make yourself presentable for his Lordship. The Inquisitors command your presence," the unkempt gaoler announces gruffly, beckoning her abruptly, almost rudely, with the index finger of his dirty left hand. Azena stares at him and shivers at the thought of when he last washed and where that hand has been since. It was the focus on such tiny things that seemed to keep her sane and helped her to ready herself for the ordeal to come.

She rises as quickly as she can and moves toward the low wooden waste pail in the corner of the cell, addressing the gaoler with her head bowed: "*Por favor, Señor*. Please allow me a moment of privacy." The gaoler stares at her, scowling. He grunts and takes a step back outside into the corridor closing the cell door behind him.

Azena attends quickly to her physical needs, straightens her clothing, gaining strength with every passing moment. She puts her hands into a small bowl of water, using the wetness to wipe her face and with two hands, pushes back the thick dark hair on each side of her forehead. She is calm; almost unnaturally calm.

Feeling revived, she calls to the gaoler: "I am ready Señor."

The gaoler re-enters the dusty cell. Azena offers up her wrists. He chains them roughly with heavy iron links. She looks at the chains and sees how they are polished shiny in parts by constant use; but where the links interlace, they are greasy from the sweat, grime and exfoliated skin residue of the many hundreds of inmates hands they have manacled. Some would have been calloused and worn; others finer, whiter and usually trembling – but mostly sweating from fear of the ordeal ahead. Yet Azena's hands were strangely cold and dry, calm with not even a hint of a shake. She was ready.

BEGINNINGS                                      Gary Heilbronn

Not even the vicious shove between her shoulder-blades that the gaoler judiciously bestowed, as if to punish her for making him wait those extra seconds, affects her tranquil, uplifted state of mind. But it does send her stumbling forward, almost tripping. She only avoids crashing to the floor by a show of that agility which she'd possessed since a young child. It is the young child she now sees in her mind, playing running and chasing games with her siblings and other clean and happy local children. As in those times; she is barefooted though her feet have lost the toughness they had then acquired and the skin where her toenails had once been still stings with sensitivity.

Nonetheless, the pleasure she feels from the flashes of memories of those long gone times is immense and profound and she all but forgets where and in what unenviable straits she now finds herself.

The path to the interrogation rooms passes along the corridor that runs from the cells through the larger, untidy guard's chamber. From there, cleaner and brighter corridors lead both to the left and to the right. Off to the left there is an assembly area and also an open courtyard from which other corridors lead towards several other openings and to freedom.

"But it is to the right that I must go" Azena thinks to herself, as she heads along that dimmer corridor leading deeper into the old stone building that houses the tribunal's guards as well as its dungeons.

Her thoughts remain detached as she reflects on her surroundings. She is familiar with this place.

"This building is an annex to the old Church of Our Lady of the Pilar" she thinks, almost aloud, dispassionately. Her calmness is uncanny.

"It was rebuilt," she continues "if legend is to be believed," knowing that she believes the legend, "on the site where in the year 40 AD, the Blessed Virgin Mary appeared to St James the Apostle. She was standing atop a pillar of marble."

Azena seems oblivious to her circumstances.

The image of the scene appears in her mind's eye and seems to inspire her and she breathes in deeply, straightening her shoulders.

Azena knew this legend well. It told of St James who had come to this far off land preaching the gospel of Our Lord. He had been praying on the banks of the Ebro River when Our Lady appeared to him and presented him with a wooden pillar and her statue. She instructed him to build a church on that very spot, in her honour.

"That chapel was built right here" she whispers. "It was the first ever dedicated to the Virgin Mary", she says almost aloud and with pride. But for her trouble she receives another violent shove in the back that forces her to stumble. She quickly recovers.

"How fitting," she reflects to herself, "that now, just weeks before the Fiesta del Pilar, I stand here and call upon our patron saint, the Blessed Virgin," she says; silently mouthing the words of her prayer under her breath, "for the strength to overcome this evil enemy of the gospel of God preached by Our Lord Jesus Christ."

It was as if she was slowly working herself up into a religious passion and her heart pounded as if imbued with some divine force.

As she stumbles onward, the passion subsides, but the ruminations continue to absorb and distract her.

Her mind clearly elsewhere, Azena makes her way unhurriedly, almost unconsciously, though helped by regular but half-hearted shoves from the gaoler, towards the inquisitorial interrogation rooms. At the entrance of a large chamber she stops briefly, before her gaoler again pushes her, more roughly this time, through the entrance.

He is keen to make a good impression on the officials of the inquisition now seated several paces across the room behind a long, heavy oak wood table. Though it is long enough to seat at least six persons on one side of it, the table is surprisingly narrow, as if it was never intended that anyone should be seated opposite those sitting behind it. It had been placed judiciously in front of a large high window decorated with colourful stained glass representations of Jesus on the cross. Dusty, dull beams of sunlight penetrate through the stained glass and into the chamber. Azena stares up at the image of Jesus and it fortifies her against the ordeal she knows is to come.

Over to the right of the heavy table is the door leading to a somewhat smaller windowless room. It is the torture chamber, housing the 'potro', otherwise known as the 'rack'; and near it is the 'garrucha' or 'strappado' used to suspend victims from a tower by their wrists tied together behind their backs. There were other implements of torture. A favourite of the inquisitors was the 'toca' or 'waterboard', used to simulate drowning by stuffing a cloth in the victim's mouth and pouring water on to it. It needed very little space, no more than a small table placed in the corner of the room with a bucket full of water below it.

It was in this room that Azena's toenails had been extracted slowly, one at a time with an instrument resembling a smaller version of blacksmith's tongs. This device had been resorted to after several sessions on the rack had done nothing to loosen her tongue and make her confess her sins and those of her husband's family, who the inquisitors believed to be religious hypocrites and 'crypto-Jews'.

Azena stops and is once again half pushed towards the inquisitors until she stands just a few steps before them, in front of the massive table and feels the crashing blow of the gaoler's fist on her shoulder. She falls, hearing his sneering voice, seeking the favour of his masters:

"On your knees, heretic and blasphemer, consort of a crypto-Jew!"

The gaoler stands back, feeling well-pleased with his performance. He towers over his charge, waiting, and only moves when after a time the 'fiscal' or prosecutor, sitting at one end of the table, speaks sternly to him:

"That will be all. Remain at the door until you are needed."

He retreats feeling righteous and almost smiling.

## Fifty-Eight

Azena kneels before the tribunal of inquisitors. The prosecutor who had spoken to her gaoler was already known to her. He had supervised her previous interrogations and even the torture she had already endured. He was a thin, sharp-nosed man, with sunken cheeks and burning dark eyes. His head was shaved clean. He had an aura of pitilessness and cunning about him. The sort of man that children shy away from in the street, if they see him coming; and who, despite his markedly unimpressive physique and stature, rogues and brigands would think twice about, before choosing as a potential victim, even in a dark alleyway.

He spoke again:

"You are Señora Azena de Valdés y Carvajal?" It was not really a question.

Azena lifted her head and stared at the man who had already caused her so much physical suffering:

"You know who I am. You have already stretched my limbs and torn out my toenails and know I have nothing to confess. Why do you keep me here and torture me? Is it just for your pleasure?" Her eyes blazed but she lowered her head.

"Señora," another, older and softer voice addressed her. It was the man seated at the middle of the table of tribunal inquisitors. She thought that he must be the Inquisitor-General. In a tone that was a mockery of compassion, he said:

"You must bear your suffering as did Our Savior, the Lord Jesus Christ, when he was condemned and tortured to appease the Jews of Jerusalem. He carried his cross along the 'via dolorosa' before heavy nails were driven into his feet and hands and he was raised up on that cross. If you have been chosen as the bearer of such pain not often accorded to sinners in this life, feel honored that it is you who is being tested by Our Lord. If your faith is strong and your words are true, the Lord will free you of all suffering. That is God's will."

Azena kept her head bowed but spoke through almost clenched teeth and with vehemence, almost spitting out her words.

"Who are you to say that it is God's Will that my toenails be ripped from me and my limbs be almost torn asunder? Where in the Holy Book is it said that these are the ministrations of the servants of a loving God?"

One of the men behind the vast table shifted uncomfortably in his seat. It was the 'calificador' whose task it was to advise the tribunal on religious matters. But the older man, who had just spoken, glared at the woman and his twisted mouth betrayed what seemed like the beginning of a sneering smile, though it lasted less than a second and he replied:

"Your tongue will only bring you more pain, Señora, though we can always remove it for you if you cannot hold your counsel."

Azena had turned slowly and raised her eyes to face the ugly older man. She was now sure he was the feared Inquisitor-General himself, Toma de Torquemada, a hated man who had started his life as a cook at the Dominican monastery in Valladolid three hundred kilometres due west of Zaragoza; a religious centre where Isabel of Castile and Ferdinand of Aragon were married in 1469. De Torquemada had somehow worked himself into a position as advisor and confessor to that lady who had become Isabella, Queen of Castile; and in that trusted position he had planted the seeds that launched the new inquisition with himself at its helm. He was a brutal, scarred and puffy-faced man with dark, vacant eyes that Azena sensed immediately to have never shown a spark of human kindness. He was indeed the Devil's emissary.

"It would be an insult to any animal or even to a crow" she thought "to compare its beady black eyes with these empty, opaque windows to the inner workings of Inquisitor-General's evil mind." Azena knew instinctively that this man could not and did not have a soul.

"Is it possible?" she thought again to herself, as she only half-listened to his threats, "that any man fashioned in the image of the Almighty, could be born into this life without a soul? Even the vicious, mean-spirited 'fiscal' does not have about him that aura of the absence of any humanity at all. Hateful and cruel he is, but he does not carry that look of pure evil. Would it be a sin to cause the death of such a being? To crush a cockroach would be more sinful than to erase the life-force that this entity has somehow evilly usurped."

Azena was kneeling directly before the Inquisitor-General; though there was still the wooden table between them. The table was heavy, but relatively low and narrow. She moved her knees on the hard stone floor, inching herself even closer to the edge of the table while raising her hands palms together as if in prayer and as if a suppliant for the compassion of the black-cloaked men sitting in her judgement.

Thinking that she was pleading disgustingly for some kind of mercy, the ugly Inquisitor-General leaned slightly backwards away from her, raising his fatty chin, thick nose and inhuman gaze upwards as if recoiling from an unpleasant smell.

Under her long robe, Azena had brought her left foot forward, flexing her knee to its maximum and placing her foot flat on the ground just in front of her while maintaining the appearance of kneeling. Judging that she had come as close as she might safely do, she deftly brought forward her right foot to place it on the floor under her crouching body and in almost the same movement sprung with all her force towards the unsuspecting Tomas de Torquemada, her bent elbows straightening to give her arms greater speed and strength and her hands still in front of her as if in prayer with her wrists still manacled.

She moved with such speed that de Torquemada had barely opened his mouth to voice surprise when the strong, sharp, long fingernails on the index, middle and ring-fingers of her right and left hands, projected forward by her uncoiling body, pierced the soft wrinkled skin on both sides of his throat. They penetrated deeply, her victim's body was already backed up against the upright support of his heavy wooden chair; unable to recoil further and supporting the penetration of her sharpened nails through the soft skin as she curled her fingers, rounding them as if to rip out his trachea.

Dark thick blood spurted instantly from the severed jugular vein, splattering Azena's face, arms and shoulders. She almost delighted in the warm sensation she experienced. As de Torquemada writhed and twisted back and forth, pinned by her hands still joined at his throat, the gush of dark red fluid flew from side to side dousing the startled 'fiscal' and 'calificador' to each side of this Devil incarnate. Blood and saliva bubbled up through his throat and out of his now wide-open mouth, his eyes bulging and bloodshot. Azena could have sworn that she saw a vicious devilish image escape from his mouth before she felt the slicing force of the gaoler's sword across her left shoulder near her neck and she felt, or did she see, her body spread out slowly across the inquisitor's table. Anna could see it from her vantage point above the woman's body, as her image of the sight dimmed.

The heavy flat sword had slashed a gaping wound almost severing Azena's head from her body. It was as if the dark red stain on the side of her neck stood out as a target for the blow and it sent buckets of blood spewing out on to the table and around the other inquisitors now scrambling away from the carnage. Azena's body lay lifeless. The 'calificador' sprung back quickly, trying to hold his hand across the wounds to the Inquisitor-General's neck. The 'fiscal' screamed out orders for attendants to come and take de Torquemada's still convulsing body to his chamber and tend to his wounds.

Unlike Azena, who was now at peace, Toma de Torquemada's eyes still vaguely registered what was happening around him. Blood still pumped through his brain though more slowly with every passing second and he knew he had lost control of his limbs even as the attendants carried him away from the blood-soaked scene.

The shaken 'fiscal' had quickly taken command of the incident and caring not to share any responsibility for his superior's injuries, had, on pain of death, ordered those who witnessed any of the events to keep their silence.

§

Later that night hasty preparations were made and the following day, the Inquisitor-General's closed carriage and his grand retinue left Zaragoza for his palace in the then majestic fortified town of Avila, some four hundred kilometres to the south-west, in the kingdom of Castile.

There, his peaceful death was announced to the public some days later. Few mourned his passing. The Pope had already been petitioned to restrain de Torquemada's excesses. Whether he had indeed survived Azena's attack long enough to return alive to Avila can never be known for sure, though it is more likely that he died there in Zaragoza or en route for the south.

His assassin's body was secretly carried out of the city and thrown in the nearest woods for the wolves to devour. Her family was never informed of her death and no rumours of that day's momentous events were ever heard to circulate in the city; though they marked the beginning of the end to one of the most evil chapters in the history of the Spanish inquisition.

# TRACKING DOWN EXILES
*Bayonne and Paris, France 1959*

## Map of Spain and France

## Fifty-Nine

January 1959 in Bayonne was superb. Almost two weeks of continuous sunshine had chased away the winter chill. Maria had enjoyed a wonderful and sunny Christmas with Anna. She'd come home for a ten-day visit; arriving on the 21st of December, the winter solstice. Solstices have been celebrated for millennia, but these days only a few lost souls still practise pagan religions and their rituals are often performed in secret. For Maria and Anna, the winter solstice marked the official beginning of winter in the northern hemisphere and the day of the year brightened by the fewest hours of sunlight. But during those few hours, the southern sun seemed to work harder than ever.

Much further to the north, in less hospitable parts of Europe, cold grey skies dampened many spirits. Overcoats, scarves and umbrellas retrieved from storage were being kept handy for three, four or perhaps even five months to come. Already, icy winds had rushed cruelly across from the steppes of Russia with such cold and constant force that they were felt as far away as Holland, Belgium, many parts of France; and even, on occasion, in northern Spain. But as usual, the Mediterranean coast was spared their worst effects, as was the Basque region in the south-west corner of France's Atlantic coastline. There the sun shone brightly, if not with its full force.

Throughout the northern winter, the Bayonne region and the nearby coastal centres of Anglet, Biarritz and Hendaye are some of the most hospitable spots in France. Sometimes they benefit from the slightly warmer Atlantic waters in the Bay of Biscay. But those waters can be rough in winter, blown up by westerly winds; the winds that also clear away the occasional heavy grey clouds to reveal an expanse of bright blue winter sky. And often, the smaller winter sun still manages to warm up the coastal region around Bayonne and even the wooded foothills and plains to each side of the Pyrenees Mountains for hundreds of kilometres inland from the coast.

BEGINNINGS                                      Gary Heilbronn

So far, the winter had been warm and dry in Bayonne. It had not even been cold in the centre of the old town itself, where shadows cast by even the low buildings block all but the midday sun's warmth from some of the narrow lanes and backstreets. The outside tables of the street cafés along the banks of the shimmering river Nive and indeed any other sunny spots scattered around the old town, were quickly occupied by locals and the occasional tourist still hoping to bask in the warmth of the winter sun. By ten in the morning, they were already there; enjoying its warming rays, though the sun was still far from its highest point in the sky.

In winter, people in France often say that 10am is really only 9am 'in the sun' or according to 'mean solar time' – Greenwich Mean Time (GMT), as some would call it. Immediately after the war, the French government quickly abandoned the practice introduced by the German occupying forces of adding two hours to 'mean solar time' to align French time with 'Berlin time'. Pre-war 'legal time' was re-instated. Clocks were set to just one hour ahead of GMT for both summer and winter, even though Greenwich and Paris are both on approximately the same longitude and it would be thought that they should be on the same time. It's being further south that makes all the difference. And it wouldn't be until three decades after the war that summer time in France would be decreed to be two hours ahead of 'mean solar time'. What's time anyway?

By late January, those happy residents of Bayonne lucky enough to be soaking up the warmth of the winter sun would have expected to have suffered a few serious cold spells and even seen some decent snowfalls. But so far, the white shroud of winter blanketed only the peaks and upper reaches of the nearby Pyrenees mountain range. Only traces of snow were apparent on the lower slopes.

At any time, the Pyrenees are an impressive chain of mountains, often visible from as far north as Toulouse on a clear day; usually snow-covered for all winter and sometimes well into the spring. The mountains rise quickly up from the Atlantic coast forming a majestic backdrop to the city of Bayonne before ranging eastwards to establish the length of the modern land border separating republican France from what was then nationalist Spain. At the same time, the mountains' western peaks serve to divide the culturally unified Basque people into two national entities.

Anna was to turn twenty a few months after her Christmas visit. More than a year and a half ago, she had completed the final year of her *Lycée* studies, called *Terminale*. She had taken easily to the maths-oriented school system in France, showing all the zeal and conscientiousness needed to excel.  Three years earlier, on completing College – the first four years of the seven years of secondary schooling – she'd been selected to follow the special classes for candidates of the *École Normale Primaire*, which at that time trained primary school teachers. But that wasn't how she saw her future so she continued with a general Baccalaureate, excelling in the examinations with a *mention très bien* – a very high grade achieved by only the top one or two percent of students. She was then offered a place in the preparatory course for those seeking entry into the prestigious *École Normale Supérieure* – perhaps rather inappropriately named, since it was open only to students of well above normal capacities and provided training for secondary school teachers, academics and researchers. But she refused it as she had also been accepted into the first year at 'Sciences-Po', another elite tertiary institution.  Sciences-Po's focus on studies in politics, economics, law and sociology aligned pretty much with young Anna's intellectual interests as well as with her growing political conscience.

The 'École Libre des Sciences Politiques', to give it its full name, had been founded in 1872 as an elite private tertiary educational establishment designed to improve the training of the political leaders of France. It had evolved and after the Second World War, in 1945, it was significantly reformed under President De Gaulle by the creation of the 'Fondation national des sciences politiques de Paris' and the 'Institut d'études politiques de Paris'. From then on, it operated largely under the direction of the State.  Entry into Sciences-Po was very selective. It had become one of France's most prestigious *hautes écoles* or *grandes écoles* which are of higher status than universities. Only a tiny percentage of women gained entry to Sciences-Po at the time.

Despite or perhaps because of the war and all the upheavals in the following decade or so, France at the end of the 1950s was in many respects still a deeply conservative country. So it was a considerable achievement for Anna to obtain a place in 'Sciences-Po'. It looked like the beginning of an illustrious career.

At just eighteen years old, Anna had left Bayonne and her mother to go to study in Paris – the extension of 'Sciences Po' campuses to other regions of France came much later – but she had looked forward to this. She was already a mature young woman with a strongly independent spirit. Indeed, she fully embraced this new chapter in her life. Her mother had no choice but to accept this rupture, though it tore at the very core of her heart as such separations have done for many mothers. The first few months that Anna was away were difficult for Maria, but she was fortified by the inner knowledge that her daughter could look after herself very well. Perhaps too well, Maria sometimes thought.

Anna had found the first year studies rather challenging; but she worked hard and had been successful. By the time she had completed her first year away and returned for the mid-1958 summer vacation, then departed again for Paris, Maria was almost used to her daughter's long absences, but she had few friends and still missed Anna greatly. Her daughter's brief Christmas visit restored Maria's spirits but it would be many long months before the summer when Anna would complete her studies at 'Science-Po' and be back home. And who could know where her future might be after that.

# Sixty

Throughout the 1950's life in France had been better than in the tougher immediate post-war era. Still, the decade that was now coming to a close had also been difficult at times. Aside from a continually weak economy, there were serious political tensions. There was wide public distrust of all politicians and serious instability in France's political institutions. The 1946 constitutional changes had created the era known as the *Quatrième République* (Fourth Republic) and it had been troubled. Under it, the country had been run by a succession of coalition governments, with twenty different Prime Ministers in a little over a decade and a President who was not much more than a figurehead. The regime was frail and unpopular.

At the same time, many members of the French establishment still felt humiliation and bitterness over France's failure to regain control of the country's pre-war colonies in Indo-China. Colonialism continued to be popular in Europe and the costly loss of Vietnam and Cambodia had been followed by civil disturbances and insurrection in other French colonies from Madagascar, off south-east Africa, to Tunisia, but particularly in Algeria.

As the decade passed, the situation in Algeria only seemed to be going from bad to worse.

Algeria meant more to France than just a colony. It was an important French territory in North Africa, just across the Mediterranean Sea and due south of continental France. It had been administered as part of France since the Second Republic was created in 1848; a little less than two decades after the French army conquered Algeria. However, a century later, the many Muslim Algerian soldiers who'd fought for France in the Second World War returned home dissatisfied with a political system that gave the Christian colonists six times more political representation than indigenous Muslims were allowed. Worse still, self-government was an illusion. Even though the governing council was an elected body, it possessed only advisory powers. This inequity fostered powerful popular moves for independence and persistent violent dissent.

Even in mainland France, political deadlock had developed over the increasingly heated issue of Algerian independence. Then, in May 1958, Algeria was gripped by a right-wing military coup and the military's influence even extended north into the French island of Corsica. The military command in Algeria threatened to try to take over mainland France unless the aging General De Gaulle was once again put in charge of the country. It would have meant civil war. De Gaulle was still a respected figure, but he'd withdrawn from political life years earlier. This all too real threat of a further military coup and civil war brought about the final downfall of the Fourth Republic that De Gaulle had himself helped create at the end of the Second World War.

Quick action was taken and in mid-1958 the government asked the old General to return from retirement and become Head of State. A cynic might have drawn a parallel to the return of old *Maréchal* Pétain to power in 1941. De Gaulle agreed, but only on condition that there would be a new constitution with stronger presidential powers. This was accepted and his return to office heralded in a new French Constitution creating a more stable and permanent Fifth Republic

However, the Algerian crisis was far from over. De Gaulle had returned under the popular banner: "Vive l'Algérie Française!" or Long Live a French Algeria! He sought to perpetuate Algeria's status as just another *département* or administrative region of France. It was an unrealistic plan that would prove quickly to be unworkable. What was referred to as the Algerian War of Independence had already begun in 1954 and it was only in 1962 that it would finally end with complete Algerian independence. But that was later.

These various political crises were unfolding against a domestic background of an increasing social division between the left and right of the political spectrum; though there may be little difference between both extremes. The Soviet Union-backed French communist party continued to entrench its considerable political power and control over unions and workers' movements in the nation's major industries. At the same time, right wing political and para-military groups were finding many adherents, especially in the ranks of ex-military, army and the police forces.

One of the bastions of right wing sentiment was the French riot police or the CRS (Compagnie républicaine de sécurité), which paradoxically, had its origins in the 'Forces républicaine de sécurité' (FRS), founded in 1944 by the controversial communist activist Raymond Aubrac. His appointment as Liberation Commissioner in Marseilles with wide-ranging executive powers turned out to be problematic. It was an era of some of the worst mob violence and excesses of the French liberation. During the liberation, the beatings, public humiliations and other excesses that occurred in Paris and other parts of the country were bad enough, but in Marseille and the surrounding region there was a reign of terror involving multiple killings, torture and unjust imprisonments. In January 1945, De Gaulle had Aubrac replaced. To his credit; Aubrac had immediately liberated the inmates of a work camp at Mazargues where thousands of Vietnamese workers imported from the colonies had been kept in deplorable conditions for several years during the war. This marked the beginning of his long friendship with Vietnamese communist fellow traveller Ho Chi Minh, a political figure who would return to haunt post-war France in the 1950s and the rest of the western world in the 1960s and early 1970s. Indeed, the troubles and political activism of Vietnamese in the work camp of Mazargues and elsewhere in France continued for several more years. The power of the communists in France at that time and the complexities of the post-war period were such that Aubrac would have a highly successful future career, notably as a China specialist in France's administration.

So it was perhaps understandable that more than a decade after the war's end, deep divisions, conflicts and undercurrents of anger, distrust, hatred and violence still existed in the community.

§

BEGINNINGS                                    Gary Heilbronn

Maria, like many people, tried to stay aloof from such poisonous political issues, though in her heart she suspected that both the communists and the extreme right had had a hand in the betrayal and capture of Max so many years before. But being herself a refugee from fascism just across the border, she kept her suspicions to herself and hoped only to live peacefully in obscurity and protect what was left of her small family.

As the 'fifties decade ended, Maria was in her mid-forties. She had finally resigned herself to an acceptance of the injustices that war and political upheaval always bring to ordinary people.

But it was not so for Anna and her friends with purer convictions. They could not help but be appalled by the hypocrisy and political compromises entered into by a government that seemed to have allowed many of those complicit in the worst atrocities of not only the Second World War, but also the Spanish Civil War, to escape punishment and even prosper while innocents suffered like pawns in the power-plays of gangsters and fanatics.

When Anna passionately raised such points, as she often did, Maria's response was the same:

"But has it not always been so?"

Yet Anna was far from convinced that nothing could be done. To Anna and her friends, it seemed that suffering and injustice were everywhere in the world. And for many young French people, especially those of Basque origin, this was most manifest in the politics of nearby Spain, still under the conservative authoritarian rule of General Franco.

It was common knowledge that throughout the two decades following the end of the civil war in Spain, the victorious nationalists, under Franco, had continued to persecute and oppress their republican opponents. To avoid Franco's secret police, many of the republican leaders had 'gone underground', not only in their homeland but also across the border in France. But with the passage of time they were reorganizing and re-surfacing.

Already, back in 1945, various Basque factions and exiled leaders of political parties had met in Bayonne to sign an agreement creating organized resistance councils. However, in the post-war years until

1951, resistance was largely passive with sit-ins by young activist catholic priests and strikes. But there were always those who were convinced of the need for more violent action. Some even planned robberies to secure much-needed funds for formative terrorist harassment, sporadic bombing campaigns and assassinations. While in those early post-war days, the unholy alliance of Catholic extremists and Marxists may have been historically intelligible within the Basque independence movement, but it was doomed to fail. In due course, the leftist and anti-religious precepts set out in Frederico Krutwig's book, <u>Vasconia</u> would become a bit part of the philosophical basis of the Basque separatist movement.

Not surprisingly, during these years the response level of the Spanish Guardia Civil's corps of secret police was being gradually elevated to meet the growing underground political opposition. Forays into France by undercover Guardia agents seeking out militants who might pose a threat were denied though an open secret, especially to the Basque exiles. But this undercover police activity was not official and could not be proved; nor was there proof of the close co-operation that existed between right-wing factions in both countries.

Through her contacts in Bayonne who had links with the Basque separatists, Maria and Anna had learned that in 1954, a group of Basque students at the University of Duestro near Bilbao had set up a separatist group called *Ekin* and its agenda soon evolved from mere distribution of propaganda to direct action under the banner of the ETA – *Euskadi Ta Askatasuna* or Basque Homeland and Freedom. However, it would not be until 31 July 1959 that activists who were increasingly unhappy with what they perceived as the moderate stance of the Basque Nationalist Party, in exile since the Civil War, formally turned ETA into an armed nationalist and separatist organization.

The fact that Anna found herself present at this meeting and even more so, the reason for her presence, would remain unknown, except perhaps to one or two of the persons intimately involved, although none would ever even guess the full drama of those circumstances.

## Sixty-One

Maria passed her days quietly in Bayonne, carrying out her duties at the Museum and missing Anna's lively presence after her departure for Paris. She had few friends. For the first year Anna was away, she had written to her mother every Friday, posting her letters on Saturday at the local post office so that they would arrive usually with the following Monday's mail delivery. Maria was comforted by this regular contact; it let her know that all was well and that her daughter was happy and working hard at her studies. What more could Anna do?

Anna's only outside activity that she spoke of was a martial arts course. Apart from playing Pelote to a high standard, she'd practised martial arts for several years in Bayonne and now threw herself into the classes in Paris with considerable passion. It helped channel her energies and in particular, it satisfied her need for physical exertion. It was a need that was otherwise difficult to fulfil in the big city of Paris, especially as the weather wasn't as good as it was in Bayonne. Of course Anna's natural athletic ability, physicality and strength made her an adept martial arts student, and she quickly acquired considerable expertise.

From the beginning of her second year away, Anna corresponded less frequently with her mother and there was a touch of anxiety in Maria's heart as she read between the lines of her daughter's more sporadic letters. Anna rarely mentioned her social life nor spoke of her increasing involvement with young political activists who spent most evenings in the dark smoky cafés that dotted the backstreets of Paris' legendary *Saint-Germain-des-Prés* district. These hangouts were a magnet to bright and politically motivated young people as well as to the Parisian intellectual community.

*Saint-Germain-des-Prés* is quite close to the 'Sciences-Po' buildings and where many of the students live. It's at the centre of Parisian life. To its south lies the elaborate *Jardin du Luxembourg* where the magnificent Senate building is situated, and the *Jardin des*

BEGINNINGS                                    Gary Heilbronn

*Plantes* is just a little further to the east, past the Faculties of the Sorbonne University. A little to the north of *Saint-Germain-des-Prés* is 'les Beaux-Arts' – the *École National des Beaux-Arts* – and directly opposite it, on the northern or *'rive droite'* side of the river Seine, stands the renowned *Musée du Louvre*. The *Assemblée Nationale* at the *Quai d'Orsay* and the offices of several French Government Ministries are off to the west, further along the *Boulevard Saint Germain*.

In such an environment and in view of her studies, Anna could hardly help but be immersed in the deeply enmeshed worlds of Parisian culture, politics and intellectual debate. In fact, she was both stimulated and appalled by it.

Many of Anna's classmates at 'Sciences-Po' came from what could be described as 'establishment' backgrounds. But there were a few students; some a little older, who leaned more towards anti-establishment views and humanist values; especially those then espoused by the writer Albert Camus. At just forty-five years of age, Camus was awarded the 1957 Nobel Prize for literature, mainly for his writings opposing capital punishment. But there was also the influence of intellectuals such as Simone de Beauvoir and Jean-Paul Sartre who seemed to embrace a period of political engagement throughout the 1950's in Paris. These giant personalities of literature and philosophy frequented the *Café de Flore* and *Les Deux Magots* on the wide and bustling *Boulevard Saint-Germain*; both were well-known gathering places of the Parisian intellectual and literary elite. Some years earlier, de Beauvoir and Sartre had fallen out with Camus who had publicly rejected communism and perhaps for family more than political reasons – as he was brought up in North Africa – had sought a compromise solution to calls for Algerian independence.

After Anna had conscientiously devoted herself to her studies in her first year in Paris, she had begun to widen her horizons in her second year there. In the winter months of early 1959, she often sat and listened to the passionate intellectual and political discussions raging in these smoke-filled cafés, sometimes late into the night. Although she admired the writings of the intellectuals and philosophers, she could not help but feel an edge of contempt for all their talk about political oppression.

"It's just talk and no action" she thought aloud to herself.

She could not hide a hint of bitterness and more than a touch of anger that these idle intellectuals did little more than 'trade-in' on the work of real political activists; the people who risked their lives and their freedom by fighting for their beliefs. Ironically, some years later Sartre would himself renounce his 1964 Nobel Prize for literature asserting that literature was a bourgeois substitute for real commitment. But that was later.

Among the more politically active students inhabiting the Parisian intellectual underworld at that time were several of Basque origin, though like Anna, they were also French citizens. Some had been contacted by older Basque republicans-in-exile; people who were members and supporters of the ousted Basque government and who had twenty years beforehand fled from their homeland into France. They were amongst the half a million republican sympathizers who were exiled in 1938 and 1939; many of whom had been placed in internment camps. Some were even deported to Nazi extermination camps in Eastern Europe at the hands of the Vichy government and their Nazi masters.

More than a decade after the end of the war, a few of those exiles who still harboured the dreams and hatreds of their youth, resurfaced or returned from comfortable lives in France, in America and other parts of Europe. They came back to work for the Basque cause from relatively safe bases in France. Some were now approaching middle age and had become heroes to the young student activists. Perhaps naively, none thought to question their motives or even to ask where the older men's funding was coming from, as they deftly pursued the politicizing of their young protégés.

Unsurprisingly, it was not long before the activities of these little Parisian cells of Basque activists came to the attention of Franco's secret police. Their agents made regular attempts to infiltrate the cells, identify their leaders and if need be, eliminate them. They acted in secret and bodies of victims were rarely found.

BEGINNINGS                                              Gary Heilbronn

Not many of the younger Guardia officers spoke euskara well enough to perform this task without arousing suspicion, but a few of the older, more senior officers who'd spent part of their younger lives in the Basque country spoke the language almost as well as true-born Basques. One such man operated under the name of Juan Herrerro, though it was of course not his real name and he was, in fact, a colonel in the *Guardia Civil*'s secret police. He also spoke near-perfect French – he was not a man devoid of talents and was even considered to be rather charming when the occasion required. He was not the sort of man who had many friends but was an efficient, ambitious and if necessary, ruthless, officer who pleased his superiors and had risen steadily through the ranks.

Herrerro was still slim and strong and somewhat more than medium height, with dark-hair. He had a tanned almost swarthy complexion and a heavy beard growth that meant he often shaved twice a day. His only distinguishing feature was a long straight narrow scar on his right temple, caused by a bullet that had grazed his head back during the dying days of the Civil War. He never spoke of it. He was bitter and even a little humiliated that it had been a wound suffered not in the heat of battle but from the cowardly action of a hidden sniper – an attempted assassination when he was minding his own business on guard duty on a quiet border crossing into France.

How he despised the people behind such random attacks and how ferocious had been his revenge in the days that followed. With what even his soldiers had thought was excessive zeal, he'd conducted a series of raids on local villages seeking out republican partisans. Few of the sympathizers to the cause who still lived there had escaped his wrath. Many of the others died agonizing deaths.

Herrerro now found himself in Paris. He was not a lazy man; far from it. Although now in his very late forties, he exercised regularly. Though perhaps not as fit as he was in his twenties, what he had lost in fitness and speed, he had gained in guile and cunning.

It was not surprising that there were women who found him very attractive. A number of the affluent and easily-impressed female 'hangers-on' in the cafés where Parisian intellectuals congregated had found something  exciting in his steely, almost sociopathic, empty eyes and had no difficulty luring him into brief and often violent romantic liaisons. They usually learned their lesson quickly and soon faded out of his life or were discarded. Yet there seemed to be an endless supply of such women; although after a while, the word seemed to get around about him and it was only the newcomer or the wilder, thrill-seeker who focussed her attention on him. At least he did not smoke and stink of those cheap cigarettes; the ones whose pungent, eye-watering fumes permeated the night air and eroded the lungs of the regulars in these cafés as they sipped happily away on their tall murky *verres de Ricard* or deeply purplish *vin rouge*. They seemed not even to care that the tannic red wines were too young to enjoy and lacked delicacy.

## Sixty-Two

Undercover agent Herrerro was good at his job. He made sure that he was not too frequent a patron of any particular café. He visited them all at different times, even the cheaper student hang-outs. He usually sat at or near the bar, listening, making sure not to watch anyone too closely, but glancing furtively at the other customers. His mind was working in overdrive to decide if anyone's face was familiar or if it matched the often badly focussed, grainy photos and sketches of 'persons of interest' that filled the old files in the Guardia secret police's Headquarters in Barcelona. Before his departure to Paris, he had spent several weeks based there just memorizing the faces and the personal details of known and suspected Basque dissidents.

It was probably inevitable that before long Herrerro would chance upon the little café that Anna tended to frequent. She usually arrived later on those cold winter evenings after having completed the revision of her class work or having exhausted herself at martial arts training. And so it was to be, on a Friday night in late January 1959.

The experienced undercover officer had been maintaining surveillance of a small group of Basque students there. He'd seen them meeting occasionally with an older man who he thought resembled a sketch of the face of one of those exiles that he'd committed to memory. The man was much older now, but Herrerro was pretty confident that he'd identified the likely organizer of a cell of possible activists. The older man was now marked for elimination, but in the meantime his circle of contacts had to be identified and fully checked-out.

As it happened, the young students he had been meeting were part of Anna's broader circle of friends and when she entered the café and noticed them sitting at a round wooden table well away from the bar, she naturally went over to greet them.

"Salut Anna" she heard. She was greeted by the smiling fresh-face of a young man with curly dark hair.

"Come, sit and have a drink with us" he said

The others also welcomed her warmly, although there was one slightly older young man who she did not know.

"Sure, I'd love to" she replied politely. There was no-one that she'd planned to meet and although these boys were not her close friends, they had similar backgrounds and family circumstances to her and so she was happy enough to sit with them. The young man she did not know was introduced casually to her as Yann. It seemed of so little consequence then, but sitting with them this evening would turn out to be a decision that would change the course of her life.

The boys had been at the café for some time and having consumed a few glasses of rosé wine, they were already in a lively mood, laughing and joking, perhaps making a little more noise than they would have done if their discussions were more serious and of a more political nature.

The older man who often sat with them in the café was not there that night. He was a smallish, grey-haired and discreet Basque exile. He usually directed the course of their discussions and their anger away from the contemporary Algerian crisis and the militarist tendencies that they perceived in the French government under the Fifth Republic, and more towards the unhappy state of the Basque people under the fascist Franco regime. As that latter cause was a little more distant for these young men, the anger they felt was usually quieter and their reactions somewhat more subdued.

Nonetheless, they were always so passionate and so self-absorbed that they failed completely to notice the interest that their little group evoked in a few of the cafés other patrons; men seated in the shadows or more anonymously around the edges of the bar surreptitiously sipping small glasses of *pression* – lager pumped from pressurized beer kegs beneath the counter. These half-hidden watchers were undercover police and informers of various complexions, usually well-disguised as students, out-of-work intellectuals or aspiring writers and artists. They seemed to fit easily into this environment. So only those obsessively suspicious by nature – or perhaps with a learned response to danger and more acutely aware of the threats that lurked in unexpected places – would have noticed the furtiveness in the glances of the men charged with their surveillance and the often over-careful attempts to appear wholly uninterested in the objects of their attentions.

It was just after quarter past nine that night, when a trim figure of a little more than medium height, with a swarthy complexion and penetrating dark eyes sidled into the dingy café. He skirted the central room staying half in the shadows and sat quietly down at the corner of the bar furthest from where Anna's friends' table was situated. He softly ordered a coffee when the bartender passed by and seemed absorbed in reading a few straggling pages of a newspaper that remained on the bar-top surface.

Glancing around the room without perceptibly looking away from the newspaper, he noticed the young men who'd previously been in the company of the older Basque exile he'd been keeping under surveillance. Moving slowly, his eyes settled on a shock of long, thick dark hair on the back of the head of a woman seated at their table. For some indiscernible reason his gaze lay on the back of her head for longer than he would normally permit. Something in his mind, working seemingly in slow-motion, rekindled a deep feeling of hidden emotion and flicked back to memories of that day when he had so ignominiously earned the scar on the side of his face.

"How strange," he thought. It seemed like ages since he had recalled those events. But Herrerro knew to trust his instincts.

As his frozen gaze lingered, the dark-haired head turned slightly to the left, revealing an attractive, healthy though rather pale young face. It was a face that he did not recognize at all; yet it was somehow familiar. Thick lazy curls covered the small round, rosy stain on left side of her neck. But even if he'd seen it, would he have known what it meant; would it have made a difference? His mind focussed, he checked his gaze and peered down at the pages of the newspaper in front of him. But it was not before Anna had felt a chill of fear and hatred that instantly gave birth to something cold and steely within her. It heightened her senses.

BEGINNINGS  Gary Heilbronn

She had experienced such feelings before, usually in connection with vivid dreams of ancient battles and of peoples fighting for survival, though she didn't fully understand the feelings. Her eyes moved quickly around the room, stopping briefly on a face or figure here and there until finally coming to rest on the swarthy man sitting at the bar, seeming to be so absorbed in his newspaper.

Her mind was intensely focussed, working fast, as if the world was moving in slow motion. Barely seconds had passed before she returned her regard to her young friends as if nothing had happened, joining in their conversation with guarded, now slightly forced animation. She had not noticed that the young man who her friends had introduced to her as Yann had also been aware of the interest that the dark complexioned man at the bar had been showing in them, and especially in Anna.

Indeed, he had watched Anna as her demeanour tensed and she had studied the now seemingly indifferent man at the bar. Yann felt slightly uneasy but said nothing.

Otherwise, the evening passed uneventfully. Herrerro was too experienced at undercover work ever to act precipitously. He studiously avoided looking in the direction of the Basque students' table but kept a lookout towards the door to make sure he didn't miss their departure. He had already, on previous evenings followed the boys to their various tiny apartments and rooms, but the presence of Anna presented him with a new and unexpected target. He had no reason to suspect her participation in any terrorist cell but she unnerved him and he could not be quite sure why that was. But he trusted his instincts and they told him that this girl was of considerable interest. He ordered a *pression* from the barman and slowly sipped his beer, making it last as long as possible. He sat on it for over an hour; somewhat to the barman's annoyance.

Anna was also feeling a little anxious from what she had experienced earlier in the evening. As the hours passed, she glanced a few more times in the direction of the swarthy man but at no time did he meet her eye; nor did she catch him looking in her direction. Anna drank only soft drinks and nothing was dulling her senses when she decided to leave the café a little after 11pm. She debated in her own mind whether or not to ask the boys to escort her home but decided she was most likely better off without them. She lived less than ten minutes away and knew the area intimately. Normally she would rather not walk home alone but tonight was different. She wanted to have her wits about her and having their company would only distract her.

"*A bientôt, les gars*" she said eventually, bidding her friends goodbye and rising. She moved quickly towards the door. The boys began to shuffle in their seats and start to stand up but she had already left. They sat again; shaking their heads. "That Anna was a strange one" the younger boys all thought to themselves. She couldn't even wait to properly say goodbye to each of them. Three fleeting kisses on the cheeks was the usual practice amongst the young in Paris and for many of those young men, it was the closest they would get to experience the feel of their female classmate's soft, slightly perfumed skin. But quickly their party mood returned and she was almost immediately forgotten; except by Yann who discreetly kept one eye on her as she left and the other on the swarthy man at the bar.

Anna went towards the restroom as if to stop over there but seemed to change her mind and was quickly out the door. On instinct she decided to walk in the direction opposite to the small studio apartment where she lived.

Before she reached the corner where she intended to turn to see if she was being followed, Herrerro had exited the café and hidden himself in a shadowy shop entrance. From there he was able to see Anna walk away but without her being able to see him. He stayed there long enough to see her turn the corner then poke her head briefly back around, but lower down, at about thigh height. She had obviously crouched down before looking back. He smiled in appreciation of her skills or perhaps just animal instincts. She had either been well trained in counter-surveillance or she was 'a natural'. Given her young age, he thought that the latter was more likely. But in that instant, his interest in her multiplied.

Anna's instincts were good but not up to a level that would enable her to shake off such an experienced surveillance agent as

# BEGINNINGS                        Gary Heilbronn

Herrerro.  On the other hand, he knew he had to be extra cautious and he followed her discreetly in the shadows.  He was not surprised when he noticed her double back towards the café when she was confident that she had not been followed and then he kept a safe distance until he saw her enter the old building where her studio apartment was situated.  He waited outside until he saw a light go on in a window on the third floor.

He then went swiftly to the building door, entered without difficulty and looked for the row of residents' letter boxes.  They were near the staircase and he made a note of the several of the names, one of which was Anna's.  He could now have these names checked out and would be back later to keep her discreetly under surveillance.  He was not in a hurry but he knew somehow that she would be important to him and his work.  With all his interest in Anna, Herrerro had failed to see that he himself had been followed.  Yann had quietly excused himself to his friends, citing the need to work on his thesis, and a few moments after Herrerro's departure, he had followed very discreetly at a safe distance and keeping to the shadows to ensure that Anna was all right, though she did not even know she'd been followed.

Yann, however, was very concerned by what he had witnessed that evening.

Nor did Anna forget this encounter in the café, but the weeks passed and she did not see the swarthy man again.  She even went intentionally to the same café at the same time to see if he would be there.  He wasn't, and she sat briefly with her friends again, Yann included.

Gradually she let her guard down just a little but could not stop herself keeping up a certain vigilance; though she sometimes thought it was verging on paranoia.  Yet she knew deep down in her heart that there had been a turning point in her life and that the safety and security which she had felt here in Paris and for all of her years growing up in Bayonne may now be a thing of the past.

## Sixty-Three

The months passed. Anna concentrated on her studies. It was the last year of her-two year course at 'Sciences-Po' and she wanted to get good grades in her final examinations. She rarely went to the cafés in *Saint-Germain-des-Prés*, but spent more and more of any spare time she did have, in training at her martial arts classes.

Perhaps, all that training was an unconscious response to her increased anxiety. The physical demands of the classes calmed her and increased her confidence in herself. She trained three or four times a week. She was starting to attain a good level of proficiency and the free-fighting sessions that she increasingly excelled in began to make her feel that she could handle herself well in any physical confrontation. None occurred. It was as if even those arrogant young men looking for weakness and easy sexual conquests, who often cross the paths of attractive young women, sensed that she was not to be trifled with.

At that time she allowed herself to socialize only once each week and even less than that with her young Basque student friends. Yet the intensity of her disgust with the fascist elements that she saw in both the right and left political camps and the injustices they practised seemed only to increase. Her mother had talked of the persecutions and killings carried out by the fascist Franco regime in Spain; as well as the nazi deportations and the extermination of Jews, gypsies, communists, Spanish republicans and dissidents of all complexions. But Anna had not really understood what fascism was. Now, her studies focussed her mind on this concept. She found that there was much controversy over the definition of 'fascism' and she thought long and hard about the different views.

Of course, there were apologists for the fascism of the Second World War dictators: Mussolini, Hitler, Franco; and other extreme right wing groups. And they were strangely still popular with some people, despite being discredited by the horrors of the Second World War. Notably, there was Charles Maurras, President of the strongly catholic, monarchist and anti-semitic group, Action Française, who in a seemingly chilling and cynical appeal to ordinary workers, tellingly described 'fascism' as: *a socialism emancipated from democracy*. This group had supported *Maréchal* Pétain and the collaborationist Vichy regime during the German occupation of France, but had been condemned by the church and outlawed after the liberation. Doubtless, Maurras was talking about the 'national socialism' of the Nazis and not the 'socialism' of its chief political competitor, the communists, though both these groups rejected the economic exploitation practised by the bourgeoisie and saw the working class as their power base.

The Marxists, on the other hand, argued that fascism was the last attempt of the ruling class to preserve its grip on power with the aid of funding from big business. In his book, Fascism: What is it and How to Fight it, Leon Trotsky painted a more purist picture of fascism, explaining that:

*The historic function of fascism is to smash the working class, destroy its organizations and stifle political liberties when the capitalists find themselves unable to govern and dominate with the help of democratic machinery.*

At nearer to the middle of the politico-economic spectrum, Franklin Delano Roosevelt, thirty-second President of the United States from 1933 to 1945, during the heyday of fascism in Italy, Spain and Germany and those terrible war years, had said in his 1938 Message to Congress which had been republished in Time Magazine on 9 May 1938 and elsewhere, that:

*The first truth is that liberty of a democracy is not safe if the people tolerate the growth of private power to a point where it becomes stronger than their democratic state itself. That, in its essence, is fascism – ownership of government by an individual, by a group, or by any other controlling private power.*

"Was this not" Anna asked herself "a strangely prescient statement in view of the rise of the military-industrial complex and the 'fourth estate' – the press? Perhaps democracy is an illusion."

After reading widely on the topic and with all these views in mind, she hazarded her own definition of fascism: "In essence, fascism is an authoritarian form of government through which a privileged social and economic class seeks to maintain its privileges by actively persecuting or denying democratic equality to other segments of the society usually because of their beliefs or social and economic circumstances."

"Maybe this definition is too general," she thought "as it seems to be exactly the political structure that both capitalism and communism adopt in practice."

"But maybe that only proves the validity of the definition!" she told herself. "This seems evident," Anna thought to herself, "from the ways that the multi-national companies from the USA and elsewhere had profited from supplying and supporting the Spanish nationalists and the German Nazis at least up to the time when their home countries were forced into the Second World War. It was evident too," she thought, "from the way the Soviets had infiltrated the French resistance movements during the war and then how, after the war, they had enslaved the people in the 'Soviet bloc' countries".

In Anna's young eyes, fascism was still alive and well and all too common in the modern world.

"Has nothing been learned from the horrors of the last three decades?" she continually asked herself.

But instinctively she knew only too well what the answer was. It was that fascism, in its many forms and guises, devoid of any moral foundations and bereft of any limits on the methods used to achieve its ends, is and always has been one of the most implacable vehicles for the acquisition and perpetuation of power and wealth in the world.

It was a force that was always just below the surface of civilized behaviour and if left unchecked, would all too quickly show its ugly disingenuous face and practise its violent, repressive tactics.

# Sixty-Four

Finally, Herrerro received the information he had been waiting for.  The anonymous brown envelope he held contained a report from the central intelligence files of the Guardia Civil in Madrid and it was surprisingly brief.  It had taken some considerable digging into the archives for the security officers back in Spain to locate any information on the girl who might be one of the several possible names Herrerro had taken from the letterboxes in Anna's apartment building.  He also sent a photograph that he had managed to take surreptitiously on one of his irregular surveillance expeditions to the building.  He had noticed that she had lowered her guard of late but he had nonetheless been careful.  Herrerro was sure that she had not seen her stalker.

Perhaps unwisely, Maria had not changed her family name when she escaped to Bayonne.  She'd used a fake identity to cross the border but was concerned that records had been kept of those people who crossed over, so she immediately started using her proper name Maria Abene y Perea.  Soon afterwards, to avoid attracting attention and with the virtual certainty of the death of her husband, Alberto, she dropped his name and her daughter had been registered with the local authorities and brought up simply as Anna Abene, one of the names that Herrerro had noted down from the letterboxes on the ground floor of the old apartment building in Paris.

So it wasn't long before the Guardia files were unearthed on a woman identified as Maria Abene, with details of her marriage to Alberto Perea, his subsequent political activities and his execution near the end of the civil war.  It also noted the suspicion that Maria had fled the country through the Hendaye border crossing and had disappeared in France with the aid of republican sympathizers.  The photograph Herrerro had sent back to headquarters had confirmed the identification.  It was very similar to the sketches in Maria's file. Anna very much resembled her mother when she was young.

A copy of those sketches of Maria, profile and frontal view, were included with the report sent to Herrerro. He visibly paled when his eyes scanned the sketches that he removed from the neat brown envelope. The scene on the old iron bridge at the Hendaye border crossing some twenty years beforehand flashed vividly into his mind.

"It was she. It was the woman who'd caused him to be shot and his face to be scarred for life. It was she who was responsible for the humiliation that he carried for most of his adult years, more than two decades of having to explain that not only had he been scarred by a terrorist's sniper's bullet, but that he had failed in his duties. He had failed to carry out even such a menial task as to prevent a pregnant woman slipping through his border control."

He smiled grimly and his dark eyes blazed. He knew that his moment of vengeance approached.

He did not question why it was that he felt so deeply humiliated. A psycho-analyst might have looked more closely at his psyche for an explanation of how he felt and his burning need for revenge. To him, it just seemed that it had taken forever to come to this point and inadvertently, he caressed the small, finely sharpened bronze-bladed knife that been passed down to him by his grandfather. It was of primarily ornamental and sentimental value – though sentiment was a luxury he did not permit himself. But he carried it always and had used it rarely; only on occasions when the pain he inflicted on his enemies had been of special, personal, almost spiritual significance.

§

Warmer, sunnier days were now more common in Paris and spring was in full bloom by the time Anna had completed her second year 'Sciences-Po' examinations. It was a relief and she was full of love for life, enjoying the crisp early morning air as she jogged over the bridge across the river Seine and through the *Jardin du Luxembourg*. Later, on her way home, she'd bask in the warmth of the mid-morning sun while enjoying a light breakfast outside one or another of the pavement cafés in the *Rue de Seine*.

Despite a slow start, she had studied more than in the previous year and had little concern about having done well enough to pass. But it was still a relief to have the examinations over with. Anna was looking forward to heading back home to Bayonne in a couple of weeks' time when she'd sorted out a few things in Paris. She planned to leave her small studio apartment and move elsewhere so she would need to find a place to store the few belongings she'd be leaving behind. There wasn't much. Personal things she would take with her. She had not corresponded very regularly with Maria over the last several months and of course, she'd avoided giving any indication to her mother of the disquiet she'd felt during that time. She didn't want to worry her. Now that the pressure of studies was off, Anna felt free to resume her visits to the local cafés and to socialize with her friends again on a more regular basis. So it was only for the second time since that worrying evening in late January, that Anna was again sitting with exactly the same group of young Basque friends in that same café. She was relaxed, but all that changed when she caught a glimpse of the swarthy middle-aged man whose scrutiny of her had caused her such concern all those months ago.

Her heart sank as the intense anxiety that she had gradually succeeded in shedding over the last months returned. Her breathing was laboured and she had some difficulty in keeping control of her emotions. She closed her eyes, looked down and began to breathe deeply and evenly. After a few moments, the anxiety subsided and she felt even more calm and clear-headed than usual.

When she eventually looked around again, the man had disappeared. It was a sobering experience. Anna resolved not to spend more time than necessary in the capital and to return home to her mother as soon as possible. She felt that she needed to alert her friends. But what should she say? She had only her anxieties and suspicions. Surely they were not so naïve as to imagine that there were not some police informers and undercover agents around. At last she decided to speak.

"Did it ever occur to you guys that there may be police informers and people like that in here?  I've just seen the same man watching us as I saw some time ago."

"Really, where is he?" the youngest said, looking quickly around the café.  But he was nowhere to be seen.

"Nah.  It's probably just some old guy who thinks you're cute," laughed another student called Javier.  He had said he came from Biarritz and was sitting next to the other older, quieter young man she barely knew, called Yann.  She looked at him quizzically. "Why was he so dismissive of her concerns?"  Was he all he seemed?" she thought.  Or maybe she was becoming paranoid.

"Well, don't say I didn't warn you." she said just a bit derisively as she got up to leave.  Yann watched her go but did not speak.  He knew she was right.

Herrerro was quietly overjoyed to have seen the young woman again in the company of the Basque boys in that little café and he left the café immediately.  If anything, it confirmed his suspicions that she was indeed likely to be involved with the possible terrorist cell that he'd been keeping under regular surveillance.  With the new sighting, he felt that now he could call on friendly contacts in the French intelligence community to find out more information on the young woman.  They'd have access to government files and educational records and very soon he'd know all he needed to know about her.

Of course, there was no formal agreement for cooperation between the French secret service, the *'Direction Générale de la Police Nationale'* and its Spanish counterpart, but informal relations existed, often merely between individual agents who helped each other out unofficially.  Such undocumented mutual assistance was easily tolerated by both agencies and their ministries.

## Sixty-Five

Anna discreetly and with perhaps prescient finality organized her affairs in Paris. She tidied everything up as quickly as possible and took the train back to Bayonne in late May. It was just in time for her twentieth birthday. Maria was overjoyed to see her home early, meeting her at the Bayonne railway station, the *Gare de Bayonne*, housed in its mid-nineteenth century edifice near *Place Perreire* on the northern side of the city. The railway station was in the *Quartier Saint Esprit* not far from the centre of the town and the confluence of the river Nive with the much larger river Adour. The area was an immigrant quarter and still retained its historic character.

In late Spring, the sun shone brightly and there were several degrees difference in temperature between Paris and Bayonne. The warmer weather suited Anna and especially Maria whose upbringing had been in the still hotter climes of northern Spain. Anna had all but left behind her, all the anxieties of the past few months and was beginning to feel safe back on her home ground. She quickly renewed contact with her old friends and within the first week home had even returned to her martial arts training at her old club. Her friends there watched her admiringly, impressed with the progress she had made.

Maria was feeling more content than she had for some time though she inwardly suspected that Anna had not told her everything about how her life was going in Paris. Was she not completely happy there? Perhaps she had a boyfriend who she was reluctant to speak about. "After all, she's a young woman now," she mused to herself. She resolved to broach the subject before too long but was reluctant to impinge on her daughter's private life. More and more there seemed to be a secret place in her daughter's life that no-one else could enter – not even her mother. Yet she was finding it increasingly difficult to stay silent. She need not have worried. It was Anna who brought up the subject at the dinner table at the end of her first week home.

"You know Mother, I've been wanting to talk to you" she said softly.

"What is it, dear?" Maria responded a little anxiously. She started to imagine all sorts of things.

"You know that there are quite a few other young people of Basque background studying with me in Paris. Most are boys." Anna said slowly. Maria began to suspect that she was right in thinking that there was indeed a boyfriend on the scene.

"Is there someone special, my dear?" she said brightly.

"No. It's nothing like that." Anna replied a little annoyed.

"Oh, I'm sorry, dear." Maria replied. She spoke kindly.

"Listen mother, I don't really know what's going on, but twice when I've been in a café with a group of Basque students, I've had the strangest intense feeling that someone has been watching me. It's really been rather disconcerting."

"Oh my dear!" Maria began coldly, an emptiness opening up in her stomach. She knew only too well the feeling of being under surveillance and she was worried.

"Are you sure?" she said much more intensely.

"Did you actually see anyone suspicious?" Maria's mind was now back in 'security mode' – a state she had virtually forgotten about since the end of the Second World War in Saint-Sever. But years of being continually under threat both over the border in Spain and then during the last war had made an indelible mark on her psyche. She was all of a sudden very afraid but her senses were keen.

"You really need to be careful mixing with these boys. I've no doubt that there are Franco's spies everywhere, even in Paris and these people are assassins. Promise me you'll stay away from these boys and where they go. Do you know if they have contact with the Basque underground? That's what this is probably all about." Maria said matter-of-factly.

Anna was somewhat surprised. She had never thought of her mother as having any knowledge of such matters.

"And to be this cool about it all," she thought to herself. Anna began to be impressed and started to see her mother in a new light. Talking like this with Maria helped to relieve her anxieties somewhat.

"That must be it. I'll make sure I stay away from them and those cafés" Anna replied more brightly and changing the subject, said. "Well, I have several weeks' vacation now and I really plan to have a good time here. Perhaps we can go away together somewhere if you have some holidays?"

"That would be lovely. I'll try to arrange it." Maria said happy with the new direction of the conversation.

It was so good to have her daughter back home and feel that they were close once again. Pleasant thoughts ran through both their minds as they imagined where they might go on holiday together.

## Sixty-Six

Herrerro had little difficulty in convincing his contact in the Direction Générale to obtain background information on Anna. The French secret service was as keen to avoid harbouring foreign political activists as their Spanish counterpart was in locating and breaking up these cells. Within days, Herrerro had full details of Anna's home address, her mother's job and what they had been doing for the last two decades. He was not that concerned with the last part as all indications were that they led a quiet life and had no involvement with politics, although Maria's work with the Basque museum did raise some questions. It was suspected as being a possible meeting place for Basque activists but no clear evidence existed for this.

Within a few days, Herrerro had obtained clearance from his superiors to leave Paris and travel to the south-west. He was in no particular hurry but with the Parisian summer approaching, everything was slowing down there, including political activities. Tourists were beginning to drift into the city and congregate in the restaurants, cafés and around historical sites; changing the atmosphere of the place and driving most Parisians to their country houses or into a reclusive retreat in their own apartments.

It was mid-June before Herrerro stepped off the train in Bayonne's central railway station. Unusually, the sky was a little overcast and it had been raining. He had never really liked this part of France. Perhaps it held too many uncomfortable memories. So many of Spain's republican sympathizers had escaped into the region, though fortunately, he mused with some satisfaction, they had not been welcomed too kindly and many had been interned before being freighted off by the Nazis to work camps and even an early death.

"The Vichy Government had not really been that bad," he reflected.

"Serves these Republicans right" he thought coldly to himself, "the fewer of them that survived, the fewer I have had to worry about now." He seemed oblivious of the fact that it was 1959 and twenty years had passed since the exodus of the defeated Republicans from Spain. To him, like some of those exiled Republicans, the deep division between the two sides was still fresh in his mind.

Herrerro took a taxi from the railway station across the Adour River to the Grand Hotel on the *rue Thiers*. It did not take long for him to settle into this old-fashioned, discreet but comfortable hotel in central Bayonne. He soon obtained a map of the town from the hotel reception and as evening was approaching, he set out to familiarize himself with the area surrounding the address he had been given for Maria. He knew that the information he had obtained from the *Direction Générale* was not necessarily accurate nor was it up-to-date and it was important that he try to verify it by actual, visual sightings of either woman. If they could not be sighted, he could always try to follow Maria from her workplace at the Basque Museum. As it was, Herrerro was to be caused little inconvenience in this respect.

It was on his return visit the following morning that Herrerro sighted Maria leaving for work. His stomach churned as he saw her face. She was obviously older than he remembered but he was sure it was the same woman. He nonetheless decided to follow her and trailed her inconspicuously to her place of employment to be doubly sure of her identity. He saw that she was still an attractive woman and there was a certain elegance about her that he'd already remarked in her daughter when he'd observed the young woman surreptitiously in Paris. But the mother no longer had the fresh glow of youth that the younger woman had in ample supply.

Smiling to himself, he thought how much pleasure he would take in destroying both the elegance and the youthfulness of this pair of traitors. Such was his hatred. But so far he had not caught sight of Anna.

"Perhaps she's not at home and is spending time elsewhere," he mused. "Either way," he thought, "it will just be a question of time before both of them feel the full measure of the punishment I have in store for them."

He returned to his hotel. He was feeling uncomfortable. He poured himself a large whiskey. It was not like him to let his emotions impinge on his professional duties, but more and more, these two women pre-occupied his thoughts and challenged his cool professionalism. He couldn't believe that he was becoming obsessed with them.

§

Indeed, Anna had been out of town for a few days. She'd received a telephone call from one of her friends from 'Sciences-Po' in Paris and had been invited to spend a few days at the family beach house of another of her classmates just opposite the waterfront on the *Boulevard de la Mer* at *Hendaye Plage* – almost as close as you can get to the Basque country in Spain and still be in France.

Anna was a little reluctant to accept the invitation as the friend whose beach house it was, was the student who had made light of her anxieties about being under surveillance in the café in Paris earlier in the year. She remembered she'd told her mother she'd stay away from them. But she had been re-assured when it was made clear that there would be as many as a dozen of her Paris classmates at the beach house. And there would be a mixture of males and females, though some of the young women were not her classmates at 'Sciences-Po', where there were only a small percentage of women students. Of course, her classmate's parents would also be there but that would not interfere with the group's plan to celebrate the successful completion of their studies.

At that time, the usual undergraduate degree at that prestigious institution took two years to complete, though many students stayed on to continue their studies there or undertook different postgraduate courses at other educational or research institutions. Anna had no doubt that she would obtain her degree but had not wanted to decide finally what she would do next until she was sure of her ranking in the class. Ranking was so terribly important in the

French education system and would make a difference as to which of the several institutions that she'd applied to would indeed offer her a place. The results were to be released while she would be with her friends at the beach house and the plan was that they could all celebrate together. In these circumstances she felt that there was no way that she could refuse the invitation, even if it did cause her a little anxiety.

On the other hand, she was also a little intrigued by this young man and his family and was interested to find out more about them. Perhaps she would discover just how far they could be trusted.

# DAYS OF RECKONING

*Coastal Basque Country, France and Spain 1959*

## Map of France and Spain

## Sixty-Seven

The warm springtime days in Bayonne passed pleasantly for mother and daughter. Maria went to work at the Basque Museum and Anna was enjoying the time she was spending with her mother and catching up with old friends. Some evenings they went out to restaurants or cafés. Others they spent at home, but always they both revelled in each other's company It was as if Maria had found a soul-mate where once she had a young daughter. So it was with a little disappointment that she learned that Anna would be going away for a few days with her friends. Yet she was determined to put on a brave face and be happy for her daughter, even when she learned that Anna would be with her classmates when the final exam results were released.

Of course the official letter would come a day or two later, but they had arranged to obtain their results by telephone from a friend in Paris who would copy them down from the notice board when the ranking list was posted at 'Sciences-Po'.

It was just before 11am on Friday 19th of June when Anna telephoned Maria at work to let her know that she had been very successful in her examinations and was ranked in the top ten students for that year. This was indeed a cause for celebration. It had been a brief call as Maria was at work and private calls were discouraged. Anna assured her mother that she would be home on Sunday about lunchtime and would have a long talk with her then.

Maria was naturally elated and proud and could not wait for her daughter's return. The weekend would be the official start of summer for 1959 and ten days or so later she would be able to be off work and on vacation for the month of July. So they could go away together. They had hesitantly discussed going into Spain for a visit so that Maria could show Anna where she had been born and where their family had once lived so happily and so well.

Late the previous year, Maria had bought a second-hand Renault 4CV motor car – the first car she had ever owned – and their plan was

BEGINNINGS                                       Gary Heilbronn

to drive around the northern coastal region of Spain for a fortnight or so. The car was blue-grey and shaped like the little Volkswagen 'beetle' cars that were so popular in Germany. But of course, no-one in France would buy a German car. The memories of the war were still too fresh. The choice of destination for the holiday had not been easy. Indeed, Maria had not been back to Spain in over twenty years and Anna had never set foot in the country though they both spoke perfect Spanish and euskara – as well as French and passable English. It had taken a lot of courage for Maria to consider returning to Spain even though both she and Anna now held French identity cards and had even been able to obtain passports.

Indeed, things had also changed in Franco's Spain. An end had come to the period of international isolation during which more than fifty thousand men and women opposing the nationalists had been executed – and these were just the legal executions carried out in the decade between 1939 and 1949. Many others were undocumented, even apart from the tens of thousands of executions carried out 'legally' during the civil war.

In 1953, Franco renewed relations with the Vatican and signed a treaty with the USA which included the establishment of American naval bases in Spain. In 1955, Spain was accepted into the United Nations and in 1958 it became a member of the World Bank. Much was also being made of a visit to Spain by US President Dwight Eisenhower planned for December 1959. Although it was suspected that many Nazi war criminals were still living in Spain – where they had earlier sought sanctuary as there were no extradition treaties in force with other European countries – and that Franco's campaign against political opponents still continued in secret, most countries had renewed diplomatic and trade relations with Spain.

On a more human level, for some years already, people had been visiting Spain again as tourists. So it was not necessarily a perilous voyage to undertake. But Maria was still anxious about it.

Unlike her mother, Anna was not at all worried about the trip to Spain and had been more concerned to have a good time on her visit to the beach at *Hendaye Plage* with her friends. In addition, she hoped to find out what she could about her rather mysterious classmate in case he turned out to be a threat or some kind of informer or undercover agent. In fact, little occurred during the few days that she and her friends spent at the beach that could shed any light on this matter and it had slowly receded from her thoughts. He was perhaps just a little immature.

On the other hand, Anna had discovered that she loved the beach and the heat of the sun. It was such a change from Paris. She spent as much time as she could basking in the warmth of the early-summer sun. And the water was perfect; a bit fresh, but crystal clear and calm; ideal for swimming.

Surprisingly, Anna also enjoyed the company of her soon to be ex-classmates and perhaps strangely, felt rather drawn to the classmate, Javier, who she'd previously had doubts about. As well, she found his parents to be particularly friendly and they seemed to have taken a liking to her. That Friday night, around the dinner table after several celebratory drinks, Javier's mother was sitting next to Anna and confided quietly:

"You know Anna, we too were Basque exiles ... on our arrival in France in 1939, we were interned at Gurs, about a hundred kilometres east of Bayonne. Did you know about the camp at Gurs?" she enquired.

Anna nodded her dissent, looking intently at the older woman.

"It was one of fifteen camps that had been quickly built in southern France to receive the half a million Basque and other refugees from Franco's Spain" she said. "But by May 1939, there were already nineteen thousand people crowded into the camp at Gurs; and with little food, clothing and medicines. So conditions in the camp rapidly deteriorated".

"Oh my God, Markesa" Anna replied – Javier's mother had told her to call her by her first name – their family name was Ibarrin. "I knew that my mother had a hard time when she arrived but it was nothing like that; though she never talks about it."

"You see," Markesa replied, "the refugees were effectively trapped in the camps being unable to leave unless they had a home to go to or a job outside, though some of them, especially the Catalans, were transferred to camps elsewhere to the east, nearer to

Perpignan or were released to family members. Javier and his father and I – the little boy was just under a year old at the time – had remained there for almost twelve months, when out of the blue, almost another thousand Basque refugees who were living freely outside the camps were arrested and interned there on the orders of a pro-Franco Basque politician who had been appointed to the French *Ministère de l'Intérieur*. It was surprising that your mother avoided that. Perhaps it was because she had a permanent job".

Markesa continued, "Anyway, that was in May 1940, but all of a sudden on 26 June 1940, four days after the armistice with Germany had been signed, the local administrators of the camp took a hurried decision. They allowed most refugees to leave just before the arrival of the occupying German soldiers. We assumed that it was that they feared that the Germans would return the refugees to the custody of the nationalist forces in Spain."

Anna felt so relieved that her mother had avoided those hardships but was pleased that at least some of the French bureaucrats at the time had shown enough courage to act against the Nazis. That brightened her spirits immensely as a big part of her felt French as well as being Basque. After all she was born in Bayonne and her mother had always insisted that she should feel part of her country of birth.

As they sat and talked, Javier's father, Karlos, came over and listened. When Markesa had finished speaking, he took up the story.

"Before the war, I was a young medical doctor in Bilbao; that was where I studied medicine and met Markesa. I had never been mixed up with politics, but my work involved me in treating republican sympathizers and caring for injured soldiers. All of a sudden, I was considered to be an enemy of the Franco regime. Eventually we had no choice but to flee to France with our young family. I did what I could to treat the sick at the Gurs camp and on our release at the end of June 1940, I was fortunate to quickly find friends amongst the Basque refugees in Biarritz. They looked after us and helped me start up a small medical practice. We were lucky to be able to sit out the war quietly near Biarritz. It was not easy but we were relatively safe and after it was over, I took a post at the Bayonne hospital." He paused. "Like you and your mother, we too owe a lot to France."

"But what happened to the camp at Gurs?" Anna demanded. She spoke abruptly with the impetuousness of youth.

"That's another distressing story," Karlos replied, his eyes showing sadness. "During the war, the camp at Gurs had become an internment camp for Jews with as many as six thousand sick and displaced people being held there. A thousand of them died in the camp and another four thousand were sent to concentration camps, mainly Auschwitz. So for four more years, Gurs was far from a happy place despite its tranquil rural setting and views of the Pyrenees".

He continued. "After the liberation, Gurs was used to house German prisoners and collaborators, but it was closed at the end of 1945. Later, on the site of the camp, a memorial was established to the Basques and Jews who suffered and died there. It is surprising how little-known all this is", he said with a slight shaking of his head.

"I had no idea of the existence of these internment camps in France for the Basque exiles." Anna replied. She was touched by Javier's family's story and how it seemed to parallel that of her mother, though they seemed to have had a much harder time when they had escaped from Spain. She'd never really spoken to Maria about what had happened to her. She only knew that she once had an older brother who had died before she was born and that her father had died sometime before that. Her mother had never told her the details except that the nationalists were to blame. She really did not seem to want to talk about it and Anna had never pressed her.

But now she wondered to herself half aloud: "Should I now broach the subject with my mother? Perhaps we'll talk when we're on holiday".

Sitting nearby, Javier's mother overheard her, and she replied kindly: "I'm sorry to say that the pain will never leave her but she must tell you her story. You need to know. And she needs to relieve herself of the burden that she's carried alone for all these years."

Anna was touched. Like most young people, she had never before given much thought to how her mother might feel about what were likely to be very traumatic events in her past.

"How could I have been so uncaring?" she chastised herself.

But she and her mother had lived so closely together for so long and with no close family or friends around them, such matters seemed never to be raised. It was only now, in sharing these confidences with another woman of her mother's generation that she felt a deep yearning to know of her mother's suffering and renew the intimate bond that since her birth had slowly faded into the background.

## Sixty-Eight

Maria had been to work at the museum on Saturday morning and on her return home was thrilled to see that a letter from Sciences-Po had arrived, presumably containing her daughter's exam results. But she would not think of opening it before Anna returned. Had her daughter not telephoned her the day before, she would have been in an unbearable state of anxiety. In the afternoon, she had cleaned and tidied the apartment and shopped for ingredients to make a wonderful celebratory meal. Oysters from Arcachon Bay and *foie gras* from the Landes, both just to the north, followed by roast lamb that she would cook after church the next morning, so it would be ready when Anna returned from the coast. She'd even bought a half bottle of sweetish Jurançon wine to drink with the *foie gras* and a bottle of good Bordeaux for the lamb and cheese, if indeed they were still hungry after the main course. She knew Anna would appreciate the meal. She always had a hearty appetite. Maria smiled at the thought.

"She eats like a young man" she said softly to herself. "Perhaps it's because she's always doing so much physical exercise". Her thoughts hovered for a time over the image of the daughter who was her life.

That Saturday night Maria slept soundly.

She rose early on the Sunday morning. Although any religious fervour she had experienced as a child had long since faded in Maria's heart, she often went to the local Catholic Church. It was not so much to hear what the priest had to say, but to pray for those who she had loved and lost – her parents, Alberto, Toma and even Max – as well as for the daughter who remained with her and who she cherished beyond all else. To say that she would give her own life for her daughter was beyond an understatement of how she felt. The short time in church always seemed to have this rather morbid effect on her and this day was no exception.

**BEGINNINGS** Gary Heilbronn

The cooking had been left for Sunday morning after church, and she had quickly prepared the meal and placed the lamb and vegetables in the oven.

At around eleven-thirty on that Sunday morning, she heard a knock at the door. It was unexpected, though she no longer trembled when this occurred. But people rarely visited without having made an arrangement beforehand and it was a bit early for Anna to arrive.

"That must be Madame de Leon from next door. She sometimes drops by after church." Maria said quietly to herself. She liked her neighbour.

"She'd always been so kind but discreet," Maria thought to herself. Maria was just finishing setting the table for lunch. She glanced at the table, satisfied with what she saw; then calmly moved towards the door.

§

Unlike her mother, Anna rose a little late on that Sunday morning. There had been a lot of celebrating done on Saturday night and she and her friends went to bed well after midnight. Although a few of the young men had drunk more than they were used to and were still asleep, Anna had been happy though reasonable and had consumed only a couple of glasses of white wine. But there had been dancing and singing and lots of laughing. Even Javier's parents had participated although they had gone to bed much earlier than the young people.

Javier's mother was up and in the kitchen when Anna came in. The young woman had already washed and dressed. She smiled at Javier's mother. She found that she liked the older woman more and more.

"Good morning, Markesa" she said happily. "I'll just have a quick bite to eat before taking off. I have to rush to catch the bus back to Bayonne."

"Oh, don't worry my dear, there's no rush. I have to drive to Bayonne anyway this morning. I can take you," replied the older woman kindly.

# BEGINNINGS  Gary Heilbronn

To be offered a lift home was a pleasant surprise and a relief for Anna. She had begun to feel stressed about making the bus and now she relaxed a little. The day was again beautiful. The sun shone down brilliantly and the sea was calm and looked like a sheet of glittering blue glass all the way to the horizon. She loved the *côte Basque*.

"Will you have time to stop off and meet my mother; I'm sure she would be very pleased to meet you." Anna said eagerly to the older woman. She had quickly come to admire Javier's mother and thought that it would really be a good idea for her to meet her own mother. She worried that Maria lived a somewhat isolated existence especially now that she was away so much.

"That would be very nice, the older woman replied. "I'll just have the time to stop very briefly. I need to go into town to collect some things before coming back here to the beach house."

Anna sat at the kitchen table and poured hot milk on the chocolate powder in her breakfast bowl. There was fresh bread and home-made blackberry jam on the table and a few croissants that had been warmed up in the oven by Javier's mother. It was a delicious breakfast. After she picked up the last crumbs of the croissant and put them in her mouth, Anna sat back and sighed. She had been reluctant to come to visit with these friends, but was now sad that she was about to leave. She knew that a new chapter of her life would be starting now that her undergraduate studies were completed. She wanted to talk about the future to her mother. But there'd be plenty of time for that. She rose, took her bowl, plate and cutlery to the sink and washed and left them to dry there on the drying rack.

"Thank you so much for breakfast and for everything. I've had such a wonderful time here," she said sweetly and sincerely to Javier's mother. Politeness had been a habit that Maria had drummed into her daughter from an early age.

"I'd better go and get my things ready to leave." Anna said.

"We need to go about ten-thirty," the older woman called out, almost interrupting her. She was busily organizing things in the kitchen as Anna turned to leave. She had half an hour to get packed.

# BEGINNINGS

Gary Heilbronn

Anna quickly but quietly gathered her things and packed them into the small alligator skin suitcase that she had borrowed from home. There was plenty of space for all that she needed, even her beach towel and sheets. She had sometimes seen the suitcase in her mother's closet but it seemed never to be used and so she took it. She had not even bothered to ask permission as she knew that her mother was not going anywhere right then.

The two girls who shared the room with were still fast asleep and so she left quietly without waking them. Out in the living room, one or two of the young men from her class were up and looking a little worse for wear. Anna bid them *au revoir* not knowing how long it might be before she would see them again, and asked them to say goodbye to the others on her behalf. They agreed somewhat sleepily. She went outside and found Javier's father, Karlos, standing at the driver's-side door of the car with Markesa sitting in the driver's seat.

Anna thanked Karlos cheerfully for his kind hospitality, put her old suitcase into the car and climbed into the front passenger seat. Markesa was ready to go and within a few seconds, they had pulled out and were heading north on the *Boulevard de la Mer*.

Anna revelled in the drive up along the coast along the *Route de la Corniche* and up through the town of Saint Jean-de-Luz. The coastline was so rugged and green and bordered by a sparkling blue sea stretching as far as the eye could see. Soon the road turned inland as they headed towards the Biarritz airport and north-east towards the township of Anglet and on to Bayonne. It was not that far, but the roads were narrow and not that good and they passed through a number of villages, slowing them down. As they drove, they chatted cheerfully about Anna's studies, her hopes for the future and her classmates.

It was about eleven-thirty when they parked the car just up the street from the building where Maria had now lived for more than a decade. Both got out. As Anna took her the alligator skin suitcase from the back seat, Javier's mother said:

"Lucky we're early; I'll be able to stay for at least ten minutes. I don't have to be at my next stop until after midday."

"Wonderful!" replied Anna as they walked towards the front door of the old stone building.

## Sixty-Nine

In the instant that Maria had lifted the latch and opened her front door with a friendly smile, expecting to see the face of her second-floor neighbour, a fist shot forward, fingers enclosing her throat, choking the breath from her and forcing her backwards. She gagged for breath and her eyes bulged. With both her hands, she clawed at the sinewy left wrist of the swarthy-complexioned man, struggling in vain to unlock the grip of his fingers from her throat. But his grasp was immovable and the thumb of his left hand pressed deeply into her throat between the trachea and the oesophagus, stifling almost any sound from her vocal chords, restricting her breath, choking her, making her almost faint.

With two steps forward, he was fully in the room. He was a professional and completely in control. He had clearly done this sort of thing before; though this time it was different. This was personal. He had watched Maria return from church and after a short wait, could not resist the impulse to take his revenge without further delay.

Using his right hand he lightly pushed the door shut behind him. It closed with little more sound than would have been expected if Maria had closed it herself. Only seconds had passed. Through eyes now wide with fright and surprise, she saw the face and the image of what she thought was a ghost, or was it the devil. The fierce dark eyes empty like those of an animal burned with cold hatred. She squinted at the long sickle-shaped scar on the right-hand side of her assailant's forehead and understanding trickled into her thoughts as the blood-flow to her brain slowly diminished. She knew that face and she recognized the smell of hatred and revenge that flooded the room. But revenge for what?

"What have I done to him?" she thought, "compared to what he has done to me." The images of that horrible morning back on the old metal bridge and all that blood flicked through her dimming consciousness and everything became fuzzier as she drifted into darkness.

Herrerro followed her body backwards with his right hand behind her back, holding her fragile body close as she collapsed slowly and silently towards the floor. He held tight his grip on her throat not wanting her to regain consciousness. Not yet anyway. His hold on her slowed and controlled her fall. There was almost no sound. The intensity of the initial attack had receded, the adrenalin in his veins subsided and he began to notice the delicate form of her throat and the fine, elegant lines of her face.

"She's still a beautiful woman" he thought with a wry smile.

Her head and shock of loose dark curls had fallen back freely as her seemingly lifeless body had drifted backwards onto the floor. She now lay there on her back, arms lying limply at her side. Herrerro relaxed a little his terrible grip on her reddened, swelling throat. He did not want her dead yet. He crouched over her, his left knee now on the floor and the other leg half bent astride her slim body. He gazed at her intently as if concerned by her plight. But the gaze lasted too long. He was peering questioningly at her drained face and shuttered eyes with what could only be blank indifference. He was completely oblivious to her as a human being. It was as if she were another species. She was no more than his vanquished and captured prey and he the patient predator still uncertain if his victim was still alive and might suddenly put in that last futile effort to escape.

After several moments gazing at her, he drew in a deep breath and threw his head back as if about to unleash an animal cry of satisfaction and pride following a kill. Instead he fully released the grip on the prostrate woman's throat and with his left hand grabbed roughly at the buttoned v-neck of her light summer dress and in a flash of movement ripped it downwards at the same time tearing asunder the cups of her laced white bra revealing her still heaving breast and the soft white flesh all the way from her reddened throat to her hips. Now kneeling astride her slightly spread thighs he bent down, sniffing like a curious animal at the brownish nipples on her breasts, registering the fragrance of a perfume that seemed somehow familiar. With his right hand he grasped the elastic waistband of her ample shiny pinkish panties ripping outwards revealing the flatness of her lower abdomen and the soft surprisingly straight strands of fine hair decorating the slightly protruding pubis. The slow rise and fall of her ribcage and stomach showed that she was still breathing. He rounded his back, bringing his face slowly down her body close to the soft skin, past the vertical depression of her hidden navel in the centre of her slim waist, still sniffing almost noisily, erratically like a wild animal.

At this instant, the front door swung abruptly open. There, framed in the doorway were two female faces, wide-eyed with shock. As the blood drained from their cheeks, both their mouths opened almost in slow motion, inhaling gasps of disbelief at the scene before their eyes. Anna dropped the familiar suitcase she was carrying with a light thud. The dark face below them turned slowly to its left looking upwards over the left shoulder of the crouching form to confront the newcomers; smiling slightly as if imagining the extra pleasure that these two more victims would bring to the moment. It seemed as though minutes had passed as the two women's eyes locked with those of the crouching, swarthy, evil-eyed man astride Maria's limp white body. In reality it was less than a second or two that passed.

"Please come in," he said sneeringly. He needed them off-guard and quickly in the room. The younger woman he recognized from the café in Paris. The older was a little familiar but would pose no threat. He knew he could quickly overpower them both and his thigh muscles tensed, his legs already beginning to extend beneath him, preparing to pounce. His eyes lowered and fixed on the alligator-skin suitcase; then widened as memory of it and where he had first seen it, flowed back into his brain.

Sensing the danger, the older woman at the door let out a stifled scream just as Anna sprang forward unexpectedly, with a cry of aggression and with a speed that Herrerro registered only in the blink of an eye. Instinctively and without even a thought, she had seen that her enemy was momentarily distracted and that she had merely a split-second to react.

Her arms outstretched with hands reaching for each side of the head that was already turned almost to its extremity towards the women at the door, she slams the palms of her hands together crashing on each side of the head, shocking him briefly, then pushes her thumbs, fortunate to have found their targets, directly and deeply into his ear canals. Her nails puncture the skin releasing spurts of blood and forcing a grunt of pain from the crouching man's throat.

The blow had only stunned him momentarily and his arms flail out at her; but her grip is secure and as the remaining fingers on each of her hands close tightly on the sides of Herrerro's closely cropped head, she flexes her biceps, retracting her arms, bringing the man's face almost into her chest. He glimpses the bright reddish-brown birthmark close by; and an array of women's faces flash briefly before his confused eyes.

He began to recover and she feels the force of his sudden attempt to rise and to turn his head back away from her and to face Maria; but she holds the head tightly and throws the weight of her still moving body in an anticlockwise direction behind the crouching form, twisting the straining neck below that evil face, finishing her trajectory low, crouching close to the floor on her feet at her mother's side.

A few seconds delay and Herrerro's moment of vulnerability and inattention would have been past and irrespective of Anna's fighting skills and strength and even with the older woman's help, there would have been little chance of overpowering this well-trained and athletically built intruder.

It is such instantaneous judgements and actions that tip the balance between life and death.

## Seventy

After a second, Anna released the flopping head now bizarrely twisted and facing almost directly behind the slowly sinking body, the strength ebbing from its limbs. As the vertebrae at the top of Herrerro's spine had snapped, the cracking sound he heard resounding in his brain reminded him of the report of a rifle. It took him back to the moment that he saw as his terrible humiliation although his shame had now strangely disappeared. It brought back to him those events so long ago on the old metal bridge at the Hendaye border crossing when he'd first noticed and then come so physically close to the now unconscious woman lying beneath him.

The light left his eyes and he relived the scene in his mind, imagining that he saw her body strangely rising up from the floor to meet his own as he toppled heavily onto her half-naked torso. The impact of it shook Maria into consciousness. Coughing and breathing heavily, she opened her eyes to the sight of her assailant's head lying inert beside her own, but like her own, his was facing oddly upwards as if examining the ceiling with an unblinking gaze. She closed her eyes again. It was all too much for her.

Anna began to push and pull Herrerro's heavy corpse off her mother's body. Javier's mother had not yet moved from the open door. She jumped forward and helped pull the dead-weight of the limp body to one side. This done, she returned to the door and closed it quietly, instinctively knowing that no good at all could come from making this scene public. Hopefully the neighbours had heard nothing. Basque exiles sought anonymity and lived in constant fear of silent ambush by Franco's spies or his secret police; and she knew that this man who lay dead before them had the appearance of one of those deadly assassins.

"Will they ever be free? Had nothing really changed over the last twenty years?" she thought aloud.

She started to go through the dead man's pockets, looking for identification and clues to why he was here and trying to do what he had just been prevented from doing. Anna was pre-occupied with reviving her mother, still inert on the floor.

"Mother! Mother, are you alive? Are you all right?" she cried loudly though just a few inches from her mother's ashen face, her hands shaking her mother's limp shoulders.

"I ... I think so," came the shaking reply, Maria's eyes blinking against the bright light of the day. Anna hugged and comforted her mother, at the same time trying to arrange her clothes to cover her partial nakedness.

Things were bad; "but they could have been so much worse!" Anna thought aloud. "They were both alive and Maria seemed unharmed though badly shaken."

"It's nothing short of a miracle that we've all escaped almost certain death at this man's hands" Javier's shaken mother gasped, echoing Anna's thoughts. Then, just loudly enough for the others to hear she exclaimed excitedly, "this man is clearly one of Franco's assassins. Look what I found in his pockets!" She produced his wallet and identity cards.

"There is also this," she said as she held up a sheet paper with sketches and photocopies of Maria and Anna. "And look here. It's a report on Maria from the secret files of the Guardia Civil and another on you, Anna, from the French secret service. And look at this knife!

They looked at each other, worry showing vividly on their faces.

"We must be careful." Javier's mother spoke hurriedly with emotion. "The police must not be called. No-one else must now of this. You will no longer be safe here. They know where you live." She took a few breaths. "I'll get help. Do you have a telephone?"

"But who are you?" Maria exclaimed, looking towards Javier's mother. She had no idea that Anna would be arriving with a visitor.

Anna looked up towards Markesa, trying to regain her composure. The sight of Herrerro's knife had made her head spin, dozens of visions of the dagger, sometimes simple and plain, other times ornately adorned but still clearly identifiable, were flashing through her mind.

She spoke haltingly. "This ... this is Markesa ... Markesa Ibarrin; ... the mother of my friend Javier," she explained to her Maria.

"We can trust her. We must trust her." Maria struggled to get to her feet, trying to pull her torn and dishevelled clothes around her. But the effort was too great. She began to tremble and sob quietly, sitting back onto the floor.

"The 'phone is on the low cabinet ... over there against the wall" Anna indicated to the other woman.

"Who are you calling?" she asked anxiously.

"Don't worry. It is just my husband. He'll arrange for friends to help us," she said reassuringly; but Maria looked up towards her, obviously worried.

"Don't be afraid. I'll not betray you," she said comfortingly, "but help may take some time to arrive."

Maria was relieved but kept her guard up. So many years of keeping a low profile, avoiding trouble and the notice of other people was hard to shake. However, she saw that she had little choice but to trust her daughter's new friend. She managed to get up shakily and Anna helped her to the sofa and sat down beside her. They looked at the inert body on the floor. Maria was staring at him but she seemed distant, as if lost in her thoughts.

"Do you know this man?" Anna asked her mother. But there was no reply.

## Seventy-One

The short telephone conversation was completed and Markesa turned to face Maria and her daughter. She came over towards them, sitting down opposite on an old armchair. She spoke quietly.

"We must wait here. Everything is being organized, but it may take some hours. Maybe we'll even have to wait until dark."

After a few minutes sitting in silence, Anna asked her mother again,

"Do you know this man? I'm sure he is the man who was watching us in the café in Paris."

The two older women looked towards Anna. Her mother had tears in her eyes. Javier's mother seemed composed but gazed quizzically at Anna, now very interested in what the young woman had said.

Suddenly agitated, Markesa blurted out,

"What! You've seen this man before? Who were you with in this café? Was my son there? Who are you really, Anna? Where did you learn to kill like this?"

"Yes, Javier was there too, as were several of our friends. They may all be in danger so we must warn them" Anna replied, "I already tried to in Paris but they didn't take me seriously." She avoided answering any of the other enquiries. In truth, she had no answer to the last two questions and indeed, posed them again and again to herself in her thoughts.

"I know who he is!" Maria said more quietly, almost to herself. "Or at least I knew who he was a long time ago." She looked up at them.

"He has been the Devil in my nightmares for twenty years. He is responsible for the death of your brother, Toma," she sighed, gazing intently at her daughter, "though it was not he who struck the blow that killed my little boy."

Her eyes lowered almost ashamed, as if acknowledging her own share in the responsibility for her infant son's death; then she quietly related the story of her escape from San Sebastian, at least that part she remembered clearly, up until she was carried to safety by the French frontier guards. It took several minutes.

"Since that day I have never seen this man's face in my waking hours. And now he is here; dead at my feet. And though I sought no revenge, I can say that his death grieves me not in the slightest."

The three women looked at each other, tears in their eyes. Anna had never before heard the full story of her brother's death. She could not have imagined it to have been worse. And after all this time, to find this man here, she thought. And what he tried to do to her mother. He had doubtless somehow recognized her from that sighting of Anna in Paris and had followed her here.

Anna felt responsible for all this. But in a small corner of her heart, she felt that this was somehow meant to be. Perhaps it could never have been any different. She picked up the dagger that Javier's mother had placed on the floor with the other items taken from Herrerro's pocket. She fondled it with familiarity. The thought of thrusting the dagger into the dead man's heart and twisting it sideways crossed her mind, but she put the thought aside.

"And now, I have truly avenged my tiny brother's death!" she said softly. A sad smile almost crossed her face. So many thoughts rushed through her brain that she felt almost faint. But she pulled herself together.

"Now is not the time for weakness" she said to herself. Indeed, now was not the time to disappear into a world of her own, a world where she felt strong and was feared by her enemies. Time enough for that later. She was at last clearly conscious of who she was and what it was to have a past.

The women sat there together hardly speaking. The lunch that Maria had prepared had been forgotten, but the unmistakeable aroma of the roast lamb began to permeate the apartment. It was Anna who finally said:

"There is nothing else we can do now. I think we should eat while there is time. There may be more difficulties ahead of us. Today is the beginning of a new chapter in all of our lives. Forget this evil, wasted life lying on the floor. He can no longer harm us; or anyone else for that matter."

She stopped for a moment.

"I would even raise a glass of wine to toast his departure" she said matter-of-factly.

The others sat back, momentarily shocked by the hard edge in the young woman's voice and the cold words she had uttered, though it was not the first time Maria had heard her daughter speak like this. But maybe she was right. They knew she was right. This man's life was worthless and his death deserved. He had lived only to cause harm to others. His death rather than his life was the cause for celebration.

Anna went to a closet and brought out an old blanket, throwing it over Herrerro's body. Cover the rubbish, they all thought.

Then, Maria and Anna served the food and wine while Javier's mother sat at the table chatting to them. Maria was becoming more relaxed with her visitor and new friend. The fresh oysters and *foie gras* were delicious with the slightly fruity Jurançon white wine; and the roast lamb superb with the Bordeaux red. They all ate heartily and cheerfully toasted Herrerro's death and their lucky escape; and not just once, but several times.

It seemed not to bother them overly that his cold body was covered over just a few metres away. It was as if the mound on the floor was just a pile of old blankets. The conversation became jovial; perhaps to compensate for the moments of almost debilitating fear and liberating anger that they'd all felt just such a short a time before.

## Seventy-Two

It was already dark when once again there was knocking at the door of the second floor apartment. The three women had been resting while waiting for help to arrive. They were instantly alert and waited. Two knocks in rapid succession, followed by a single knock and loud coughing. That was the signal that had been agreed by Javier's parents so the women would know that at the door there were indeed friends who'd come to help them. Herrerro's body still lay where it had been pushed to so that Maria could extricate herself from under its awful dead weight. The dishes from the table had been cleared and washed some hours ago.

Javier's mother opened the door. Anna looked towards the door and was shocked. Along with Javier and his father, there was another man. It was Yann, the older student from the café in Paris. All of a sudden, Anna was tense and afraid.

"What's he doing here?" she said, gesturing towards Yann and rising to her feet as if ready once again to pounce on an enemy.

"It's fine! Don't worry! Yann is completely trustworthy. We have known him since he was a boy and he has studied to be an advocate as well! We'll need his legal advice" Javier's father replied calmly as they came in the door and closed it quickly after them.

The three men came further into the apartment and looked at the body on the floor. Javier's mother introduced them to Maria and Maria gestured to them to sit. It was Yann who spoke first:

"You must all tell me precisely what happened. First you, aunty!" he said to Javier's mother. Then you Maria, and afterwards Anna, as it was you, I understand who delivered the blow that killed him."

Anna was surprised. Yann had called Javier's mother 'aunty'. Was she really his aunt? Her mind raced. "What was going on here?"

Slowly, they all related their versions of the events and the three men sat silently taking it all in. They could not hide their amazement at how quickly and efficiently Anna had disposed of the assassin.

When Anna told her story, she also showed them the wallet and documents that had been taken from Herrerro's pockets; but she kept the old dagger apart; she wanted it for herself. She knew somehow that it belonged to her. How the assassin had come to have it she could not know. But she felt it was her birthright and she would keep it safe.

When they had finished their stories, including the tale of the incident at the metal bridge at Hendaye so many years ago, Anna noticed that Yann was silent. What was said seemed to have a profound effect on him. He then carefully read and re-read the Guardia Report and also the more unofficial scrap of paper from the French *Direction Générale*. After that, he spoke slowly.

"The first thing I will say is that if we contact the police things will very likely go badly. While it is true, Anna, that you have saved your mother and probably the lives of yourselves as well, we cannot prove that this man threatened your lives in any way. So we have no chance of proving that you killed him in 'self-defence'. It would be different if he threatened to kill you. We cannot even prove that he was certainly going to kill your mother, so to kill him to protect your mother would be likely to be taken to be using more force than was necessary to prevent a crime. So from a strictly legal perspective, if this goes to trial you may be convicted of some offence and it could even be murder." He stopped so they could all take this in.

"Then, add to this the evidence that would come out in a trial about your Basque republican background, this man's position as a member of the Spanish secret police and even if he is acting illegally, the police and the court are going to favour him and be suspicious of you and be reluctant to believe you. Even if they do believe you, there could be serious repercussions. You certainly would not be able to maintain your anonymity here and that would be dangerous for you both. There are not many choices, but you have to decide if you want to call the police or deal with this quietly."

"But Yann, what about the Guardia and the French secret police?" Markesa responded.

"... Won't they be looking for Maria and Anna? They have files on them. They'll surely want revenge!"

"First, we should consider Maria's position, as Anna is the killer. ... I am sorry Anna," Yann said looking at her, "but to the police you are just that; and your situation is completely different to Maria's. She is a victim. She has physical injuries. But look carefully at these papers" Yann replied. "This document from the *Direction Générale* is clearly unofficial. It is likely that the request for information about Anna was made verbally and also very unofficially. I very much doubt that they will follow up at all. This man is not their agent. As to the Guardia's Report; the Guardia do not know where Maria and Anna are. All they know is that an agent in Paris has requested details of Anna and what they provided is wildly out of date.

For all we know, this man has asked for information on a lot of people and told his superiors very little. They know that he travelled to Bayonne for some reason and that is all. Indeed, he seems to have come here more on a quest for personal vengeance than on official business. But they don't know that. If he disappears without trace or turns up dead over the border, they would not come looking around here for a woman they have had no information on for over twenty years. But to be on the safe side, perhaps it would be better if you, Maria, move elsewhere and change jobs."

Maria's eyes widened; her shoulders slumping disconsolately. Realizing the effect of his words, Yann spoke again:

"But maybe this is not critical. Yes, there are risks but there have always been risks in our situation."

He stopped for a moment and looked closely at the others. Yann started to speak again, this time hesitantly.

"There is one other thing that I think I must tell you." They all looked at him somewhat surprised. "I will not tell you the whole story now, but I was there that day when Toma was killed."

If the listeners were already surprised by what he had been saying, shock now showed on their faces at this last revelation. Maria gasped in disbelief.

"So, you see, I have a personal interest in this affair. It was my father who fired the shots that killed the soldier and wounded this man who now lies dead before us! I saw it happen. I am part of the story." They were all dumbfounded. This was also news to Javier and his parents. They had no idea of this part of Yann's background.

Anna was the first to respond.

"Then it is to your father that both my mother and I owe our lives, for surely we would not be here today had he not taken the decision to shoot these men. Just as I have, today, made the decision to take the life of this man before us."

Anna paused for a moment.

"I have just said that decisions were made to do these things, but in fact, neither of us had any real choice in the matter. Yet the result is the same. People died and people lived. But failure to act would have been disastrous for us."

Anna stopped and was silent for a moment.

"Can we know where your father is to thank him for our lives?" Anna said, looking towards Yann.

"I am sorry, but he has been dead now since shortly after this incident. This man who lies before you and his henchman murdered many republican sympathizers in the region after this shooting at Hendaye happened. Though we do not know for sure who killed him, my father was one of the many victims. My mother and I left soon after for France and were interned at Gurs, where we met the other people here today. So Anna, today, you have in a way avenged my father's death as well as that of your brother."

Maria interrupted: "It grieves me to hear of the terrible retribution exacted on our people and your father by this man, though I can only rejoice in your father having saved my life and the life of my unborn child." She sighed and continued.

"But what of Anna now? What should she do?"

"Anna is more in danger here than you as there is more of a trail leading to her if someone does come looking for this assassin" Yann replied.

"If she is to be safe, she must prepare a rapid departure, never to return or at least, not for twenty years or more, and she must make a life elsewhere in the world."

Maria paled visibly on hearing these words.

"If she decides to do this, we will take the corpse of this man and arrange for it to be carried far out to sea and thrown overboard. Perhaps like that, his body will never be discovered. If Anna comes with me, we will help her make her way abroad and perhaps someday we will see her again."

He stopped and was quiet.

"Anna, it is for you to decide" Yann said.

"There is no choice" Anna replied coldly, "I must go."

Anna came over and hugged her mother. It seemed that personal loss and flight for freedom was an inevitable part of both their histories that they would never be able to escape. They stood there locked in an embrace while the others busied themselves wrapping up and preparing Herrerro's corpse.

"I know you must go" Maria said regaining her composure. "I too have had to flee for my life. Take with you only what is essential to make a new life. The small alligator-skin case will be big enough. It served me well when I needed to escape, just as it served my mother, and grandmother and so many of their mothers before them. It is time it was yours."

Maria broke down sobbing again as they left.

Now to have lost everyone she has loved seemed just too much to bear. She tried to console herself: at least she would know that Anna is safe and has a life and perhaps, one day they'll see each other again.

## Seventy-Three : Epilogue

Late the same night, the body of the Guardia agent known as Juan Herrerro was tipped off the back of a Basque fishing trawler some fifty miles out to sea. It slid quietly into the water making barely a splash. The body was weighed down and slipped quickly below the surface of the unusually calm waters of the Bay of Biscay.

Under cover of darkness he had been loaded into the van that Javier and his father and Yann Zuidilla had arrived in. The drive to the fishing port of Saint Jean de-Luz had been without incident and the body was transferred on board a fishing boat belonging to a friend when there was no-one around. All had been arranged in advance and the fishing trawler slipped quietly out of the harbour on a nearly moonless night.

After almost unbearably tearful farewells, Anna had left with Yann and the other men. She had gathered enough of her belongings, her passport and identity card as well as her official school and 'Sciences-Po' examination results to allow her to found a life elsewhere. Maria had given her all the savings that she kept secreted away in the apartment. She was distraught on Anna's departure, but had decided that it was best to continue her life as it had been, at least for the foreseeable future. She knew that she would have the support of new and trusted friends who might somehow fill the void that her daughter's long absence would be sure to leave in her life.

After dark on the following evening, the blue and white Basque fishing boat pulled into a busy port just near Santander, on the Basque coast of Spain. No-one took any notice of the boat and the two passengers who disembarked. Later that night the passengers took a bus the hundred or so kilometres back to Bilbao, where Yann had many contacts. They stayed in Bilbao for some weeks, waiting for the proper documentation for Anna to be able to take the ferry to England and to hear from friends who would help her when she arrived there.

During that time, Anna spent a great deal of time with Yann. She even accompanied him to a secret meeting of Basque students who had for some time been frustrated by the inaction of the Basque Nationalist Party. After much debate, they agreed to form a new organization known as Euskadi Ta Askarasuna (ETA) or Basque Homeland and Freedom. This was at the end of July 1959. Anna was no more than a spectator and did not speak at the meeting but understood the frustrations of the founding members.

They agreed that the new group's first assembly would be in Bayonne the following year but there was no chance Anna would attend. Nor would many even remember that she had been at the founding of a group which would in time become infamous.

Yann, however, had to continue his life and his work in Paris and though he would be at the next ETA meeting in Bayonne, he would have less and less to do with the group as the years passed and he saw that his combat for justice for his people must take a different path to that of his friends in ETA.

While together in Bilbao, Anna and Yann had become very close. It was a relationship which could have no future, they had agreed, but they discussed many things. He had told her of how Javier's family, Karlos and Markesa Ibarrin, had taken him in after his mother had died in the Gurs internment camp and how he had been released just before the Nazis arrived there. They were his only family now. They also spoke of their own personal futures and the struggles to come. Yann told her of his studies and his almost complete doctoral thesis on 'Crimes against Humanity during the Spanish Civil War' and how it had been inspired by his father's words on that day when they had seen Maria on the old metal bridge at the Hendaye-Hondarribia border crossing. He told her of his hope to work with the United Nations or some similar organization to reform the laws protecting prisoners of war.

His words were inspiring to Anna and they even discussed what further studies and work she could undertake in England, or elsewhere, to advance the cause of their people and the oppressed in whatever way possible.

Eventually, the time for Anna to depart arrived. It was with tears and sadness on the part of both Anna and Yann that they parted in mid-August and Anna took the ferry to Plymouth from Santander. Yann and his friends had many contacts in England amongst the Basque refugees who had left as children more than two decades before to escape the civil war but had not returned. Often, they stayed away because they had nothing to return home to. Their families had died and their property had been confiscated. He knew that Anna would be well looked after there and that her future would be one that she chose to make for herself, wherever her life would lead her.

¤¤¤

If you really enjoyed "BEGINNINGS: Where A Life Begins" please, please go back to Amazon or wherever you got it from and write a short review - even a sentence will do - and give it a 4 or 5 star rating! (3 stars or below means you didn't really like it that much). It'll help me get more readers!!

You can follow me on Twitter @GaryHeilbronn
or check out my blog on
http://garyheilbronnauthor.wordpress.com/
or keep up with what I'm writing on my Facebook Author Page:
Bitly.com/1gDnMJJ

BEGINNINGS                               Gary Heilbronn

# Background: Science and History

### Some Background

Birth and death are surely unique events in our lives whatever religious or spiritual beliefs we hold. In the course of our existence, we will inevitably find ourselves grappling with the seemingly haphazard nature of either or both of these events. While birth is the ultimate co-operative act, we can only conjecture as to what independent role a newborn baby plays in the events that mark the beginning of its life. Death, on the other hand, whether peaceful or traumatic, must be experienced alone; even if we are surrounded by spectators and whether or not they are affected by the event they witness.

Being born (the process from conception to successful delivery into the world) is random and largely accidental. Dying is inevitable but also random as the circumstances of a death – time, place, manner, and so on, also seem to be accidental or arbitrary. Even if there are reasons for a death, does it really matter? Are they not just explanations for why the death occurred at that particular time or place, or in those circumstances? Yet some deaths are deliberately caused or are dictated by self-preservation or by revenge. These motivations were very important in the past but are they any less relevant in the modern world? Similarly, violence and violent death were ever-present features of life in the past, but are these facets of life really that less commonplace in the modern world? So even if a death is directly caused by the act of another person, is the death or its circumstances any less arbitrary?

It may be that being killed by accident, in self-defence, in battle or gratuitously or with murderous intent has the same effect on the victim; but does it have the same effect on the "killer"? Whether or not the perpetrator had a choice seems to be of little or no relevance as one still has a choice even when acting in self-defence. Likewise, it seems to be irrelevant whether or not guilt or remorse is felt as some people feel guilt for many things they do while others feel nothing. Religious beliefs aside, if killing or being killed are no more than arbitrary events in any life, or if in some strange way, they have a meaningful or explicable place in our own lives or in the greater scheme of things, are questions will which always elude rational responses.

§

**The Science**

The inspiration for the historical themes and part of the underlying subject of this story is found in research into Mitochondrial DNA: that type of DNA which is only passed on from mothers to their children. Thus, it is a peculiarly female phenomenon and variations and markers in MtDNA are used by scientists to trace maternal genealogy down through the centuries and indeed through millennia. To some extent, the same can be said for the role of Y chromosomes in tracing male genealogy. Variations and mutations in MtDNA and Y chromosomes can and do occur from time to time, but are rare. These variants establish markers that can be a distinct and identifiable element of the genetic makeup of women and men living many hundreds of generations ago, but can be identical with that of many adults and children alive today. That links actually do exist and lineage can be traced is a reality, though it seems almost science fiction.

All this raises another question: just how complex and meaningful are these genetic links and what are their implications? Could they be, in some people, the basis for the transmission of some form of insight, knowledge or some degree of genetic memory? If so, how much memory can we have of lives lived in the past by other people; people with whom we have intimate genetic links? This may be mere insight into those ancestor's lives or some empathy or identification with them, or possibly even an ephemeral sharing of moments in the lives of those ancestors that can exist through these genetic links.

While we all share genetic links, not everyone is aware of them and some people may be more sensitive to these links than others, just as there are a number of documented cases of children with an uncanny knowledge of the lives of persons who have passed on well before they were born. Additionally, there seems to be certain ethnic groups where this genetic link may be purer, more acute or identifiable and more direct than for others. Notably, these include certain families of Lebanese origin, whose ancestors included the Phoenicians and Canaanites living in the great middle-eastern melting pot of civilization at the time of the genesis of monotheism and other major cultural advances some five thousand years ago. In this part of the world, hatreds and 'tit-for-tat' violence have also trickled down through generations over thousands of years, perhaps founding many of the apparently irrational conflicts still going on today. There is also the Basques, a people from the eastern corner of the north coast of Spain and south-west France, whose ethnic identity and genealogy have been insulated and isolated through millennia by simple but significant geographical and cultural barriers. The unique nature of the Basque language and ethnicity, with their roots in the dimness of their own antiquity may be emblematic of modern Basque social conflict with its controversial origins and complicated and often fratricidal extremes.

Though these two ethnic groups may be completely different, both groups, their descendants and their histories provide a significant back-drop and moving social context within which to explore the implications of genetic memory links between women and men alive today and their far-distant, long-dead ancestors.

§

### The History

In this tale, which is as much about human identity and what makes each and every individual who they are, as it is about the grander themes mentioned above, there are appearances and cameos by a number of the great personages from history, both ancient and modern. Likewise, there are references to places, events and peoples which are or were once real, though sometimes little-known or now almost lost in the mists of history. In the quest to bring these peoples and events to life, every effort has been made to achieve reasonable historical accuracy and truth, despite the vast range of European and Middle Eastern history that is canvassed. Doubtless there will be some who disagree with the version of historical events and characters which form the background to the storyline throughout this book. There are of course many gaps in our knowledge of many historical events and there are various areas of controversy. These have provided fertile ground for the interaction of our fictional characters and their stories within the wider world of such historical events. If there are historical inaccuracies in respect of matters where there exists clear and uncontroversial agreement amongst reputable historians or if there are unequivocal factual errors as to places and peoples, then I, as author, take full responsibility for them.

This is, after all, primarily a work of fiction.

G.H.

www.ingramcontent.com/pod-product-compliance
Lightning Source LLC
Chambersburg PA
CBHW030430300426
44112CB00009B/941